GOVERNMENT REGULATION OF BUSINESS INCLUDING ANTITRUST
INFORMATION SOURCES

MANAGEMENT
INFORMATION
GUIDE : : 11

GOVERNMENT REGULATION OF BUSINESS INCLUDING ANTITRUST

INFORMATION SOURCES

Beatrice S. McDermott
Freada A. Coleman

[
Librarians
Dewey, Ballantine, Bushby
Palmer & Wood
Winthrop, Stimson, Putnam
& Roberts
]

A Comprehensive Annotated Bibliography of Works Pertaining to the Antitrust Division, Department of Justice, and to the Major Regulatory Agencies of the Federal Government

GALE RESEARCH COMPANY · BOOK TOWER · DETROIT, MICHIGAN

OTHER BOOKS IN THE

MANAGEMENT INFORMATION GUIDE SERIES

THE DEVELOPING NATIONS—A Guide to Information Sources Concerning Their Economic, Political, Technical and Social Problems. Edited by Eloise ReQua and Jane Statham, Library of International Relations. Covers all aspects of the difficult situations confronting both the less-developed nations and those who would be of assistance to them.

STANDARDS AND SPECIFICATIONS INFORMATION SOURCES—A Guide to Literature and to Public and Private Agencies. Edited by Erasmas J. Struglia, Consumers Union of the U. S. Deals with the standardization activities that pertain to the development, coordination, and application of rational standards.

PUBLIC FINANCE INFORMATION SOURCES. Edited by Vera H. Knox, The Tax Foundation. Thoroughly documents the economics of government—the collection of revenues and their disbursement.

TEXTILE INDUSTRY INFORMATION SOURCES—An Annotated Guide to the Literature. Edited by Joseph Kopycinski, Lowell Technological Institute. Covers the literature of America's ninth largest industry.

REAL ESTATE INFORMATION SOURCES. Edited by Janice B. Babb and Beverly F. Dordick, National Association of Real Estate Boards. Directs users to information on more than a thousand important real estate topics.

BUILDING CONSTRUCTION INFORMATION SOURCES. Edited by Howard B. Bentley, "Architectural Forum" and "House and Home" magazines. Covers building industry information sources concerning both major basic problems and lesser matters of every-day concern.

PUBLIC UTILITIES INFORMATION SOURCES—An Annotated Guide to the Literature and Regulating Bodies. Edited by Florine Hunt, Public Service Electric & Gas Co.

TRANSPORTATION INFORMATION SOURCES—An Annotated Guide to Publications, Agencies, and Other Data Sources. Edited by Kenneth Metcalf, Henry Ford Museum.

BUSINESS TRENDS AND FORECASTING INFORMATION SOURCES—An Annotated Guide to Theoretical and Technical Publications. Edited by James Woy, Mercantile Library, Free Library of Philadelphia. Unique feature is a glossary to terms, with precise but simple definitions.

PACKAGING INFORMATION SOURCES—An Annotated Guide to the Literature, Associations, and Educational Institutions Concerned with Containers and Packaging. Edited by Gwendolyn Jones, Librarian, St. Regis Paper Company.

Library of Congress Catalog Card Number 67-25294

$8.75

Copyright © 1967 By

GALE RESEARCH COMPANY

CONTENTS

FOREWORD 7

INTRODUCTION 9

ACKNOWLEDGMENTS 11

Section 1 - ADMINISTRATIVE LAW AND ADMINISTRATIVE
AGENCIES 15
    Texts 16
    Government Publications 23
    Miscellaneous 25

Section 2 - CIVIL AERONAUTICS BOARD 29
    Texts 29
    Government Publications 32
    Miscellaneous 37
    Periodicals 39
    Trade Associations 40

Section 3 - ANTITRUST DIVISION OF THE DEPARTMENT OF
JUSTICE AND THE FEDERAL TRADE COMMISSION. 43
    Basic Materials 44
    Texts 45
    Government Publications 95
        Landmark Investigations 96
        Reports and Studies by Congressional Committees, Federal
        Administrative Agencies and Departments of the Government . . 98
        Investigations of the Federal Trade Commission 99
        Congressional Reports and Studies 99
        Reports and Studies of Government Departments and Agencies . . . 119
    Bibliographies 120
    Periodicals and Services 121

Section 4 - FEDERAL COMMUNICATIONS COMMISSION 125
    Texts 125
    Government Publications 128
    Miscellaneous 130
    Periodicals 131
    Trade Associations 133

CONTENTS

Section 5 – FEDERAL POWER COMMISSION 137
  Electric and Gas Utilities 137
    Texts 137
    Government Publications 142
    Miscellaneous 146
    Periodicals 149
    Trade Association 150
  Natural Gas 150
    Texts 151
    Government Publications 152
    Miscellaneous 153
    Periodicals 155
    Trade Association 155

Section 6 – INTERSTATE COMMERCE COMMISSION 159
    Texts 159
    Government Publications 165
    Miscellaneous 170
    Periodicals 172
    Trade Associations 173

Section 7 – SECURITIES AND EXCHANGE COMMISSION 177
    Texts 177
    Government Publications 185
    Miscellaneous 189
    Trade Association 190

APPENDIX 193
    Legal Bibliographies 193
    General Sources 194
    Economic Periodicals 201

AUTHOR INDEX 205

INDUSTRY INDEX 217

GOVERNMENT REPORTS INDEX 225

FOREWORD

Management processes continue to grow more complex and the range of factors relevant to contemporary decision-making mounts apace. Inevitably, the volume of published information and the number of institutions and agencies which aid in the identification of factual material, increases correspondingly. The variety of materials, publications, and institutions useful in providing the factual basis for informed management judgments varies considerably from one field to another. Often, the businessman, government official, student, and librarian will lack a comprehensive and organized inventory of the resources available for fact finding in a particular field. One inevitable consequence is that the opportunity to apply appropriate factual information to the problem-solving process may be lost.

The "Management Information Guide Series" is being developed expressly in order to overcome this deficiency in basic business research tools. Each volume is edited by one or more individuals known to be expert in the subject matter of the field as well as in the information resources applicable to the problems of that field. Each is devoted to a topic of broad interest to business and professional personnel. Each work in the series is designed to direct the user to key sources by arranging, describing, and indexing published sources as well as the programs and services of organizations, agencies and facilities, which in combination make up the total information scene of each of the fields covered.

Paul Wasserman
Series Editor

INTRODUCTION

Today, practically every business operation is confronted with some form of regulation by federal, state and even municipal government. These governmental relations with business are largely exercised on a day-to-day basis by the administrative agencies. The authors, librarians for large law firms and members of the New York bar, therefore believe that there is a need for a comprehensive bibliography of works on the "big six" administrative agencies, and the Antitrust Division of the Department of Justice.

When this source book was first planned, the editors considered covering such subjects as taxation, labor and banking. However, materials published in any one of the above fields were found to be so voluminous that the work would have comprised many volumes. Thus, it was necessary to limit the scope of the book. In so doing, the editors decided to confine coverage to material relating to the Antitrust Division of the Department of Justice and to six of the largest independent agencies: the Civil Aeronautics Board, the Federal Communications Commission, the Federal Power Commission, the Federal Trade Commission, the Interstate Commerce Commission, and the Securities and Exchange Commission.

In addition to texts, periodicals, bibliographies, and trade associations, many government publications, including reports of Congressional committees (made after extensive hearings and investigations) are listed in the succeeding chapters. These studies, which may appear only as committee prints, often contain valuable findings, recommendations, statistical and historical data.

This is a selective work, generally limited to publications federal in scope and issued since 1950. Material covering certain phases of state regulation can be found in some of the Commerce Clearing House loose-leaf services, or may often be obtained by writing directly to the respective state commissions. Addresses and titles of these commissions may be found in the BOOK OF THE STATES, described in the Appendix.

It is hoped that this source book will prove helpful to the lawyer, librarian, and student faced with the problem of determining what materials and recognized authorities are available in the fields covered. Although legal publications are stressed, the editors have tried to include some leading economic books on government regulation of business, particularly in the section on Antitrust.

Beatrice S. McDermott
Freada A. Coleman

November, 1966

ACKNOWLEDGMENTS

We wish to express our gratitude to the following institutions in New York City which most generously permitted us the use of their collections and library facilities: the American Gas Association; the Association of the Bar of the City of New York; the Brooklyn Public Library, especially its Business Library; the Edison Electric Institute; the Graduate School of Business Administration of New York University; the New York County Lawyers Association; the New York Law Institute; the New York Public Library; and Pan American Airways.

Those who lent us a helping hand with our work were Professor Cyril L. McDermott, Law Librarian at St. John's University School of Law, who read the manuscript and made many helpful suggestions; Edith C. Stone, Librarian of the Simmons-Boardman Publishing Company, who reviewed the material on the Interstate Commerce Commission and made valuable additions; Cornelius B. Allen, Librarian of the New York University Graduate School of Business Administration, who suggested leading economics periodicals; Charles O. Svenson, an attorney with the firm of Dewey, Ballantine, Bushby, Palmer & Wood, who read the section on administrative agencies; R. Max Pershe, Librarian at the University of Puerto Rico, who read the section on the Civil Aeronautics Board; and Albert Johnson of the New York University Graduate School of Business Administration, whom we consulted with regard to our coverage of government regulation of business from an economist's viewpoint, and who also contributed the materials in the field of economics included in the introduction to the textbook section of the section on antitrust.

Although the majority of annotations have been taken from the preface,

ACKNOWLEDGMENTS _____

foreword, introduction or the table of contents of the various items listed, several are quoted from book reviews. We wish also to thank the authors and publishers who so kindly granted us permission to use these annotations.

The ENCYCLOPEDIA OF ASSOCIATIONS, Volume I, "National Organizations of the United States," 4th edition, 1964, published by the Gale Research Company in Detroit, was the source of information on trade associations.

Section 1

ADMINISTRATIVE LAW AND ADMINISTRATIVE AGENCIES

Section 1

ADMINISTRATIVE LAW AND ADMINISTRATIVE AGENCIES

The administrative agencies of the federal government have been the object of several studies as their number and power have grown.

In 1947, during President Truman's administration, the first Hoover Commission was established to study and investigate the organization and methods of operation of the Executive Branch, and to recommend organizational changes to promote economy, efficiency and improved service. It was chiefly concerned with the structural reorganization of departments and agencies, and with inter-agency relations.

The second Hoover Commission, under President Eisenhower, dealt more with the functional organization of the Executive Branch, and with policy questions. Its recommendations were largely based on an examination of related functions within the entire Executive Branch. A number of reports were submitted to Congress, some of which resulted in the passage of legislation.

In 1953 President Eisenhower called a conference, which became known as the President's Conference on Administrative Procedure. It held hearings, conducted studies, and prepared reports and recommendations. As its final action, in 1955 it recommended the establishment of a permanent conference.

In 1960, President-elect Kennedy asked James M. Landis, former dean of the Harvard Law School, to prepare a report on the administrative agencies and their problems. This report was submitted to him on December 26, 1960, and was entitled "Report on Regulatory Agencies to the President-elect."

On April 13, 1961, by Executive Order 10934, the Administrative Conference of the United States was created to assist the President, the Congress, and the administrative agencies and executive departments in improving administrative procedures. The order provided that the conference was to conduct studies of the efficiency, adequacy, and fairness of the procedure by which federal executive departments and administrative agencies determine the rights, privileges, and obligations of private persons and protect the public interest.

A final report summarizing the activities of the conference was submitted to President Kennedy on December 15, 1962, together with a letter of recommendations for the future. In addition, the committees set up by the conference made a number of individual reports, which were separately issued. A selection of these reports was printed as a Senate Document.

Public Law 88-499, approved August 30, 1964, set up the permanent Administrative Conference of the United States in order to provide permanent machinery whereby the federal agencies, with assistance from non-government authorities on administrative practice, will be able to make recommendations to improve government procedures by cutting down time and costs while preserving due process of law. The conference will stand in a similar relationship to the agencies as the Judicial Conference stands to the federal courts.

TEXTS

Bar Association of the District of Columbia. Junior Bar Section. FEDERAL ADMINISTRATIVE PRACTICE MANUAL. Washington, D.C.: 1964. 186 p.
> A revision and expansion of the 1956 edition. Covers thirty-two federal agencies. Contains a summary of each agency's organization, procedures and statutory authority.

Bar Association of the District of Columbia. Junior Bar Section. A MANUAL ON TRIAL TECHNIQUE IN ADMINISTRATIVE PROCEEDINGS AND ILLUSTRATIVE FEDERAL ADMINISTRATIVE AGENCIES. Washington, D.C.: 1958. 131 p.
> The introduction to Part I, by Judge E. Barrett Prettyman, states: "Almost universally the great task of trial counsel in an administrative proceeding is to produce a written record in which appear, as clearly as the ability of counsel permits, the facts which lead to the results he desires. The accomplishment of that task requires a trial technique which differs in material respects from that of the usual courtroom trial." Part I covers preparation for the trial, the hearing, and the preparation of the brief. Part II contains a resume of statutes, rules, regulations, and typical procedures of some illustrative federal administrative agencies.

Bennett, H. Arnold. THE COMMISSION AND THE COMMON LAW. A STUDY IN ADMINISTRATIVE ADJUDICATION. New York: Exposition Press, 1964. 127 p.
> The author, a professor of public law, takes up the role of the Interstate Commerce Commission in the development of the freight-forwarding industry in the 20th century.

Bernstein, Marver H. REGULATING BUSINESS BY INDEPENDENT COMMISSION. Princeton: Princeton University Press, 1955. 306 p.
> The objective of the present study is threefold: (1) to evaluate critically the role of the independent regulatory commissions; (2) to develop a more realistic concept of the process of governmental regulation; and (3) to appraise the independent commission as an agent of governmental regulation at the national level.

Blachly, Frederick and Oatman, Miriam E. ADMINISTRATIVE LEGISLATION
AND ADJUDICATION. Washington, D.C.: Brookings Institution, 1934.
296 p.

>   At the time this book was written, there were some sixty different
>   administrative tribunals in the federal government, making judicial
>   decisions affecting private rights. These did not proceed accord-
>   ing to any single form, nor did they follow any uniform proce-
>   dure, and they did not fit in as integral parts of a coherent and
>   intelligible system. In addition, there was a large number of
>   authorities with sub-legislative powers.
>
>   The volume, which is the result of a ten-year study in adminis-
>   tration, attempts to analyze the above situation in the light of
>   valid principles of public administration. The authors have sought
>   to determine how technical efficiency and speed in working out
>   legislative detail, and economy of time and effort in the admin-
>   istration of legal rules, may be accomplished, while providing an
>   intelligent method of control and a just and impartial system of
>   administration.
>
>   An excellent source for those researching the history of federal
>   administrative agencies.

Blachly, Frederick and Oatman, Miriam E. FEDERAL REGULATORY ACTION
AND CONTROL. Washington, D.C.: Brookings Institution, 1940. 356 p.

>   This book describes briefly the organization, legal status, and
>   relationships of the federal administrative system. Examines var-
>   ious plans advocated for improvement of this system. Its object
>   is to contribute toward an understanding of the many legal and
>   administrative problems to be solved if federal intervention in
>   the economic realm is to be both efficient and legal.

Boyer, William W. BUREAUCRACY ON TRIAL: POLICY MAKING BY GOV-
ERNMENT AGENCIES. Indianapolis: Bobbs-Merrill, 1964. 184 p.

>   The author gives an analytical description of the administrative
>   decision-making process. He views this as having five stages:
>   the initial stage; the preliminary drafting; public participation;
>   final drafting; and internal review.
>
>   The relationship of the legislature and public and private interest
>   groups with the agency is also taken up.
>
>   An independent office of administrative procedure is proposed,
>   together with better standards for delegating responsibility to
>   agencies.

Cooper, Frank E. ADMINISTRATIVE AGENCIES AND THE COURTS. Ann
Arbor: University of Michigan Law School, 1951. 470 p.

>   This work does not discuss the problems of administrative organi-
>   zation and agency management. It does describe the standards
>   which the courts impose on administrative agencies, controlling
>   and limiting their power. It brings together the leading cases
>   in which the courts have laid down the principles which govern
>   frequently litigated questions between the agencies and the

parties with whom they deal; and describes the criteria and techniques of administrative adjudication within these standards set by the courts.

Material is grouped under the following major headings: place of administrative agencies in the judicial system; underlying constitutional questions; procedure in adjudication of cases; rule making; and judicial review.

Cooper, Frank. STATE ADMINISTRATIVE LAW. Indianapolis: Bobbs-Merrill, 1965. 2 vols.

This is a study sponsored by the American Bar Foundation and the University of Michigan Law School. The purpose was primarily to analyze the statutory and case law of the several states bearing on problems of administrative procedure. The analysis was made in light of the provisions of the Revised Model State Administrative Procedure Act, as drafted and promulgated by the Commissioners on Uniform State Laws in 1961.

It also tries to give an up-to-date analysis of the laws in areas not covered by the Revised Model State Act, such as the delegability of legislative and judicial powers.

Davis, Kenneth C. ADMINISTRATIVE LAW AND GOVERNMENT. St. Paul: West, 1960. 547 p.

This book, designed for political science instruction in administrative law, does both much more and much less than a book on the same subject for law school instruction. It does more in that it emphasizes some of the fundamentals of our entire legal system, with less narrowing to the special problems of administrative law. It does less in that it eliminates or minimizes those aspects of law study which have little value apart from the vocational training of the practitioner.

Davis, Kenneth C. ADMINISTRATIVE LAW TREATISE. St. Paul: West, 1958, with 1965 pocket supplements. 4 vols.

"These four volumes include thirty chapters, ranging through the familiar topics pertaining to the creation of administrative power, the manner of its exercise, and the possibility of judicial review of the end product. Each chapter begins with a general statement of the problem to be examined, with suitable historical and philosophical observations. Then comes a penetrating discussion of pertinent statutory and case materials, enriched by discerning references to the works of scholars and official investigators. Finally Davis pithily presents his own conclusions." Walter Gellhorn, Betts Professor of Law, Columbia University. 59 Col. L. Rev. 214.

Davis, Kenneth C. ADMINISTRATIVE LAW TEXT. (Hornbook series). St. Paul: West, 1959. 617 p.

This book is exclusively for law students.

The two forerunners of this book are a volume published in 1951, designed for everyone, not especially for students, and a four-volume treatise published in 1958, designed primarily for practitioners and judges. The present book is essentially an adaptation of the treatise.

Davison, James F. and Grundstein, Nathan D. CASES ON ADMINISTRATIVE LAW. Temp. rev. ed. Washington, D.C.: Lerner Law Book, 1964. 359 p.

Forkosch, Morris D. A TREATISE ON ADMINISTRATIVE LAW. Indianapolis: Bobbs-Merrill, 1956. 856 p.
> This book is designed for use in teaching. It deals with both the substantive and procedural aspects of administrative law. Some of the major topics discussed are: judicial control and the bases for delegations; requirements of notice and hearing for administrative proceedings; delegation of powers; licensing; non-adjudicatory functioning of the administrative agencies; notice; hearings (pre-testimony requirements and procedures, testimony procedure, and post-testimony procedure); orders; review (agency and judicial).

Friendly, Henry J. THE FEDERAL ADMINISTRATIVE AGENCIES. THE NEED FOR BETTER DEFINITION OF STANDARDS. Cambridge: Harvard University Press, 1962. 180 p.
> The Oliver Wendell Holmes lectures, delivered at the Harvard Law School in February 1962 by the author, a judge of the United States Court of Appeals for the Second Circuit.
>
> Judge Friendly discusses the Interstate Commerce Act, national labor relations, the licensing of radio and television broadcasting, and the certification of competitive domestic air routes. He concludes with recommendations for a better definition of standards.

Gellhorn, Walter and Byse, Clark. ADMINISTRATIVE LAW, CASES AND COMMENTS. 4th ed. Brooklyn, N.Y.: Foundation, 1960. 1256 p.
> This new edition contains a greater amount of textual material than prior ones. The text is intended to give a straightforward explanation and to sharpen issues.

Heady, Ferrel. ADMINISTRATIVE PROCEDURE LEGISLATION IN THE STATES. (Michigan Governmental Studies no. 24). Ann Arbor: University of Michigan Press, 1952. 137 p.
> Table of contents includes chapters entitled: I. Improvement of Administrative Procedure; II. Survey of Developments in Representative States; III. Administrative Rule Making; IV. Administrative Adjudication; V. Judicial Review of Administrative Action; and VI. Evaluation of State Administrative Procedure Legislation.

Jaffe, Louis L. JUDICIAL CONTROL OF ADMINISTRATIVE ACTION. Boston: Little, Brown, 1965. 792 p.

A systematic account of the relation between the agencies and the courts. It treats all major aspects of this relationship, such as primary jurisdiction (competing original jurisdictions between agencies and courts), enforcement, and other aspects. While most of the book is devoted to federal law, state law is considered as well.

Jaffe, Louis L. and Nathanson, Nathaniel L. ADMINISTRATIVE LAW. CASES AND MATERIALS. 2nd ed. Boston: Little, Brown, 1961. 932 p.

The major topics discussed are: the constitutional position of the administrative agency; the scope of judicial review; administrative discretion in formulating policy; administrative jurisdiction and the right to invoke it; the administrative power to investigate; notice and hearing; the process of decision; enforcement of administrative decisions; and the right to judicial review.

Extensive textual material is supplemented by case reports, which are often followed by notes.

McFarland, Carl and Vanderbilt, Arthur T. CASES AND MATERIALS ON ADMINISTRATIVE LAW. 2nd ed. New York: Matthew Bender, 1952. 763 p.

This work consists largely of source material, with some text. The larger part deals with the federal government, but a substantial portion takes up state administration.

Major topics discussed are: regulatory functions; powers and procedures; judicial controls; and administrative law in action.

Musolf, Lloyd D. FEDERAL EXAMINERS AND THE CONFLICT OF LAW AND ADMINISTRATION. Baltimore: Johns Hopkins Press, 1953. 203 p.

The author, a political scientist, discusses the following topics, among others: regulatory administration and the common law; the genesis of the examiner; examiners and the separation of functions; and staffing the office of examiner.

Nelson, Dalmas H. ADMINISTRATIVE AGENCIES OF THE USA, THEIR DECISIONS AND AUTHORITY. Detroit: Wayne State University, 1964. 341 p.

This work brings together the material on the scope of the court-like authority which federal administrative agencies have acquired; examines the ways in which decisions, in pursuit of such authority, are enforced; and tries to determine whether such decisions are administratively and judicially reviewable.

New York University School of Law. THE FEDERAL ADMINISTRATIVE PROCEDURE ACT AND THE ADMINISTRATIVE AGENCIES. Ed. by George Warren. New York: New York University School of Law, 1947. 630 p.

Proceedings of an Institute conducted by the New York University School of Law February 1-8, 1947.

The Institute was designed to give an opportunity to government personnel, attorneys at law, and the faculties of law schools, to hear outstanding experts discuss the act and describe its application to the more important federal administrative agencies.

Parker, Reginald. ADMINISTRATIVE LAW. Indianapolis: Bobbs-Merrill, 1952. 344 p.

This treatise is confined to general administrative law. The author thinks of administrative law as law that "protects" not only citizens but the government as well. It shows the limits placed on the individual and the executive branch of the government.

Pfiffner, John M. and Presthus, Robert V. PUBLIC ADMINISTRATION. 4th ed. New York: Ronald, 1960. 570 p.

The authors, political scientists, have designed this text for university and college students. It takes up the following major topics: the environment of public administration; the functions of the administrator; organization; personnel administration; financial administration; administrative law and regulation; and administrative responsibility. The regulatory agencies, the regulatory process, and judicial review of administrative action are discussed in chapters 26, 27 and 28.

Prettyman, E. Barrett. TRIAL BY AGENCY. (The Henry L. Doherty Lectures, 1958) Charlottesville: Virginia Law Review Association, 1959. 60 p.

Judge Prettyman gives students a richly detailed study of a case in a "formal adjudicatory proceeding before an administrative agency."

Redford, Emmette S. ADMINISTRATION OF NATIONAL ECONOMIC CONTROL. New York: Macmillan, 1952. 403 p.

The author, a political scientist, tries to show the features of the administrative system in use in economic control. He also takes up those general aspects of administration which are required for understanding this problem.

Some of the major topics discussed are: administrative tools and techniques -- instruments and operating methods; the problem of the interest groups; organization; safeguards; and the effectiveness of administrative control.

Redford, Emmette S. NATIONAL REGULATORY COMMISSIONS, NEED FOR A NEW LOOK. College Park: University of Maryland College of Business and Public Administration, Bureau of Governmental Research, 1959. 23 p.

A paper delivered by Dr. Redford on April 17, 1959. It briefly analyzes the performance of the regulatory commissions to indicate possibilities for modification in the existing system to make it more effective, and to indicate the adequacy or inadequacy of the commission system for new tasks in economic regulation.

Schulman, John. ADMINISTRATIVE AGENCIES. New York: Practising Law
Institute, 1956. 43 p.
> This monograph is written by a general practitioner for lawyers
> in general practice. Its limited object is to propose a method
> of approach to a practical problem and a habit of thinking which,
> if adopted, may ease the way for the practicing lawyer in the
> field of administrative law.

Schwartz, Bernard. AN INTRODUCTION TO AMERICAN ADMINISTRATIVE
LAW. 2nd ed. London: Pitman; New York: Oceana, 1962. 272 p.
> The author takes up the administrative process; delegated legis-
> lation--delegations of power and procedure, and safeguards; ad-
> ministrative justice; adjudicatory procedure--right to be heard,
> and processes of proof and decision; judicial review--availability
> and scope; tort liability; and estoppel and privilege.

Schwartz, Bernard. THE PROFESSOR AND THE COMMISSIONS. New York:
Knopf, 1959. 275 p.
> An account of the author's experiences as counsel to the sub-
> committee on Legislative Oversight of the House Committee on
> Interstate and Foreign Commerce. The subcommittee was investi-
> gating the federal regulatory agencies at the time.

Swenson, Rinehart John. FEDERAL ADMINISTRATIVE LAW. A STUDY OF THE
GROWTH, NATURE AND CONTROL OF ADMINISTRATIVE ACTION. New
York: Ronald, 1952. 376 p.
> This book, whose author is a political scientist, is limited almost
> entirely to the federal government. It examines the forms of
> administrative action and the means of their enforcement; the
> relations of the constitutional separation of powers to the devel-
> opment of administrative law in the United States; the review
> of administrative actions by the regular courts; and the role of
> Congress in supervising administration.

Wade, H.W.R. TOWARDS ADMINISTRATIVE JUSTICE. Ann Arbor: University of Michigan Press, 1963. 138 p.
> Five lectures, delivered by Professor Wade of Oxford University
> as the Cooley lectures, in October 1961. While primarily
> based on British administrative law, they contain some compari-
> sons between the British and American institutions.

Woll, Peter, ADMINISTRATIVE LAW. THE INFORMAL PROCESS. Berkeley:
University of California Press, 1963. 203 p.
> The author, a political scientist, investigates the hypothesis that
> the requirements of public policy and speed made administra-
> tive adjudication primarily informal in nature. He discusses the
> development of administrative law, and the role of the adminis-
> trative agencies within our legal system. Attention is concen-
> trated on the following agencies: Interstate Commerce Commis-
> sion; Federal Communications Commission; Securities and Exchange
> Commission; Federal Trade Commission; Civil Aeronautics Board;
> National Labor Relations Board; Internal Revenue Service; Veter-
> ans Administration; and the Bureau of Old-Age and Survivors

Insurance within the Social Security Administration.

GOVERNMENT PUBLICATIONS

Administrative Conference of the United States. Committee on Rulemaking.
IMPROVEMENT IN THE CONDUCT OF FEDERAL RATE PROCEEDINGS. Washington, D.C.: September 18, 1962. 57 p. (Later included in Senate Document
No. 24, 88th Cong., 1st Sess. "Selected Reports of the Administrative Conference of the United States.")
> The Committee on Rulemaking studies the rate proceedings con-
> ducted by five federal regulatory agencies: the Civil Aeronau-
> tics Board, the Federal Communications Commission, the Federal
> Power Commission, the Interstate Commerce Commission and the
> Department of Agriculture. Report is limited to litigated pro-
> ceedings involving the validity of proposed or existing rates to
> the exclusion of charges for government services and subsidy
> determinations. Summarizes various proposals which the Commit-
> tee believed would improve the speed and effectiveness with
> which federal rate agencies perform their responsibilities. Rec-
> ommendations are concerned with four sets of issues: (1) the
> general nature of the hearing which should be accorded in rate
> cases; (2) methods of reducing the number or scope of rate
> proceedings prior to hearing; (3) methods of improving the hear-
> ing itself; and (4) methods of improving the decisional process.
> A concluding section discusses broader proposals relating to
> agency personnel, organization, and effective formulation of
> policy.

LEGAL SERVICES AND PROCEDURE. A REPORT TO THE CONGRESS. Washington, D.C.: Government Printing Office, 1955. 115 p.
> This is a report of the Commission on Organization of the Execu-
> tive Branch of the Government [Hoover Commission] to the Con-
> gress. Parts II and III contain recommendations on procedure in
> the administrative agencies.

REPORT ON LEGAL SERVICES AND PROCEDURE. Prepared for the Commis-
sion on Organization of the Executive Branch of the Government by the Task
Force on Legal Services and Procedure. Washington, D.C.: Government
Printing Office, 1955. 442 p.
> Part III of this report, prepared for the Hoover Commission, deals
> with the administrative agencies, covering, among other things,
> administrative procedure and the status of hearing examiners.

U.S. Congress. House. Committee on Government Operations. SURVEY AND
STUDY OF ADMINISTRATIVE ORGANIZATION, PROCEDURE AND PRACTICE
IN FEDERAL AGENCIES. (85th Cong., 1st Sess.) Committee Print. December 1957. Washington, D.C.: Government Printing Office, 1957. Parts 1 to
11 D.
> In this publication the Committee makes available the agencies'
> own views of their powers, organization, and decision-making
> processes, as reflected in the responses to a questionnaire sent
> out by the Committee. Among the departments and agencies

covered by the report are: Department of Commerce (Part 2); Department of Justice (Part 6); Civil Aeronautics Board and Federal Communications Commission (Part 11A); Federal Power Commission and Federal Trade Commission (Part 11B); Interstate Commerce Commission (Part 11C); Securities and Exchange Commission and the Small Business Administration (Part 11D).

U.S. Congress. House. Committee on Interstate and Foreign Commerce, subcommittee on Legislative Oversight. INDEPENDENT REGULATORY COMMISSIONS. (85th Cong., 2nd sess.) Report No. 2711. Washington, D.C.: Government Printing Office, 1959. 98 p.

This report was based on the hearings which were held in 1958 to survey the work of the Civil Aeronautics Board, the Federal Communications Commission, the Federal Power Commission, the Federal Trade Commission, the Interstate Commerce Commission, and the Securities and Exchange Commission. The report contains recommendations as to legislation in connection with each commission studied and as to administrative action which should be taken by each; and sets out matters requiring further legislative inquiry. It recommends a statutory code of ethics for all federal agencies.

U.S. Congress. House. Committee on Interstate and Foreign Commerce, subcommittee on Legislative Oversight. INVESTIGATION OF REGULATORY COMMISSIONS AND AGENCIES. AN INTERIM REPORT. (86th Cong., 2nd sess.) Report No. 1258. Washington, D.C.: Government Printing Office, 1960. 95 p.

Panel discussion hearings held in June 1959, in which the following participated: members of the Civil Aernautics Board, Federal Communications Commission, Federal Power Commission, Federal Trade Commission, Securities and Exchange Commission, and Interstate Commerce Commission, practitioners before these agencies, members of the regulated industries, representatives of bar associations, trade associations, and of the Federal Trial Examiners' Conference. The highlights of these panel hearings are contained in Appendix C to the report. After these hearings, an Advisory Council of Administrative Problems was set up, composed of representatives from the six principal independent regulatory agencies, the Office of Administrative Procedure of the Department of Justice and the subcommittee staff. The aim of the Council was to produce a body of up-to-date factual information and data to be used in devising proper remedies for some of the recognized deficiencies in the administrative process. Appendix D describes the activities of the Council.

The bulk of the report deals with the adequacy of the law, rules, and policies related to the regulation of radio and television broadcasting, advertising and unfair business practices; and particularly with the rule of the Federal Trade Commission in curbing abuses, such as deceptive quiz shows.

U.S. Congress. House. Committee on Interstate and Foreign Commerce, subcommittee on Legislative Oversight. INDEPENDENT REGULATORY COMMIS-

SIONS. (86th Cong., 2nd sess.) Report No. 2238. Washington, D.C.:
Government Printing Office, 1961. 86 p.
> The report is based on an investigation of the manner in which
> the independent regulatory commissions have functioned. Ex
> parte communications are considered, together with other matters.
> Appendix E lists the publications of the subcommittee.

U.S. Congress. Senate. Subcommittee on Administrative Practice and Procedure of the Committee on the Judiciary. REPORT ON REGULATORY AGEN-
CIES TO THE PRESIDENT-ELECT [Landis Report]. (86th Cong., 2nd sess.)
Committee Print. December 1960. Washington, D.C.: Government Printing Office, 1960. 87 p.
> An appraisal of the various functions and activities of the federal
> regulatory agencies. Makes recommendations with regard to the
> following: (A) delays in the disposition of adjudicatory pro-
> ceedings; (B) costs; (C) personnel; (D) ethical conduct; (E)
> administrative procedures; (F) administrative organization; (G)
> the formulation of policy within the agency; (H) inter-agency
> policy formulation; (I) relationship of the agencies to the execu-
> tive; and (J) relationship of the agencies to the legislative.

U.S. Congress. Senate. Subcommittee on Administrative Practice and Proce-
dure of the Committee on the Judiciary. SELECTED REPORTS OF THE ADMIN-
ISTRATIVE CONFERENCE OF THE UNITED STATES. (88th Cong., 1st sess.)
Document No. 24. Washington, D.C.: Government Printing Office, 1963.
> Contains text of the final report of the Administrative Conference
> of the United States, and selected studies which constituted the
> basis for some of the recommendations made in the final report.

U.S. Department of Justice. ATTORNEY GENERAL'S MANUAL ON THE AD-
MINISTRATIVE PROCEDURE ACT. Prepared by the U.S. Department of Justice.
Leavenworth, Kansas: Federal Prison Industries, Inc. Press, 1947. 139 p.
> A general analysis of the provisions of the Administrative Proce-
> dure Act, intended primarily as a guide to agencies in adjusting
> their procedures to the requirements of the Act.

MISCELLANEOUS

ADMINISTRATIVE LAW REVIEW. Chicago: Administrative Law Section, American Bar Association. Published three times a year.
> Contains articles on various aspects of administrative law, and on
> the administrative agencies.

PIKE AND FISCHER ADMINISTRATIVE LAW. 2nd series. Washington, D.C.:
Pike and Fischer. Current.
> A service which digests and reports cases in the administrative
> law field, keyed to the relevant provisions of the Administrative
> Procedure Act. Cases are reported currently, and then cumulated
> in bound volumes. It covers both court and administrative opin-
> ions.
>
> The Current Material volume, which is supplemented biweekly,
> reports current cases. A Desk Book contains the Federal Admin-

istrative Procedure Act, the Congressional committee reports on it, comments from law reviews, and the 1964 Administrative Conference Act. The rules of practice of the following major federal administrative agencies are also included in the Desk Book: the Civil Aeronautics Board; the Federal Communications Commission; the Federal Power Commission; the Federal Trade Commission; the Interstate Commerce Commission; the National Labor Relations Board; the Post Office Department; and the Securities and Exchange Commission.

A four volume Consolidated Digest was published in 1965, with pocket supplements. It covers cases from the beginning of administrative regulation up through volume 14 of Administrative Law, Second Series (1964). It will be kept up to date with periodical supplements, incorporating later opinions and decisions. All material is keyed to the Administrative Procedure Act of 1946. A Digest Analysis and a Descriptive Word Index facilitate the location of the classification of any particular point.

Section 2

CIVIL AERONAUTICS BOARD

Section 2

CIVIL AERONAUTICS BOARD

The Civil Aeronautics Board provides federal regulation of civil aviation. Its role is twofold: (1) the economic regulation and promotion of air transportation; and (2) investigation and analysis of civil aircraft accidents and promotion of air safety. The Board awards routes to airlines, supervises rates and fares, plays an active role in the establishment and execution of United States policy governing the exchange of air rights with other governments and the working out of intergovernmental problems attendant on airline operations pursuant thereto, strives to achieve air safety, and recommends legislation necessary to implement its work.

TEXTS

Billyou, de Forest. AIR LAW. New York: Ad Press, 1964. 674 p.
    Largely a collection of source material, arranged topically.
    Bibliographical notes are included for the various topics, but
    there is no general bibliography.

Caves, Richard E. AIR TRANSPORT AND ITS REGULATORS. AN INDUSTRY
STUDY. Cambridge: Harvard University Press, 1962. 479 p.
    This study tries to analyze the market structure, conduct and
    performance of the United States domestic passenger airlines. It
    examines the detailed regulation of the industry's day-to-day
    business decisions by the Civil Aeronautics Board, and tries to
    relate the airlines' market conduct and performance both to the
    regulatory pattern and to the economic elements of market structure.
    Part I deals with market structure; part II, with public regulation;
    part III, with market conduct; and part IV, with market performance.

Cherington, Paul W. AIRLINE PRICE POLICY. A STUDY OF DOMESTIC
AIRLINE PASSENGER FARES. Boston: Division of Research, Graduate School
of Business Administration, Harvard University, 1958. 471 p.
    A study of some of the factors which affect airline management
    decisions as to what prices should be charged the traveling pub-
    lic, and of the problems which are encountered in translating
    these decisions into actual tariffs. Primary attention is focused
    on individual firms and the policy formation process within that

firm. Added to the case studies is a collection of facts on carriers and industry trends which are necessary for pricing decisions, some statistical, some descriptive. It deals almost exclusively with domestic trunkline carriers.

Davies, R.E.G. A HISTORY OF THE WORLD'S AIRLINES. London: Oxford University Press, 1964. 591 p.
  An account of the world's air carriers which fills in the gap since the publication of Oliver Lissitzyn's International Air Transport and National Policy, published in 1942. It is concerned with the airline structures, the aircraft, and the operational results of the airlines. The author also touches on some of the personalities who have helped to develop the industry.

Fixel, Rowland W. THE LAW OF AVIATION. 3rd ed. Charlottesville, Virginia: Michie, 1948. 550 p.
  The author has tried to give the legal profession a well-rounded presentation of air law in all its ramifications, keeping in mind the necessity of making it a useful working tool. Long quotations from court decisions and theorizing on what the law should be, have not been generally included.

Frederick, John H. COMMERCIAL AIR TRANSPORTATION. 5th ed. Homewood, Illinois: Irwin, 1961. 497 p.
  This text discusses regulatory legislation, Civil Aeronautics Board policies, safety in air transportation, and international air transportation policy of the United States.

Guandolo, John. TRANSPORTATION LAW. Dubuque, Iowa: W.C. Brown, 1965. 864 p.
  A discussion of the principles of law established by the Interstate Commerce Commission and the courts under the Interstate Commerce Act and related acts; by the Civil Aeronautics Board and the courts under the Federal Aviation Act and related acts; and by the Federal Maritime Commission and the courts under the Shipping Act and related acts.

  Gives full coverage to the application of the antitrust laws to common carriers.

  The book is divided into the principal subject headings under which various laws applying to each mode of transportation can be found.

  Designed to be used for a course in transportation law at the law school level, and as a primary reference for administrative law and transportation courses.

Keyes, Lucile Sheppard. FEDERAL CONTROL OF ENTRY INTO AIR TRANSPORTATION. Cambridge: Harvard University Press, 1951. 405 p.
  The purpose of this study is to analyze and evaluate the policies of the federal government toward the entry and exit of firms engaged in the air transportation business, in terms of economic performance. It tries to evaluate these policies from the point of view of their effect on the functioning of the controlled markets.

Locklin, David Philip. ECONOMICS OF TRANSPORTATION. 6th ed.
Homewood, Illinois: Irwin, 1966. 882 p.
> This work emphasizes the economic aspects of transportation. It
> covers railroad, water, and pipeline transport, with expanded
> coverage of highway and air transport.

MacIntyre, Malcolm A. COMPETITIVE PRIVATE ENTERPRISE UNDER GOV-
ERNMENT REGULATION. New York: New York University, 1964. 61 p.
> The author of this little book was formerly president of Eastern
> Air Lines. It is a reprint of the Charles C. Moskowitz lectures
> which he delivered at New York University.

> The author sets forth the story of the airline industry in the
> United States, touching on such areas as the effects of overcompe-
> tition, the role of the governmental regulatory agencies, and
> other problems facing the industry.

Nicholson, Joseph L. AIR TRANSPORTATION MANAGEMENT, ITS PRACTICES
AND POLICIES. New York: Wiley, 1951. 446 p.
> This book was written to supply information to those who look to
> the airlines for a career, for investment, or for a rapid means of
> transportation. Its object is to present a balanced economic
> analysis of the industry's policies, as well as those of the federal
> government. Chapter 8 deals with federal regulation.

Phillips, Charles F., Jr. THE ECONOMICS OF REGULATION. THEORY AND
PRACTICE IN THE TRANSPORTATION AND PUBLIC UTILITY INDUSTRIES.
Homewood, Illinois: Irwin, 1965. 783 p.
> This book resulted from a one semester course given by the au-
> thor at Washington and Lee University. It concentrates on the
> theory and practice of regulation, and on current regulatory
> problems.

> Topics discussed are: the economic and legal concepts of public
> regulation; the independent regulatory commissions; accounting
> and financial control; operating costs; the rate base; rate of re-
> turn; rate structure; service and safety regulation; regulation of
> transportation industries; public policy; and transportation.

Richmond, Samuel B. REGULATION AND COMPETITION IN AIR TRANSPOR-
TATION. New York: Columbia University Press, 1961. 309 p.
> Covers in detail much of the legal, economic and historical
> analysis involved in dealing with the question of competition
> and regulation.

Speiser, Stuart M. LAWYERS AVIATION HANDBOOK. Rochester: Lawyers
Co-operative, 1964. 576 p.
> A guide to cases, statutes, forms, regulations and law reviews.

Speiser, Stuart M. SPEISER'S AVIATION LAW GUIDE. 1962-1963 edition.
Indianapolis: Bobbs-Merrill, 1962. 264 p.

A checklist of statutes, regulations, administrative organizations, case law, law review articles, and the industry itself. Citations are given to federal statutes and regulations concerned with the aviation industry. The major part of the guide consists of a topical index to cases in the field, with their citations. A very small section gives citations to law review articles, and an even smaller section lists scheduled air carriers and principal aviation, engine, helicopter, and propeller manufacturers.

Wilson, G. Lloyd and Bryan, Leslie A. AIR TRANSPORTATION. New York: Prentice-Hall, 1949. 665 p.

The material in this volume has been used over a period of years in undergraduate and graduate courses in the economic aspects of air transportation. Part I gives the background of the development of aviation and air transportation; part II surveys the organization, services, and charges of the commercial air transportation enterprises; and part III is devoted to the regulation of air transportation and aviation by local, state and federal agencies of the government, and to the regulation of international air transportation.

Wolfe, Thomas. AIR TRANSPORTATION, TRAFFIC AND MANAGEMENT. New York: McGraw-Hill, 1950. 725 p.

This work covers the history and general framework of air transportation, government regulation and organizations, economics of air transportation, general organization of airlines, technical traffic procedures, and sales. It is designed to give an over-all picture of the industry.

GOVERNMENT PUBLICATIONS

Administrative Conference of the United States. Committee on Licenses and Authorizations. LICENSING OF DOMESTIC AIR TRANSPORTATION BY THE CIVIL AERONAUTICS BOARD, prepared by William K. Jones. Washington, D.C.: September 1962. 180 p.

This study is concerned with the licensing of domestic air transport operations by the Civil Aeronautics Board. It begins with a consideration of the substantive policies and economic factors relating to airline licensing--the needs which the licensing process must fulfill and the conditions under which it must operate. It then takes up the way in which the process is organized, the successive steps in processing formal route cases, and the instances in which operating authority is granted pursuant to informal procedures. The remainder of the study is devoted to proposals to improve the licensing process.

AIR CARRIER FINANCIAL STATISTICS. Washington, D.C.: Civil Aeronautics Board. Quarterly.

Based on CAB Form 41 reports. Compares current quarter and 12-month financial data with same periods of prior year.

ALL ECONOMIC ORDERS AND OPINIONS. Washington, D.C.: Civil Aeronautics Board. Weekly.

In addition to subject matter described in annotation under Economic Opinions below, these releases consist of orders on exemption, intervention, airport notices, interlocking relationships, agreements, mail rates, charters, etc. Selected orders are subsequently included in bound volumes of Board Reports because of precedent involved or policy pronouncements of the board.

Civil Aeronautics Board. AERONAUTICAL STATUTES AND RELATED MATERIAL. Washington, D.C.: Government Printing Office, 1963. 436 p.
> Contains the Federal Aviation Act of 1958 and other provisions relating to civil aeronautics, compiled by the Office of the General Counsel of the Civil Aeronautics Board.

Civil Aeronautics Board. ANNUAL REPORTS. Washington, D.C. Government Printing Office. 1938-
> Summarize the work of the year.

Civil Aeronautics Board. CUMULATIVE INDEX DIGEST, CIVIL AERONAUTICS BOARD REPORTS. Washington, D.C.: Government Printing Office, 1963. 1218 p.
> Indexes economic cases in volumes 1-20 of the Civil Aeronautics Board Reports, covering August 1938 to May 1955.

Civil Aeronautics Board. HANDBOOK OF AIRLINE STATISTICS, 1963 edition. Washington, D.C.: Government Printing Office, April 1964. Reissued and updated every two years.
> Data are provided for individual carriers, 1953-1962; and for carrier groups, 1926-1962. (Traffic, finances, aircraft, chronologies of events, early historical data, glossary of air transport terms, jet penetration).

Civil Aeronautics Board. REGULATIONS. Washington, D.C.: Government Printing Office, November 1, 1963. Current.
> Covers economic regulations (parts 200 to 299), procedural regulations (parts 300 to 311), safety investigation regulations (part 320), special regulations (parts 375, 376, 377, 379), organization regulations (parts 385, 386, 389), and policy statements (part 399).

Civil Aeronautics Board. REPORTS. Washington, D.C.: Government Printing Office. Vol. 1-   , 1938-
> Bound volumes of Civil Aeronautics Board decisions, opinions, and selected orders in economic and safety proceedings.

Civil Aeronautics Board. SUBSIDY FOR UNITED STATES CERTIFICATED CARRIERS. Washington, D.C.: Government Printing Office. Annual.
> A report of the Board to the Congress and the public which shows tabulations of the subsidy accruing for individual carriers, carriers groups, and the industry for each fiscal year since the formal separation of subsidy and service mail pay (1954) through the current fiscal year, plus one projected year.
>
> Text of the report includes a summary of the purpose of the subsidy, the process of determination of the subsidy; and details the bases employed in preparing all information contained in the report.

Civil Aeronautics Board. UNIFORM SYSTEM OF ACCOUNTS AND REPORTS FOR CERTIFICATED ROUTE AIR CARRIERS IN ACCORDANCE WITH SECTION 407 OF THE FEDERAL AVIATION ACT. Washington, D.C.: Government Printing Office, 1961. 113 p. Supplemented currently.

> Contains Part 241 of the Civil Aeronautics Board's Economic Regulations, comprising the Uniform System of Accounts and Reports for Certificated Route Air Carriers, with amendments as adopted by the Board to June 1, 1961.
>
> This system of accounts and reports is applicable to all certificated route air carriers holding Certificates of Public Convenience and Necessity, subject to the provisions of the Federal Aviation Act of 1958, as amended.

Civil Aeronautics Board. WEEKLY SUMMARY OF ORDERS AND REGULATIONS. Washington, D.C.: Publications Section. Current.

> Available on a yearly subscription basis from the publications section of the Civil Aeronautics Board.

ECONOMIC OPINIONS. Washington, D.C.: Civil Aeronautics Board. Weekly.

> These releases set forth matters considered, findings, conclusions, and decisions; usually include an order in such cases as route awards to domestic and foreign air carriers, mergers, mail rates, enforcement, and policy. Subsequently included in bound volumes of Board Reports.

INITIAL AND RECOMMENDED ECONOMIC DECISIONS OF EXAMINERS. Washington, D.C.: Civil Aeronautics Board.

> These releases set forth matters considered by the examiner, his findings, conclusions, and decisions in such cases as route awards to domestic and foreign air carriers, mergers, mail rates, enforcement, and policy. These initial and recommended decisions may subsequently become finalized, in whole or in part, as the decision of the board.

Federal Aviation Agency. REPORT OF THE TASK FORCE ON NATIONAL AVIATION GOALS. PROJECT HORIZON. Washington, D.C.: Government Printing Office, September 1961. 239 p.

> This report was prepared at the request of President Kennedy. It sets out goals for the period 1961-70, with recommendations as to how they can be attained. The report was prepared by a task force, supplemented by an Advisory Board composed of leaders in the aviation community, and a Technical Advisory Committee. It discusses the various types of air vehicles, airports, international aviation, the aircraft manufacturing industry, the financial posture of airlines, economic regulation of airlines, government promotion and subsidy, air carrier marketing, economics of air traffic control, safety, research and development, civil-military relations, labor-management relations, and education. The report is on a broad survey basis rather than on a technical one.

Hector, Louis J. PROBLEMS OF THE CAB AND THE INDEPENDENT REGULATORY COMMISSIONS. Washington, D.C.: September 10, 1959. 76 p.

Memorandum to the President of the United States by resigning member of the Civil Aeronautics Board in support of the following recommendations: 1. Transfer of policy-making, planning and administration from the Civil Aeronautics Board to an executive agency, such as the Department of Commerce, the Federal Aviation Agency, or a new Department of Transportation; 2. Transfer of the judicial and appellate duties of the Civil Aeronautics Board to an administrative court; 3. Transfer of the duties of investigation and prosecution to an executive agency such as the Department of Justice.

LIST OF PUBLICATIONS. Washington, D.C.: Civil Aeronautics Board. Annual.
   Lists publications available from the board, from the Government Printing Office and from the Air Transport Association.

LIST OF U.S. AIR CARRIERS. Washington, D.C.: Civil Aeronautics Board. Semiannual.
   Lists certificated and supplemental air carriers and airfreight forwarders, and lists for each its authorization, president, and address.

PREHEARING CONFERENCE REPORTS. Washington, D.C.: Civil Aeronautics Board. Irregular.
   Reports of conference on procedural steps to be followed in subsequent conduct of proceedings. Defines the issues, gives an account of the results of the conference, specifies a schedule for the exchange of initial and rebuttal exhibits, and the date for hearing. The prehearing conference report, under the rules, constitutes the official account of the conference and controls the subsequent course of the proceeding.

PRESS RELEASES. Washington, D.C.: Civil Aeronautics Board. Irregular.
   Summarize matters pertaining to the Board.

SAFETY ENFORCEMENT OPINIONS AND ORDERS. Washington, D.C.: Civil Aeronautics Board.
   These releases set forth opinions and orders of the Civil Aeronautics Board after review on appeal from action of the administrator involving suspension, revocation, modification, or denial of airman and/or air safety certificates. Subsequently included in bound volumes of Board Reports.

WEEKLY SUMMARY OF ORDERS AND REGULATIONS. Washington, D.C.: Civil Aeronautics Board. Weekly.
   Lists serial number of order or regulation, docket or agreement number, brief description, and the adopted or effective date.

U.S. Congress. House. Committee on the Judiciary, Antitrust Subcommittee. THE AIRLINES INDUSTRY. (85th Cong., 2nd sess.) Report No. 1328. Washington, D.C.: Government Printing Office, 1957. 358 p.
   This report is derived from hearings which began on February 27, 1956, and continued through June 15, 1956, during which representatives from the Civil Aeronautics Board, the Department of Justice and the Comptroller General of the United States, as well as representatives

from both certificated and non-scheduled carriers, and trade association spokesmen, were heard. They were held in response to complaints about the administration of the Civil Aeronautics Act by the Civil Aeronautics Board. The airline industry was considered a good subject for a case study of the role of competition in regulated industries, since airline regulation typifies administrative control of industrial enterprise through control of prices, regulation of entry, supervision of consolidations, and administrative inspection of records. The report takes up the present structure of the industry, the regulators, competition and entry, the Air Transport Association of America, travel agents, the International Air Transport Association, and Pan American World Airways.

U.S. Congress. Senate. Commerce Committee. AIR LAWS AND TREATIES OF THE WORLD. (89th Cong., 1st Sess.) Committee Print. Washington, D.C.: Government Printing Office, 1965. 3 vols.
This publication was compiled by the staff of the Law Library of the Library of Congress: William S. Strauss, editor-in-chief and compiler; William J. Klima, associate editor; and Ivan Sipkov, assistant editor. The text is in English and other languages. Volume 1 gives the contents for all three volumes; and volume 3, the index.

U.S. Congress. Senate. Commerce Committee. AVIATION STUDY. (83rd Cong., 2nd Sess.) Senate Doc. No. 163. Washington, D.C.: Government Printing Office, 1954. 150 p.
This study presents a detailed analysis of the hearings held from April 6 through July 22, 1954, on Senate bill 2647, to revise the Civil Aeronautics Act of 1938. It also submits a further revised substitute for the bill. The report was submitted for the guidance of the 84th Congress, taking up government organization and its effect on civil aviation; economic regulation; safety regulation; and international agreements and international air transportation.

U.S. Congress. Senate. Subcommittee on Monopoly. Select Committee on Small Business. THE ROLE OF COMPETITION IN COMMERCIAL AIR TRANSPORTATION. (82nd Cong., 2nd Sess.) Subcommittee Print. Washington, D.C.: Government Printing Office, 1952. 54 p.
Prepared by the Civil Aeronautics Board. Sets forth the Civil Aeronautics Board's views and policies, with respect to competition in the aviation industry and the entry of new companies into this field, within limitations. The Board traces the historical development of the air transport system in the United States.

U.S. Congress. Senate. Select Committee on Small Business. MATERIALS RELATIVE TO COMPETITION IN THE REGULATED CIVIL AVIATION INDUSTRY. (84th Cong., 2nd Sess.) Committee Print. April 18, 1956. Washington, D.C.: Government Printing Office, 1956. 228 p.
This document contains the answers of the Civil Aeronautics Board to a number of questions presented to it by the committee. The first question was on the significant changes in the airline industry since the Board submitted its report on The Role of Competition in

Commercial Air Transportation in 1952. Other questions were concerned with the Board's interpretation of "public convenience and necessity" as used in the Civil Aeronautics Act; what weight the board assigns to competition as a component of the public interest; how the board defines effective competition, etc.
Part III contains 1955 decisions and opinions of the Civil Aeronautics Board in six cases.

MISCELLANEOUS

American Bar Association. Section of Public Utility Law. ANNUAL REPORT. Chicago.

> Contains articles and reviews of the year's developments in the field of public utilities, which takes in air transportation.

Blaisdell, Ruth F., et al. SOURCES OF INFORMATION IN TRANSPORTATION. Chicago: Northwestern University Press, 1964. 262 p.

> A publication intended to enable the user to find the principle sources of information in several fields of transportation. It should be of use to both beginners and candidates for the doctoral degree, as well as to those who seek practical day-to-day answers to operating problems.

> Lists are presented under the following headings, each compiled by a librarian who is a specialist in the field: general sources, highways, motor carriers, metropolitan transportation, railroads, pipelines, merchant marine, inland waterways, air transportation, and missiles and rockets.

Commerce Clearing House, Inc. AVIATION LAW REPORTER. 3 vols. Loose-leaf. Current.

> Volume 1 contains the federal statutes and regulations; volume 1-A, the Federal Aviation Act, annotated, and current aviation cases; volume 2, additional aviation cases. This service also reports new developments in the field, lists state laws, and has sections on international aviation law.

HAWKINS INDEX-DIGEST-ANALYSIS TO CIVIL AERONAUTICS BOARD REPORTS. Washington, D.C.: Hawkins Publishing Co., 1965. Current.

> A service which contains a table of cases, docket citator, decision citer and definitions, words and phrases section covering all volumes of Civil Aeronautics Board reports which have been published. A topic-digest section covers both printed and mimeographed reports and orders since volume 34. This section will eventually cover the digest material subsequent to the Civil Aeronautics Board's cumulative index-digest, as well as all mimeographed reports and orders.

> A "Current Cases" section will cover mimeographed opinions and orders of the Board, before they are published in the printed volumes.

Government Printing Office. AVIATION. PRICE LIST 79. Washington, D.C.: October 1963. 36 p.

> Lists publications in the field of aviation available from the Government Printing Office. Covers civil and naval aviation, air force, National Aeronautics and Space Administration, Civil Aeronautics Board, Federal Aviation Agency, and technical reports on space.

Institute of Air and Space Law, McGill University. CATALOGUE OF AIR AND SPACE LAW MATERIALS. Montreal: July 1, 1965. 103 p.

> A listing of the materials available at the Institute's library. The listings are in the following categories: books, theses, term papers and pamphlets; documents; and serial publications.

McKinsey and Company, Inc. INCREASING THE EFFECTIVENESS OF THE CIVIL AERONAUTICS BOARD. Washington, D.C.: October 27, 1960.

> A report submitted to the Bureau of the Budget by this firm of management consultants. The report is supported by five appendices covering: the decision-making processes of the Civil Aeronautics Board; policy making and planning in the Civil Aeronautics Board; organization of the Board and its immediate staff; improving organization and operations in the bureaus and offices; and increasing the effectiveness of administrative support.

National Association of Railroad and Utilities Commissioners. PROCEEDINGS. Washington, D.C. Annual.

> Papers presented at the annual meetings of the association, which consists of commissioners on both the federal and state level, who head commissions regulating public utilities. On the federal level, the Interstate Commerce Commission, the Federal Communications Commission, the Federal Power Commission, the Securities and Exchange Commission, and the Civil Aeronautics Board are represented.

UNITED STATES AVIATION REPORTS. Baltimore: United States Aviation Reports. Vol. 1- , 1928- .

> These volumes contain an index of cases by jurisdictions, a table of cases, decisions of both federal and state courts in full text and in summary, statutes and regulations, treaties and international agreements. A cumulative digest covers 1922-1944. This includes a digest of state legislation. A second cumulative digest covers 1945-1952; and a third, 1953-1960. The third digest contains a subject index.

WORLD AIRLINE RECORD. 6th ed. Chicago: Roadcap & Associates, 1965. 496 p.

> Gives statistical and analytical information on 306 airlines. Each airline is analyzed under the following major headings: route map; management; ownership (control); operations; competition; regulation; traffic trends; subsidy; equipment; future planning; history; comment (analysis); revenues; earnings; and statistical summary.

CIVIL AERONAUTICS BOARD

WORLD AVIATION DIRECTORY. Washington, D.C.: American Aviation
Publications. Semi-annual.
Lists aviation companies and officials, covering the United States,
Canada, Europe, Central and South America, Africa and the
Middle East, Australasia, and Asia. Also included are primary
aircraft and missile manufacturers, with their addresses and officers; manufacturers and distributors of equipment; aviation fuel
and oil companies; aviation insurance, credit, and financing;
distributors, maintenance, overhaul, export and foreign services;
ferrying and airport ground services; consultants and special services; U.S. terminal airports; repair stations, mechanics' schools
and airman agency flying and ground schools; U.S. Army schools,
airline training schools; and major caterers to airlines and business aircraft. It also lists organizations, associations, and non-
profit research groups; foreign diplomatic representatives; and
aviation missions in the United States. A separate section constitutes a Buyers' Guide, listing products and companies.

PERIODICALS

AIR TRANSPORTATION. New York: Import Publications, Inc. Monthly.
Covers the entire air cargo industry for the benefit of all those
engaged in shipping and handling domestic and international air
freight, air express, and air parcel post. Contains articles and
news features.

AMERICAN AVIATION. Washington, D.C.: American Aviation Publications,
Inc. Monthly.
Contains articles on new developments in the field of aviation,
as well as news items.

AVIATION DAILY, INCLUDING INTERNATIONAL AVIATION. Washington,
D.C.: American Aviation Publications. Daily except Saturday, Sunday and
holidays.
Immediate notification of the latest developments in the field, on
all levels - governmental, courts and airlines.

AVIATION WEEK & SPACE TECHNOLOGY. New York: McGraw-Hill.
Weekly, with an additional issue in December.
Short articles on air transport, space technology, aeronautical
engineering, and other topics. Contains features entitled "Washington Roundup," "News Digest," and "Aerospace Calendar."

THE JOURNAL OF AIR LAW AND COMMERCE. Dallas: Southern Methodist
Law School. Quarterly. Vol. 1- , 1930-
Contains articles, book reviews, reports on current legislation
and decisions.

TRAFFIC WORLD. Washington, D.C.: The Traffic Service Corp. Weekly.
Very short articles and news items on the Interstate Commerce
Commission and the Maritime Administration, as well as the Civil
Aeronautics Board. It summarizes the work of these agencies
during the preceding week, listing orders issued, hearings, etc.,
as well as news items.

39

TRANSPORTATION BUSINESS REPORT. Washington, D.C.: Federal Publications. Biweekly.

A four page report designed for transportation industry executives, their legal and technical representatives, and government officials. It covers significant developments, present and prospective, and contains briefings on the effects of those developments on carriers and their users. Railroads, motor carriers, airlines, barge lines, and pipelines are covered. Sources used for information are the regulatory agencies of the federal government (Interstate Commerce Commission, Civil Aeronautics Board, and Federal Aviation Agency); the federal departments concerned with transportation, state planning agencies, the courts, Congress, and top men in government and industry.

TRADE ASSOCIATIONS

The Air Transport Association of America, 1000 Connecticut Avenue, N.W., Washington 6, D.C. is a trade association formed by the major air mail carriers in 1934 to deal with their mutual problems on a cooperative basis. It is now composed of United States airlines certified by the Civil Aeronautics Board for scheduled service over regularly established routes.

Primarily a service organization, it employs experts in traffic and sales, engineering, economics, business, and public relations.

It issues a quarterly public relations release on financial and traffic statistics for the various segments of the airline industry, and also publishes a series of reports on the large irregular air carriers, using material furnished to the Civil Aeronautics Board. In addition, it has issued an ATA manual on airports; a monthly Air Transport Advisory, which is a factual newsletter; a monthly Air Transport News; and an annual Air Transport Facts and Figures, showing statistically the growth of commercial air transportation in the United States.

The International Air Transport Association is a private trade organization of the scheduled international air carriers, designed primarily to provide a method for its members to take joint action with respect to rates and fares, and to standardize operational practices and procedures. Its members are air carriers that have been authorized to operate scheduled international services by countries eligible for membership in the International Civil Aviation Organization. It was incorporated under a Canadian Act of Parliament in 1945, and its main office is in Montreal. The Civil Aeronautics Board has approved the IATA's articles of association, and has periodically approved joint agreements promulgated by IATA's members which establish worldwide rates and fares for international air transportation. The Board's approval of these agreements confers immunity under the antitrust laws to the airlines that participate.

The Civil Aeronautics Board has no direct authority over rates and fares of United States carriers engaged in international air transportation, being limited to the removal of discrimination, after a hearing.

Section 3

NTITRUST DIVISION OF THE DEPARTMENT OF
STICE AND THE FEDERAL TRADE COMMISSION

Section 3

ANTITRUST DIVISION OF THE DEPARTMENT OF JUSTICE AND THE FEDERAL TRADE COMMISSION

In 1890 the Sherman Antitrust Act became law. The Act declared illegal every contract, combination or conspiracy in restraint of trade or commerce among the states. It also condemned attempts to monopolize any part of this trade and provided that victims of such illegality could bring civil suits to recover triple the amount of damages they had suffered.

In 1914 Congress enacted two laws: the Federal Trade Commission Act, which created an agency to proceed in the public interest against unfair methods of competition in commerce, and the Clayton Act which prohibited certain discriminatory and acquisitive practices where the effect could be shown to suppress competition.

Over the years, there have been many amendments to the antitrust laws. Of great significance was the Robinson-Patman Act passed in 1936 which prohibited price and related discrimination.

The Antitrust Division of the Department of Justice is responsible for enforcing federal antitrust statutes, and engages in both criminal and civil litigation. The overall objective of the Antitrust Division is to ensure that artificial restraints interposed by private business do not hamper our system of free enterprise.

The Federal Trade Commission is also charged with the responsibility of administering and enforcing laws in the field of antitrust. However, it has no punitive authority; its function is to prevent illegal acts through cease-and-desist orders and other means. Its basic purpose, that of keeping competition both free and fair, finds its primary expression in the Federal Trade Commission Act, as amended, and in four sections of the Clayton Act, as amended, including Section 2 (price discrimination) and Section 7 (mergers). The Commission also has the duty of investigating and reporting economic problems and corporate activity, particularly in relation to the antitrust laws and in aid of legislation.

Because of the similarity of their objectives - the maintenance of a free and competitive economy through the enforcement of the antitrust laws - the editors have included both the Antitrust Division of the Department of Justice and the Federal Trade Commission in one section.

ANTITRUST DIVISION

BASIC MATERIALS

The literature in the field of antitrust law is so voluminous that it may be helpful to point out some standard works to serve as starting points. All are fully described in the bibliography which follows.

No research in antitrust would be complete without consulting the REPORT OF THE ATTORNEY GENERAL'S NATIONAL COMMITTEE TO STUDY THE ANTITRUST LAWS.

Three introductory books, designed to orient the newcomer in the field, are: ANTITRUST FUNDAMENTALS by Thompson and Brady; AN ANTITRUST PRIMER by Kintner; and UNDERSTANDING THE ANTITRUST LAWS by Van Cise.

For general works, Oppenheim's CASES ON FEDERAL ANTITRUST LAW and Handler's CASES ON TRADE REGULATION are excellent.

Recommended materials on the Robinson–Patman Act are Rowe on PRICE DISCRIMINATION UNDER THE ROBINSON–PATMAN ACT, Austin on PRICE DISCRIMINATION AND RELATED PROBLEMS UNDER THE ROBINSON–PAT-MAN ACT, and Patman's COMPLETE GUIDE TO THE ROBINSON–PATMAN ACT.

For unfair competition, consult Callman on TRADEMARKS AND UNFAIR COMPETITION, Oppenheim on UNFAIR TRADE PRACTICES, and Handler on TRADE REGULATION.

To keep abreast of developments in the field, the ANTITRUST AND TRADE REGULATION REPORT published by The Bureau of National Affairs, Inc., and the reports for the TRADE REGULATION REPORTER published by Commerce Clearing House, Inc., should be checked each week.

Each year Milton Handler summarizes developments in the antitrust field in the October issue of THE RECORD OF THE ASSOCIATION OF THE BAR OF THE CITY OF NEW YORK.

The New York State Bar Association conducts an annual symposium on selected aspects of the antitrust law, the proceedings of which are published by Commerce Clearing House, Inc.

Twice a year the Antitrust Section of the American Bar Association issues a publication containing articles on antitrust.

The economics of governmental policies toward business is well covered by the following general works in that area: PUBLIC POLICIES TOWARD BUSI-NESS by Wilcox; GOVERNMENT AND BUSINESS by Mund; PUBLIC REGULA-TION OF BUSINESS by Pegrum; and BUSINESS, GOVERNMENT AND PUBLIC POLICY by Isaacs and Slesinger.

Some of the classic contributions dealing with the specific area of price theory include: THE ECONOMICS OF IMPERFECT COMPETITION by Robinson; THE THEORY OF MONOPOLISTIC COMPETITION by Chamberlin; and THE THEORY OF PRICE by Stigler.

Frequently, an excellent paper on the subject of economic policy and business appears in the AMERICAN ECONOMIC REVIEW, the QUARTERLY JOURNAL OF ECONOMICS, and the JOURNAL OF POLITICAL ECONOMY. THE JOURNAL OF ECONOMIC ABSTRACTS is a good source for the contents of many learned journals on economics published throughout the world.

TEXTS

Abbott, Lawrence. QUALITY AND COMPETITION; AN ESSAY IN ECO-NOMIC THEORY. New York: Columbia University Press, 1955. 229 p.
   The book's primary objective is to work out a theory of quality determination under competitive conditions.

Adams, Walter and Gray, Horace M. MONOPOLY IN AMERICA: THE GOV-ERNMENT AS PROMOTER. New York: Macmillan, 1955. 221 p.
   The major contribution of the authors is in pointing out how gov-ernment actually fosters monopoly, quasi-monopoly, and imper-fect competition by its policies. It does this in part in the case of the highways, the air waves, and the air space, by parcelling out the right to use these publicly owned facilities to certain favored trucking, broadcasting, telecasting, and aviation lines through the grant of certificates of convenience and necessity to some and the denial of such to others.

   Messrs. Adams and Gray call for a return to fundamentals. They demand that the government should cease favoring the giants, and take affirmative steps to develop a greater degree of competition.

Adams, George P., Jr. COMPETITIVE ECONOMIC SYSTEMS. New York: Thomas Y. Crowell Co., 1955. 516 p.

Adams, Walter, ed. THE STRUCTURE OF AMERICAN INDUSTRY: SOME CASE STUDIES. 3rd ed. New York: Macmillan, 1961. 603 p.
   An examination of the problems of competition and monopoly in a cross section of American industry. Includes individual indus-try studies in the light of recent antitrust cases and major Con-gressional investigations. Among the industries covered are the residential construction industry, the steel industry, the alumi-num industry, the chemical industry, the petroleum industry, the automobile industry, the metal container industry and the airlines industry.

Adelman, Morris. A & P: A STUDY IN PRICE-COST BEHAVIOR AND PUBLIC POLICY. (Harvard Economic Studies, Vol. 113). Cambridge: Harvard Uni-versity Press, 1959. 537 p.
   The basic material was the Transcript of Record and some 5200 exhibits in the case of U.S. v. The New York Great Atlantic and Pacific Tea Co.

Allen, C.L., et al. PRICES, INCOME, AND PUBLIC POLICY. 2nd ed. New York: McGraw-Hill, 1959. 501 p.

Allen, Frederick L. THE BIG CHANGE: AMERICA TRANSFORMS ITSELF, 1900-1950. New York: Harper, 1952. 308 p.

American Bar Association. Section of Antitrust Law. AN ANTITRUST HAND-BOOK. Chicago: 1958. 581 p.
> Covers fundamental phases of antitrust law including problems and solutions, substantive, procedural, and remedial aspects of the antitrust laws.

American Bar Association. Section of Antitrust Law. CONFERENCE ON ANTITRUST AND THE EUROPEAN COMMUNITIES. Proceedings held in Brussels, September 23-25, and Luxembourg, September 25-26, 1963. Chicago: n.d. 290 p.
> Because the American lawyer went to Europe to learn from his European brother, the principal participants in the meeting were European. These came from all of the six member countries and the United Kingdom, as well as from the executive and judicial agencies of the communities. As the high quality of the papers in this volume attests, the European specialists in antitrust gave generously of their time and intellect to present just as comprehensive and as detailed a discussion of antitrust problems under the treaties of the European communities as four days would allow.

American Bar Association. Section of Antitrust Law. JURY INSTRUCTIONS IN CRIMINAL ANTITRUST CASES. Chicago: 1965. 537 p.
> Beginning with the TRENTON POTTERIES case in 1923, when the Supreme Court adopted a per se rule as to price-fixing, the volume contains approximately half of the charges to juries in Sherman Antitrust Act cases. Covers most of the instructions which have been reviewed on appeal. Also included are a statement of the charge in the indictment, the verdict and judgment entered, the sentence imposed, and citations to reported opinions on appeals from final judgments.

American Bar Association. Section of Antitrust Law. MERGER CASE DIGEST. Chicago: 1964. 429 p. (Supplemented)
> A digest of 143 individual merger cases instituted by the Department of Justice and the Federal Trade Commission under Section Seven of the Clayton Act from 1914 through January 1, 1963.

American Bar Association. Section of Antitrust Law. NEW FRONTIERS IN SECTION 7 ENFORCEMENT AND JOINT VENTURES IN THE SHERMAN ACT. Two panel discussions. Chicago: August 11, 1963. 41 p.
> A report of the discussions on the topics, with footnotes to cases and law review articles.

American Bar Association. Section of Antitrust Law. REPORT OF THE COMMITTEE ON PRACTICE AND PROCEDURE IN THE TRIAL OF ANTITRUST CASES. May 1, 1954. New York: 155 p.
> This report does not attempt to set down any one procedure. It is, rather, a statement of different procedural techniques that

have been worked out to deal with the great variety of problems
that are encountered in these cases.

American Bar Association. Section of Antitrust Law. STREAMLINING THE
BIG CASE. New York: 40 p.
> Report of special committee of the section. September 15, 1958.

American Bar Association. Section of Antitrust Law. Subcommittee of Section
7 of the Clayton Act. IMPLICATIONS OF BROWN SHOE FOR MERGER LAW
AND ENFORCEMENT. Chicago. 89 p.
> Proceedings held August 5, 1962 in San Francisco.

American Enterprise Institute for Public Policy Research. PRICING POWER AND
"ADMINISTRATIVE" INFLATION, CONCEPTS, FACTS AND POLICY IMPLI-
CATIONS. Washington, D.C.: American Enterprise Institute, 1962. 63 p.
> Economic evaluation of the "administered price" doctrine.

American Fair Trade Council. DIGEST OF FAIR TRADE DECISIONS. Gary,
Ind: 1955. 93 p.

American Management Association. COMPETITIVE PRICING; POLICIES,
PRACTICES AND LEGAL CONSIDERATIONS. New York: 1958. 123 p.

American Management Association. CORPORATE MERGERS AND ACQUISI-
TIONS; BASIC FINANCIAL, LEGAL AND POLICY ASPECTS. New York:
1958. 178 p.

American Management Association. LEGAL, FINANCIAL, AND TAX ASPECTS
OF MERGERS AND ACQUISITIONS: WITH A PAPER ON THE ECONOMIC
SIGNIFICANCE OF THE CURRENT WAVE OF MERGERS. (Its Financial Man-
agement Series, No. 114) New York: 1957. 90 p.
> Material presented at the Special Financial Management Confer-
> ence of the American Management Association, held at the
> Hotel Roosevelt, New York City, October 31, November 1-2,
> 1956.

Anderson, Ronald A. GOVERNMENT AND BUSINESS. 2nd ed. Cincinnati:
South-western, 1960. 681 p.
> Since the subject of government regulation of business raises the
> question of "which government" as well as "what business," the
> first part of the book is devoted to a summary of the distribution
> of powers within our multi-unit system of government. The
> second part of the book deals with the constitutional limitations
> that restrict government in regulating business. The third part
> then treats specifically the different powers of the governments
> and the regulations that have been imposed under their authority.
> The fourth part of the book deals with the actual problems of
> administration.

Anderson, Thomas J. OUR COMPETITIVE SYSTEM AND PUBLIC POLICY.
Cincinnati: South-western, 1958. 586 p.
> This book provides a general survey of competition and monopoly
> in the American economy , and of public policies affecting the
> competitive system. It is designed for use as a text in courses
> concerned with this area of public regulation of the economy.

An innovation for this type of book is the inclusion in Part B of several chapters on the competitive and monopolistic aspects of factor markets. The growth of labor organizations and the development by them of significant anti-competitive practices justify examination at some length of those union developments substantially affecting competition, and of government policies that encourage or restrict such developments.

The book concludes with a summary of significant policy considerations and proposals on the competitive system. Presented here are policy considerations and proposals pertaining to the need for codification of federal antitrust law, the adequacy of antitrust penalties, the need for changes in antitrust administration, the wisdom of continuing the fair trade statutes, suggestions for revising our patent policy, and many other aspects of public policy affecting the competitive system.

Andrews, P.W.S. and Friday, Frank A. FAIR TRADE RESALE PRICE MAINTENANCE RE-EXAMINED. New York: St. Martin's Press, 1960. 84 p.
Criticizes the case against resale price maintenance as it has been put forward, notably in Professor Yamey's pamphlet. Contains statistical assessment of the actual importance of resale price maintenance, giving figures trade by trade. Because of the strongly competitive structure of retail trade, it is argued that resale price maintenance can persist in practice only if it brings cost-price advantages, which benefit the consumer.

Anshen, Melvin and Wormuth, Francis D. PRIVATE ENTERPRISE AND PUBLIC POLICY. New York: Macmillan, 1954. 742 p.

Association of the Bar of the City of New York. Special Committee on Antitrust Laws and Foreign Trade. NATIONAL SECURITY AND FOREIGN POLICY IN THE APPLICATION OF AMERICAN ANTITRUST LAWS TO COMMERCE WITH FOREIGN NATIONS. New York: 1957. 29 p.
Deals with the problems created when important questions of the national security or foreign policy of our country arise in connection with any effort to apply our American antitrust laws to commerce with foreign nations.

Austern, H.T. ANTITRUST IN ACTION: SOME RECENT DEVELOPMENTS IN ANTITRUST ENFORCEMENT. New York: New York University School of Law, 1960. 21 p.

Austin, Cyrus. PRICE DISCRIMINATION AND RELATED PROBLEMS UNDER THE ROBINSON-PATMAN ACT. Rev. ed. (June, 1959). Philadelphia: American Law Institute, 1959. 178 p.
This is the third edition of this important and authoritative work.

Backman, Jules, et al. ADMINISTERED PRICES, ADMINISTERED WAGES AND INFLATION. (Current Business Studies) New York: Society of Business Advisory Professions, Inc., 1958. 48 p.

Backman, Jules. COMPETITION IN THE CHEMICAL INDUSTRY. Washington, D.C.: Manufacturing Chemists' Association, 1964. 90 p.

Chapters are as follows: 1. Industrial Chemicals defined; 2. Patterns of Competition; 3. The Number of Competitors; 4. Structure of the Chemical Industry; 5. Competitive Products; 6. Price Competition; 7. Nonprice Competition; 8. Patents and Competition; 9. Foreign Competition; 10. Competition and Intercompany Relationships; 11. Summary and Conclusions. Book also contains numerous tables and charts.

Backman, Jules. PRICE PRACTICES AND PRICE POLICIES, SELECTED WRITINGS. New York: Ronald Press, 1953. 660 p.

Backman, Jules. PRICING POLICIES AND PRACTICES. New York: National Industrial Conference Board, 1961.
> The present study examines in greater detail than has hitherto been possible the pricing techniques of companies in many different industries. It begins with an examination of the pricing models that appear in economic textbooks and the unavoidability of departures from theoretical models. This is followed by a brief discussion of the nature of administered prices. Finally, the study considers various aspects of pricing, noting the interrelated roles of established company policy and day-to-day judgments in individual pricing decisions.

Bain, Joe S. BARRIERS TO NEW COMPETITION, THEIR CHARACTER AND CONSEQUENCES IN MANUFACTURING INDUSTRIES. (Harvard University Series on Competition in American Industry, No. 3) Cambridge: Harvard University Press, 1956. 329 p.

Baldwin, William L. ANTITRUST AND THE CHANGING CORPORATION. Durham, N.C.: Duke University Press, 1961. 307 p.
> The present study represents an effort to ascertain the extent to which the literature dealing with the modern business corporation, written between the 1880's and the present, contains insights into the actual form of that artificial body which may be useful in dealing with problems of antitrust enforcement.

Barger, Harold. DISTRIBUTION'S PLACE IN THE AMERICAN ECONOMY SINCE 1869. Princeton, N.J.: Princeton University Press, 1955. 222 p.

Barnard, Robert C. HOW GOOD ARE YOUR CONTRACTS? Fourth Annual Institute on Corporate Counsel. The Antitrust Structure of the European Common Market. New York: Fordham University School of Law, December 7, 1962. 19 p.

Baum, Daniel J. THE ROBINSON-PATMAN ACT, SUMMARY AND COMMENT. Syracuse: Syracuse University Press, 1964. 167 p.
> Written for the law student and the business student, as well as the general practitioner and the antitrust specialist. Intended to provide the in-depth reader with a broad background that will make further study more meaningful.

Bergh, Louis O. and Conyngton, Thomas. BUSINESS LAW. 6th ed. New York: Ronald, 1964. 1006 p.
> Chapter 78 is entitled "Preservation and Regulation of Competition."

Berle, Adolf A. THE AMERICAN ECONOMIC REPUBLIC. New York: Harcourt, Brace, 1963. 247 p.
> Chapter 10 entitled "The Free-Market Sector: Industry and Its Concentration" deals with 1. Realities of the Free Market; 2. Industry and Its Concentration; 3. Problems of Antitrust Policy-- Artificial Competition; 4. The Semi-controlled Businesses; and 5. Stability under Competition--the "Administered Price."

Bernstein, Marver H. REGULATING BUSINESS BY INDEPENDENT COMMISSION. Princeton: Princeton University Press, 1955. 306 p.
> The objective of the present study is threefold: (1) to evaluate critically the role of the independent regulatory commissions, (2) to develop a more realistic concept of the process of governmental regulation, and (3) to appraise the independent commission as an agent of governmental regulation at the national level.

Bliss, James J. and Millstein, Ira M. eds. MANUAL OF FEDERAL TRADE REGULATIONS AFFECTING RETAILERS. New York: National Retail Merchants Association, 1963. 232 p.
> Retailing no longer conforms to the simple pattern of merchandise purchases from resources and sales to consumers, an activity which presupposes two basic requisites--good management and good location. Today, distribution to the consumer is attended by a veritable network of governmental restrictions which must be understood and applied, practically and legally, if the retailer is to meet the competition of those who study and comply with legal requirements. This book fills a need for this type of information.

Boarman, Patrick M. UNION MONOPOLIES AND ANTITRUST RESTRAINTS. Washington, D.C.: Labor Policy Association, 1963. 203 p.

Bock, Betty. CONCENTRATION PATTERNS IN MANUFACTURING. SOME FINDINGS FROM AN INQUIRY INTO THE RELEVANCE OF DATA BEING USED TO MEASURE MARKET SHARES IN SPECIFIED INDUSTRIES. (Studies in Business Economics, No. 65) New York: National Industrial Conference Board, 1959. 128 p.
> A study based on the findings of the Subcommittee on Antitrust and Monopoly of the Senate Committee on the Judiciary entitled "Report on Concentration in American Industry," issued in 1957 and covering the committee's appraisal of trends between 1947 and 1954.
>
> Scrutinizes the definitions used by the committee and examines the measures and ratios it adopted in determining the degree of concentration in particular industries.

Bock, Betty. MERGERS AND MARKETS, A GUIDE TO ECONOMIC ANALYSIS OF CASE LAW. 3rd ed. (Studies in Business Economics, no. 85) New York: National Industrial Conference Board, 1964. 289 p.
> This study is designed as a guide to the economic factors taken into account in the enforcement of the merger act. The first section of the study considers the background of the act, enforcement processes, key issues, and basic defenses. The second

analyzes issues of company and market vulnerability, as reflected in the 122 complaints brought by the Federal Trade Commission and the Department of Justice between January 1, 1951, and January 1, 1964. A third section considers the economic factors entering into court and Federal Trade Commission decisions during the same period; it deals with methods of identifying the markets in which competition may be substantially lessened, and with criteria for assessing the competitive consequences of acquisitions. The Appendices show the status of each merger case as of January 1, 1964, and the basic company and market facts alleged in each case.

Bock, Betty. MERGERS AND MARKETS - AN ECONOMIC ANALYSIS OF THE 1964 SUPREME COURT MERGER DECISIONS. (Studies in Business Economics, No. 87). 4th ed. New York: National Industrial Conference Board, 1965. 128 p.

In these decisions, the Court dealt principally with questions of evidence of the potential effects of an acquisition on competition where the acquiring and acquired companies were neither direct competitors nor closely related vertically; the Court also began to explore the competitive questions raised when an acquisition involving relatively low market shares affects markets where concentration is relatively high.

The study begins by outlining the 1964 complaints and decisions, as they stand, and then goes on to consider the economic factors bearing on identification of the markets affected, the factors bearing on competitive effects, and the lines of defense that have been rejected. The final chapter explores the basic relationships between economic evidence and the requirements of the law.

Appendix A shows the status as of January 1, 1965, of new complaints brought during 1964, and of earlier complaints whose status changed during the year. Appendix B outlines the basic company and market facts alleged in the 1964 complaints. Appendix C provides citations for the decisions analyzed in the study. The appendix material is designed to fit into and supplement the corresponding appendices in the earlier (1964) edition of the study.

Bowie, Robert R. et al. GOVERNMENT REGULATION OF BUSINESS: CASES FROM THE NATIONAL REPORTER SYSTEM. Brooklyn: Foundation, 1963. 1770 p.

Brems, Hans. SOME PROBLEMS OF MONOPOLISTIC COMPETITION. Copenhagen: Munksgaard, 1950. 274 p.

Brewster, Kingman. ANTITRUST AND AMERICAN BUSINESS ABROAD. New York: McGraw-Hill, 1958. 509 p.

"While certain parts of the book have been contributed by other authors, it is essentially an individual critical appraisal of the part played by present antitrust law in foreign business operations, followed by some constructive proposals for amendment of the law. One of the most valuable features is an appraisal of the

results of interviews conducted with representatives of some
seventy business enterprises engaged in foreign operations, in-
quiring as to the effect of antitrust considerations on their business policies." Wolfgang G. Friedmann, 58 Col. L. Rev. 1311.

Briggs, Edwin W. LEGAL BARRIERS TO COMPETITION IN MONTANA STATE
AND LOCAL LAW. Missoula, Mont.: Bureau of Business and Economic Re-
search, Montana State University, 1965. 165 p.
The principal legislation studied in this report includes Montana's
Unfair Practices Act, the Fair Trade Act, the Barbers Act, the
Beauty Shop Act, and the Milk Control Act. Each act is the
subject of a detailed analysis as to its legislative and adminis-
trative history, its current status, and its effect upon the market.
The Fair Trade Act was declared unconstitutional by the Montana
Supreme Court in 1961, but continues to be of interest in view
of recent attempts to establish a national fair trade law under
the title of "Quality Stabilization."

Bureau of National Affairs, Inc. ANTITRUST AND TRADE REGULATION
TODAY. (2nd ed.) Selected Analyses from BNA's Antitrust and Trade
Regulation Report. Washington, D.C.: 1966. 341 p.
Part I. Restraints and Monopolies; Part II. Vertical Arrange-
ments; Part III. Mergers; Part IV. Price Discrimination; Part
V. Regulated Industries; Part VI. Justice Department Practice;
Part VII. FTC Procedures; Part VIII. Treble-Damage Actions;
Part IX. Deceptive Practices; Part X. Foreign Laws.

Burn, Duncan L. THE STEEL INDUSTRY 1939-1959; A STUDY IN COMPETI-
TION AND PLANNING. Cambridge, Eng.: University Press, 1961. 728 p.
No attempt is made here to describe the antitrust system in gen-
eral; but its impact on the steel industry is surveyed.

Burns, Joseph W. STUDY OF THE ANTITRUST LAWS, THEIR ADMINISTRA-
TION, INTERPRETATION, AND EFFECT. New York: Central, 1958. 574 p.
A report to the Subcommittee on Antitrust and Monopoly of the
Committee on the Judiciary, U.S. Senate, 84th Congress, 1st
Session.

Callman, Rudolf. THE LAW OF UNFAIR COMPETITION AND TRADEMARKS.
Chicago: Callaghan, 1950. 5 v.
Coverage includes government and business competition, unfair
competition and the antitrust laws, resale price maintenance, and
price discrimination.

Campbell, Alan. RESTRICTIVE TRADING AGREEMENTS IN THE COMMON
MARKET: TEXT, COMMENTARIES. London: Stevens; South Hackensack,
N.J.: Rothman, 1964. 228 p.
This book has the practical aim of enabling business interests
to know where they stand and what they must do in order to
conduct their business relations with the Common Market in
conformity with its recently promulgated law of restrictive practices and monopolies.

Cassady, Ralph. COMPETITION AND PRICE MAKING IN FOOD RETAILING:
THE ANATOMY OF SUPERMARKET OPERATIONS. New York: Ronald, 1962.

333 p.
>A study of the economics of competition and the conditioning of
>competitive behavior by various types of legal circumscriptions,
>based on actual market investigation.

Cassady, Ralph, Jr. and Cassady, Ralph, III. THE PRIVATE ANTITRUST SUIT
IN AMERICAN BUSINESS COMPETITION. Los Angeles: Bureau of Business and
Economic Research, University of California, 1964. 67 p.
>A motion-picture industry case analysis.

Chamber of Commerce of the United States. FEDERAL REGULATION OF
BUSINESS: WHERE DO WE GO FROM HERE? Washington, D.C.: 1964.
25 p.
>Panel discussion of Association's Public Affairs Conference, held
>in Washington, February 5 and 6, 1964. Among matters discus-
>sed were Hart packaging bill, Douglas truth-in-lending bill,
>temporary Federal Trade Commission injunctions, and federal
>representation of consumers.

Chamber of Commerce of the United States. MERGERS; REPORT OF THE
COMMITTEE ON ECONOMIC POLICY. Washington, D.C.: 1957. 23 p.

Chamber of Commerce of the United States. THE MERGER ISSUE IN THE
UNITED STATES. AN ASPECT OF ANTITRUST ENFORCEMENT--SELECTIVE
ACTIONS vs. GENERAL CONTROLS. Washington, D.C.: 1961. 38 p.
>Considers whether the present merger law is adequate, or if
>further broad extensions of federal control are necessary.

Chamberlin, Edward H. ed. MONOPOLY AND COMPETITION AND THEIR
REGULATION. Papers and proceedings of a conference held by the Interna-
tional Economic Association. London: Macmillan; New York: St. Martin's
Press, 1954. 548 p.
>Papers presented at the September 1951 meeting of the Association
>held in France.

>The topic afforded an opportunity for international comparisons
>and for improving the understanding of the problems of one coun-
>try by putting them alongside the same or similar problems as
>they manifest themselves in other economic, political or cultural
>contexts.

Chamberlin, Edward. THE THEORY OF MONOPOLISTIC COMPETITION: A
RE-ORIENTATION OF THE THEORY OF VALUE. 8th ed. (Harvard Economic
Studies, v. 38). Cambridge: Harvard University Press, 1962. 396 p.
>A landmark work which was first published in 1933 and consti-
>tuted a major contribution to price theory. It set off a theoreti-
>cal revolution by providing the major outlines of a price theory
>based on oligopoly and product differentiation.

>The author advanced the concept of an economy of enterprises
>made up of industries having a variety of distinctly different mar-
>ket structures, with market conduct and performance tending to
>differ significantly with those differences in structure.

>This work developed a classification of market structures which
>was the basis for later more elaborate market classifications. It

had great impact on the development of the field of industrial organization.

The eighth edition includes three new appendices: F, The Definition of Selling Costs; G, Numbers and Elasticities; and H, The Origin and Early Development of Monopolistic Competition Theory.

Chamberlin, Edward. TOWARDS A MORE GENERAL THEORY OF VALUE. New York: Oxford University Press, 1957. 318 p.

Chicago Bar Association. Special Subcommittee on Illinois Antitrust Laws. A STUDY OF THE LAWS OF ILLINOIS RELATING TO COMPETITION. Chicago: 1960. 285 p.

Choka, Allen D. BUYING, SELLING AND MERGING BUSINESSES. Philadelphia: Joint Committee on Continuing Legal Education of the American Law Institute and the American Bar Association, 1965. 191 p.
Deals with the problems facing a lawyer in a merger transaction, including not only statutory mergers but also consolidations, stock transactions, and asset purchases. In general it is written from the point of view of the lawyer for the buyer, although the problems of the seller are not neglected.

The six chapters cover: I. The Mechanics of Merger; II. The Financial Statements; III. Valuation and Payment; IV. The Contract; V. Four Legal Problems--section 7 of the Clayton Act, Rule 10b-5, sale of corporate control and sale of assets; and VI. The Tax Aspects. Appendices include: Reorganization Agreement; Checklist of Proposed Acquisitions; and Broker's Agreement.

Clabault, James M. and Burton, Jr., John F. SHERMAN ACT INDICTMENTS 1955-65. New York: Federal Legal Publications, Inc. 1966. 504 p.
Chapter One covers "A Legal Analysis of Sherman Act Indictments;" and Chapter Two covers "An Economist's Analysis of Sherman Act Criminal Cases." Contains four useful indexes as follows: I. Chronological Index of Cases; II. Index of Cases by Court; III. Index of Cases by Industry; and IV. Index of Defendants.

Clark, John M. COMPETITION AS A DYNAMIC PROCESS. Washington, D.C.: Brookings, 1961. 501 p.
This volume by a distinguished economist critically examines the dynamic character of modern competition, appraises the inadequacies of equilibrium theory, and suggests a new approach to the study and interpretation of competitive activities in the economy.

Cochran, C.L. and Ross, R. THE CASE FOR COMPETITION IN ELECTRIC POWER. Pamphlet No. 241. New York: Public Affairs Pamphlets, 1956. 28 p.

Commerce Clearing House, Inc. NEW ANTITRUST RULES OF THE COMMON
MARKET. Chicago: 1962. 48 p.
> Explanation of procedures; forms for "negative clearance" or
> exemption; regulations; text.

Conant, Michael. ANTITRUST IN THE MOTION PICTURE INDUSTRY; ECO-
NOMIC AND LEGAL ANALYSIS. (Publication of the Bureau of Business and
Economic Research) Berkeley: University of California Press, 1960. 240 p.
> This study is an attempt to analyze and evaluate the impact of
> antitrust actions on the structure, behavior, and performance of
> an industry. Another purpose is to examine the development of
> antitrust law within an industry and the effect of government
> prosecutions as an impetus to private treble-damage actions.

Conant, Michael. RAILROAD MERGERS AND ABANDONMENTS. Berkeley:
University of California Press, 1964. 212 p.
> The author, an economist and lawyer, is associate professor of
> business administration at the University of California in Berkeley.
> He has written this book as an economic criticism of the admin-
> istrative regulation of resource allocation.
>
> Among the particular topics taken up at length are: the inef-
> fectiveness of inter-railroad competition as an impetus to the
> adjustment of investment to changing demand; the economic im-
> pact of recent railroad mergers; and problems presented by the
> reallocation of resources resulting from disinvestment in fixed
> plant.
>
> Chapter III is devoted to the antitrust laws and railroad consoli-
> dation, with an economic appraisal of recent mergers.

Cook, F.H. PRINCIPLES OF BUSINESS AND THE FEDERAL LAW. New
York: Macmillan, 1951. 563 p.
> The book is a combination text and case book stressing the im-
> portant legal and economic principles that affect business in its
> relation with government. The second part surveys specific fed-
> eral legislation in the fields of restraints upon business, labor
> legislation, security legislation, and transportation.

Cook, Paul W., ed. CASES IN ANTITRUST POLICY. New York: Holt,
Rinehart, 1964. 182 p.

Cookenboo, Leslie. CRUDE OIL PIPE LINES AND COMPETITION IN THE
OIL INDUSTRY. Cambridge: Harvard University Press, 1955. 177 p.
> Contains chapter on public policy toward crude oil pipe lines.

Cotter, Cornelius P. GOVERNMENT AND PRIVATE ENTERPRISE. New York: Holt, Rinehart, 1960. 527 p.

> This book attempts to convey to the reader an understanding of how and why government undertakes to regulate business in the United States. Covers the process of policy making and the problems associated with it.

Cravath, Swaine and Moore. OPINION OF COUNSEL AND MEMORANDUM CONCERNING THE APPLICABILITY OF THE ANTITRUST LAWS TO THE TELEVISION BROADCAST ACTIVITIES OF COLUMBIA BROADCASTING SYSTEM, INC. New York: Columbia Broadcasting System, 1956. 78 p.

Cross, James. VERTICAL INTEGRATION IN THE OIL INDUSTRY. Cambridge: School of Industrial Management, Massachusetts Institute of Technology, 1953. 13 p.

Crowley, Joseph R., ed. THE ANTITRUST STRUCTURE OF THE EUROPEAN COMMON MARKET. New York: Fordham University Press, 1963. 179 p.

> Proceedings of the Fourth Annual Institute on Corporate Counsel sponsored by Fordham University School of Law, December 6th and 7th, 1962. In view of the necessity of registration of certain contracts by American corporations doing business in the market, there was an intense interest in the opinions of European as well as American specialists in the field. American antitrust laws have been subject to judicial interpretation since 1890 and there are still areas of uncertainty. Hence the prospect of trade regulation by statutory enactment, with virtually no judicial interpretation, has created apprehension among American business men and their counsel. The aim of the institute was to bring to these shores the best talent available to estimate the impact of regulation.

CURRENT BUSINESS STUDIES. New York: Society of Business Advisory Professions, Inc. 1948-

> A list of all studies, from Nos. 1 to 44, appears on pages 24-26 of Current Business Studies No. 45. The items listed below were selected for inclusion in this section because they deal with antitrust, competition, and related subjects.

> No. 1. "Basing Points: A symposium" by Corwin D. Edwards, et al. 1948. 52 p.

> No. 5. "The Economics & Legality of "'Bigness'" by James V. Hayes, et al. 1950. 60 p.

> No. 8. "Antitrust Aspects of a Controlled Economy" by Frederick M. Eaton, et. al. 1951. 53 p.

> No. 12. "Competition-Today and Tomorrow" by Melvin G. DeChazeau, et al. 1952. 59 p.

> No. 14. "Government Regulation of Business" by Blackwell Smith, et al. 1953. 48 p.

> No. 21. "Mergers and Competition: Recent Developments" by Oswald W. Knauth, et al. 1954. 39 p.

No. 24. "Costs Under the Robinson-Patman Act, the Taggart Report: A Study in the Presentation of Evidence in Administrative and Judicial Proceedings" by Gerard Swope, Jr. et al. 1956. 31 p.

No. 28. "Administered Prices, Administered Wages, and Inflation" by Jules Backman, et al. 1958. 48 p.

No. 30. "Should Overlapping Jurisdictions of Federal Trade Commissions and Department of Justice be Eliminated?" by Joseph W. Burns, et al. 1958. 43 p.

Nos. 41-43. "Federal Government Policies and Their Relationship to the Development of the United States Economy" by Stanley S. Surrey, et al. 1962. 56 p.

No. 45. "Antitrust Considerations in the Exchange of Price Information Among Competitors" by John J. Galgay. 1963. 26 p.

Davidson, Ralph K. PRICE DISCRIMINATION IN SELLING GAS AND ELECTRICITY. Baltimore: Johns Hopkins Press, 1955. 254 p.
Adopts the economic definition of price discrimination for analysis of past and present gas and electric utility rate structures. It is not concerned with the determination of the proper rate base for utilities or the proper rate of return, but rather examines the various explanations given to rationalize and explain particular rate structures chosen by gas and electric utility companies. Focuses on two questions: (1) do the implications of the theory of price discrimination "explain" or rationalize the observed differential rates in gas and electric rate schedules better than the implications of alternative hypotheses; and (2) what is the effect of the rate schedules used today by gas and electric utility companies on allocation of productive resources?

Davis, J.P. CORPORATIONS; A STUDY OF THE ORIGIN AND DEVELOPMENT OF GREAT BUSINESS COMBINATIONS AND OF THEIR RELATION TO THE AUTHORITY OF THE STATE. New York: Capricorn, 1961. 280 p.

DeChazeau, Melvin G. and Kahn, Alfred E. INTEGRATION AND COMPETITION IN THE PETROLEUM INDUSTRY. New Haven: Yale University Press, 1959. 598 p.

Dewey, Donald. MONOPOLY IN ECONOMICS AND LAW. (Rand McNally Economic Series). Chicago: Rand McNally, 1959. 328 p.
An account of what economists and lawyers have thought about monopoly since the subject first received their serious attention. The author, a teacher of economics, draws on his own store of knowledge to illustrate or test those generalizations which he considers most worthy of emphasis. The author feels that the important issues in the control of monopoly are "economic" and that economists and lawyers interested in monopoly as a policy problem cannot get along without one another.

Dewhurst and Associates, J. Frederic. AMERICA'S NEEDS AND RESOURCES; A NEW SURVEY. New York: Twentieth Century Fund, 1955. 1148 p.

This volume gives the present position of American economic
resources, production and consumption. It establishes a basis
of comparison with earlier figures and makes it possible to see
the extent of progress made.

A new and more comprehensive survey of the demands and needs,
resources and capacities, of the American economy. Major
focus is on the postwar boom, the long-range upsurge of the economy, and the significance of our expanding economy for the
future well-being of the nation. Major headings are: basic
trends; consumption requirements; capital requirements; government and foreign transactions; resources; and capacities.

Dietz, Arthur T. AN INTRODUCTION TO THE ANTITRUST LAWS. New
York: Bookman Associates, 1951. 84 p.
Intended for use in elementary courses in economics. Tries to
provide the student with an opportunity to understand the nature
of a fundamental application of economic theory to legislation
and judicial practice.

Diplock, Sir Kenneth. ANTITRUST AND THE JUDICIAL PROCESS. (Eighth
Ernst Freund Lecture). Chicago: University of Chicago Law School, 1964.
16 p.
Author is Lord Justice of the Court of Appeal in the United
Kingdom. Lecture is a discussion of the British Restrictive Prac-
tices Act, and the judicial process enforcing it.

Dirlam, Joel B. and Kahn, Alfred E. FAIR COMPETITION: THE LAW AND
ECONOMICS OF ANTITRUST POLICY. Ithaca: Cornell Univ. Press, 1954.
307 p.
Tries to answer the question of whether fair competition is "workable"--does antitrust conflict seriously with the requirements of
efficiency. Focuses attention on decisions of last fifteen years
illustrating divergent and economic conceptions of monopoly and
competition. Treats only indirectly with the traditional law of
unfair competition; misrepresentation, molestation, trade-mark
infringement, etc. Analyzes and evaluates the law we now have.

Dixon, Brian. PRICE DISCRIMINATION AND MARKETING MANAGEMENT.
(Michigan Business Studies Vol. XV, No. 1). Ann Arbor, Mich.: University
of Michigan Press, 1960. 124 p.
From the point of view of the manufacturer, a rather wide range
of differential pricing policies makes sense in terms of the maxi-
mizing goals of the firm. On the other hand, much of economic
theorizing and present legislation concerning differential pricing
suggests a course of action sharply at odds with a logical management approach. This book tries to resolve these differences.

Drayton, Clarence I., Jr., et al. MERGERS AND ACQUISITIONS: PLAN-
NING AND ACTION. New York: Financial Executives Research Foundation,
1963. 229 p.
The purpose of this book is to outline a rational approach to
mergers and acquisitions, and to thus help the reader anticipate
problems and minimize their adverse effects since adequate preparation should make it possible to deal quickly and thoroughly

when an opportunity arises or is developed.

This book approaches the subject of merger/acquisition primarily from the standpoint of the buyer, i.e., a company engaged in a program of expansion that involves merger/acquisition. Much of what is said is equally applicable to the seller, and a number of problems faced by sellers are commented upon.

Edwards, Corwin D. BIG BUSINESS AND THE POLICY OF COMPETITION. Cleveland: Western Reserve Univ. Press, 1956. 180 p.

This volume presents in revised form four lectures sponsored jointly by Western Reserve University and Case Institute of Technology. Their purpose is to summarize the governmental policy toward big business which is implied in the anti-trust laws, and state the rationale of that policy.

Edwards, Corwin D. MAINTAINING COMPETITION. New York: McGraw-Hill, 1949. 337 p.

The purpose of this book is to set forth the content of a policy designed to maintain the competitive system within the United States. It focuses on the character of a governmental program that would be appropriate to the maintenance of competition and the nature of the economic and administrative difficulties which would be encountered in carrying out that program. The author is an economist.

Edwards, Corwin D. THE PRICE DISCRIMINATION LAW; A REVIEW OF EXPERIENCE. Washington, D.C.: Brookings Institution, 1959. 698 p.

Presents a detailed review of experience under the Robinson-Patman Act, stressing particularly the litigation of economic issues and the modifications in business practices that followed. The author was formerly a staff member of the Federal Trade Commission.

Based on findings, orders, appellate decisions, and underlying public records of cases arising under the Act; and on field interviews with persons participating in or affected by these cases.

Edwards, Corwin D. TRADE REGULATION OVERSEAS: THE NATIONAL LAWS. Institute of Comparative Law, New York University School of Law. Dobbs Ferry, N.Y.: Oceana, 1965. 600 p.

History, content, and application of national laws on cartels and dominant firms are analyzed and interpreted here in terms of the legal, economic, and cultural issues involved. Developments are covered to 1963.

Eiteman, Wilford J. PRICE DETERMINATION IN OLIGOPOLISTIC AND MONOPOLISTIC SITUATIONS. (Michigan Business Reports, No. 33). Ann Arbor: Bureau of Business Research, School of Business Administration, University of Michigan. 1960. 45 p.

Elkouri, Frank. TRADE REGULATION: CASES AND MATERIALS. Englewood, N.J.: Prentice-Hall, 1957. 312 p.

Fainsod, Merle, et al. GOVERNMENT AND THE AMERICAN ECONOMY. 3rd ed. New York: Norton, 1959. 996 p.

> Examines and analyzes the assumption by government of major responsibilities for the guidance and direction of the American economy. Emphasis is placed on the political forces which influence the formation and execution of public policy. This approach does not mean that the economic analysis is neglected as every effort has been made to take account of the economic as well as the political, legal, and administrative factors which enter into the determination of public economic policies. The third edition has added new chapters on transportation, antitrust policy, coal, oil, natural gas, atomic energy, monetary and fiscal policy, and the economic responsibilities of government in the international field.

Federal Bar Association. Antitrust Committee. PROPOSED MERGER GUIDE-LINES. Washington, D.C.: Bureau of National Affairs, Inc., 1965. 29 p.

> Contains complete transcript of the panel discussion of merger "guidelines" held at the Association's annual meeting in September, 1965.
>
> Of significance is the participation of Assistant Attorney General Donald F. Turner. In his comments and answers to questions, Mr. Turner spells out additional details on the nature and function of the merger "guidelines" which he proposed.

Federal Bar Association of New York, New Jersey and Connecticut. Trade Regulation Committee. MONOPOLIES, MERGERS AND MARKETS--A NEW FOCUS. A symposium edited by Sigmund Timberg and Malcolm A. Hoffman. (Trade Regulation Series No. 1) New York: Federal Legal Publications, 1955. 76 p.

Federal Bar Association of New York, New Jersey and Connecticut. Trade Regulation Committee. SYMPOSIUM ON TWENTY YEARS OF ROBINSON-PATMAN; THE RECORD AND THE ISSUES. Edited by Sigmund Timberg. Symposium on the House Counsel and the Attorney General's Committee Reports, edited by Earle Warren Zaidins. (Trade Regulation Series, No. 3). New York: Federal Legal Publications, 1956. 210 p.

> A collection of five papers on various aspects of the Robinson-Patman Act. The introduction gives a brief history of the origin of the act. Professor Corwin Edwards' paper is a preliminary survey of the Federal Trade Commission's enforcement record during the prior twenty years. Joseph A. Seeley, assistant counsel to the Senate Subcommittee on Antitrust and Monopoly, writes of current legislative proposals and attitudes concerning the Robinson-Patman Act. Lawrence S. Apsey, General Counsel, Celanese Corporation of America, writes on the featuring of fabricators and outlets in producers' advertising as a "service" under the Robinson-Patman Act, section 2(e). Cyrus Austin writes of "Brokerage vs. Service Payments: Another Look at Section 2(c)."

Part II of the symposium also contains five papers. The first is
Milton Handler's review of antitrust developments. The second,
by John C. Stedman, is on the reconciling of patent practices
with the antitrust laws. The third is by Edward F. Howrey, on
the Federal Trade Commission and the Attorney General's Committee Report, an address delivered when Mr. Howrey was Chairman of the Federal Trade Commission. The fourth is on exclusive
dealing arrangements in buyer-seller relationships, by Reynolds C.
Seity. The fifth is on current problems of merchandising in the
face of the proportionally equal terms requirement, by Ralph E.
Axley.

Feldman, George J. and Zorn, Burton A. ROBINSON-PATMAN ACT--AD-
VERTISING AND PROMOTIONAL ALLOWANCES. Washington, D.C.: Bureau
of National Affairs, Inc., 1948. 290 p.
    The purpose of this handbook and analysis is to provide in the
    most convenient form possible all the working materials required
    for a thorough understanding of the provisions of the Robinson-
    Patman Act which deal with joint promotion of a product.

Fisher, Burton R. and Withey, Stephen B. BIG BUSINESS AS THE PEOPLE
SEE IT; A STUDY OF A SOCIO-ECONOMIC INSTITUTION. (Survey Research
Center Series, Publication No. 6). Ann Arbor: Survey Research Center, In-
stitute for Social Research, University of Michigan, 1951. 200 p.
    A technical report based on a questionnaire designed to explore
    popular attitudes toward big business. Purely a presentation of
    findings with sparse interpretations.

Fisher, W.E. and James, C.M. MINIMUM PRICE FIXING IN THE BITUMI-
NOUS COAL INDUSTRY. Princeton: Princeton University Press, 1955. 523 p.
    The story of the experiment in the setting of guaranteed minimum
    prices under the Bituminous Coal Act of 1937, which expired in
    1943. This study gives the details of the measures taken to
    translate the language of the statute into a rational structure of
    minimum prices, which would provide for the recovery of desig-
    nated costs by the producers, and for the protection of consumers.

Fishman, Leo and Fishman, Betty G. THE AMERICAN ECONOMY. (The Van
Nostrand Series in Business Administration and Economics.) Princeton, N.J.:
Van Nostrand, 1962. 822 p.
    Basic information about the nature of the American economy,
    today's important economic problems, and the principal tools
    available for analyzing, solving, or ameliorating these problems.
    Covers such topics as maintaining competition; modifying competi-
    tion; the regulation of public utilities; and other government
    policies towards business.

Fleming, Harold. TEN THOUSAND COMMANDMENTS: A STORY OF THE
ANTITRUST LAWS. (Foundation for Economic Education; Irvington-On-Hudson.)
New York: Prentice-Hall, 1951. 214 p.
    The author is a business reporter. The book is intended for lay-
    men rather than lawyers, although legal citations are included.
    Consists of a series of 28 articles which first appeared on the
    business page of the Christian Science Monitor during the summer

of 1949.

Flynn, John J. FEDERALISM AND STATE ANTITRUST REGULATIONS. Ann Arbor: University of Michigan Law School, 1964. 312 p.
> A study of the state antitrust regulations in the light of the federal antitrust and regulatory laws. Federal and state antitrust powers under the commerce clause are analyzed, and the question of federal supremacy and preemption, as well as concurrent antitrust powers of the state and federal government, are surveyed.

Forkosch, Morris D. ANTITRUST AND THE CONSUMER (ENFORCEMENT). Buffalo: Dennis, 1956. 521 p.
> Although the consumer may ultimately benefit through increased and freer competition, this is considered to be merely an indirect rather than a direct effect of the antitrust laws. The consumer may not sue for alleged injuries resulting from antitrust violations, although injury to him could establish a Sherman Act violation. How correct this limited approach to the consumer's antitrust interest is, is the overall question investigated in this essay.

Foulke, Roy A. DIVERSIFICATION IN BUSINESS ACTIVITY. New York: Dun & Bradstreet, 1956. 79 p.
> A history of the beginnings of corporate enterprise in this country. Discusses mergers, consolidations and acquisitions, and the antitrust laws. The second part of the pamphlet is a series of financial ratio tables based on financial statements for the years 1950-1954 for 78 lines of business activity.

Fuchs, Victor R. THE ECONOMICS OF THE FUR INDUSTRY: A STUDY OF A HIGHLY COMPETITIVE INDUSTRY IN A LESS COMPETITIVE ECONOMY. New York: Columbia University Press, 1955. 236 p.
> Written in partial fulfillment of the requirements for the degree of Doctor of Philosophy in the Faculty of Political Science, Columbia University. Selects two basic problems of the fur industry for study: (1) the marked fluctuations in prices, production, and sales which are characteristic of the industry; and (2) the failure of the industry to grow with the rest of the economy. The concluding chapter deals with the relationship between competitive structure and inter-industry competition. Primary emphasis is given to the years after World War II.

Fugate, Wilbur L. FOREIGN COMMERCE AND THE ANTITRUST LAWS. (Trade Regulation Series.) Boston: Little, Brown, 1958. 384 p.
> Much of the discussion in the book is based on interstate commerce cases since the application of the antitrust laws to foreign commerce is still somewhat of a frontier area of law. Where there are few foreign cases, or sometimes none, dealing with a particular practice, the writer has tried to place the interstate commerce rules in the context of foreign commerce situations so that we may judge to what extent these rules are valid in the new setting.

Fulda, Carl H. COMPETITION IN THE REGULATED INDUSTRIES--TRANS-PORTATION. (Trade Regulation Series) Boston: Little, Brown, 1961. 533 p.

This book deals with the interplay between competition and regulation in one of the federally-regulated industries, interstate transportation. This takes in railroads, motor and water carriers, airlines, and freight forwarders. The administrative decisions of the Interstate Commerce Commission, the Civil Aeronautics Board, and the Federal Maritime Board are considered.

Fuller, J.G. THE GENTLEMEN CONSPIRATORS; THE STORY OF THE PRICE-FIXERS IN THE ELECTRICAL INDUSTRY. New York: Grove, 1962. 224 p.
Story told by a reporter of the charges of price-fixing and bid-rigging involving suppliers of electrical equipment.

Galbraith, John K. A THEORY OF PRICE CONTROL. Cambridge: Harvard University Press, 1952. 81 p.
Concerned with generalizations concerning price control--price control per se, and in the context of full and limited mobilization of resources.

Giddens, Paul H. STANDARD OIL COMPANY (INDIANA): OIL PIONEER OF THE MIDDLE WEST. New York: Appleton-Century-Crofts, 1955. 741 p.
A history of the company. Chapter IV is entitled "Governmental Attacks Upon Standard" and deals with the antitrust suits brought against the company.

Glover, John D. ATTACK ON BIG BUSINESS. Boston: Harvard Graduate School of Business Administration, 1954. 375 p.
The object of this work is to examine the literature of the attack on big business, to discern any pattern thereto, and to summarize the attack on big business. Its purpose is to help businessmen formulate policies, reach decisions, and take actions better related to the reality of widespread hostility and suspicion toward big business.

The book is in four parts: Part one deals with the attack on economic grounds; part two treats of social and political criticism; part three takes up criticism on ethical and moral grounds; and part four interprets and evaluates.

Goldberg, Milton S. THE CONSENT DECREE: ITS FORMULATION AND USE. Bureau of Business and Economic Research. East Lansing, Mich.: Graduate School of Business Administration, Michigan State University, 1962. 71 p.
This study is concerned with the use of the consent settlement procedure in the settlement of antitrust cases brought under the Sherman Act. Early chapters discuss the background, nature, and employment of the consent decree in antitrust litigation, followed by a discussion of two important cases settled in this fashion. Later chapters concern themselves with the important relief provisions of other decrees. The last chapter appraises the policy concerning consent decrees, and offers some suggestions for improving the effectiveness of the procedure. The work is based on an examination of the final decrees issued in 581 civil cases brought under the Sherman Act, which included 472 consent decrees.

Goldstein, Ernest E. AMERICAN ENTERPRISE AND SCANDINAVIAN ANTI-TRUST LAW. Austin: University of Texas Press, 1963. 391 p.
> Examines the legal systems of Denmark, Norway, and Sweden, as to their antitrust laws. This analysis attempts to provide a basis for an evaluation and understanding of the administrative process and of the European administrator.

Gort, Michael. DIVERSIFICATION AND INTEGRATION IN AMERICAN IN-DUSTRY. (National Bureau of Economic Research No. 77, general series.) Princeton: Princeton University Press, 1962. 238 p.
> A comprehensive study of the inter-industry structure of the large, diversified enterprise. In order to trace the history of diversification as well as to analyze the causes which have been proposed for its development, the author's basic statistical study covers 111 of the largest companies in the country, for which the product structures in 1929, 1939, 1947, 1950 and 1954 have been compiled.

Goss, Bert C. TRIAL OUTSIDE THE COURTROOM, THE EFFECTS OF ANTI-TRUST ACTIONS ON PUBLIC OPINION TOWARD BUSINESS. Chicago: Chicago Bar Association, 1962. 20 p. Address.

Greenleaf, William. MONOPOLY ON WHEELS. Detroit: Wayne State University Press, 1961. 302 p.

Grimshaw, Austin. PROBLEMS OF THE INDEPENDENT BUSINESSMAN. New York: McGraw-Hill, 1955. 403 p.
> Material for a course in "Problems of the Independent Business-man." The case method is used. The objectives of the course are: (1) to cover systematically the various industrial and commercial groupings and the major subgroups in the American economy so that students may get the feel of one area as against another; (2) to acquaint students with the environment in which owner-managers operate and with the mass of conflicting facts, interpretations, opinions, trends, and uncertainties out of which policy and operating decisions must come; and (3) to develop in students a habit of arriving at decisions based on such limited facts as are available.

Guandolo, John. TRANSPORTATION LAW. Dubuque, Iowa: Wm. C. Brown Co. 1965. 864 p.
> The application of the antitrust laws to common carriers is one of the many areas in transportation which is becoming of increasing importance to common carriers and is not generally familiar to transportation lawyers. This topic is given full coverage in this book.

Hale, George and Hale, Rosemary D. MARKET POWER: SIZE AND SHAPE UNDER THE SHERMAN ACT. (The Trade Regulation Series) Boston: Little, Brown, 1958. 522 p.
> "The authors have endeavored with considerable success to analyze, by comparison, differentiation, and orientation, not only the legal concepts of monopoly and the varying doctrines and criteria upon which these concepts are from time to time

rested, but their economic counterparts as well.

* * *

Certainly the incisive economic approach to price discrimination, vertical integration, and exclusive arrangements is refreshing and enlightening, and on the whole this work is certainly one of the most thought-provoking, however controversial, syntheses of anti-trust law and economics yet published." Fred E. Fuller, 59 Columbia Law Rev. 220.

Hamilton, Daniel C. COMPETITION IN OIL--THE GULF COAST REFINERY MARKET 1925-1950. Cambridge: Harvard University Press, 1958. 233 p.
  A market analysis focused chiefly on price behavior. Within the limitations of the applicability of theory and availability of data, it tries to judge the character of price behavior and re-lated aspects of market production.

Hamilton, Walter. THE POLITICS OF INDUSTRY. New York: Alfred A. Knopf, 1957. 169 p.
  Five lectures delivered under the auspices of the William W. Cook Foundation at the University of Michigan during February and March of 1955. Includes a discussion of the history of government regulation of business.

Handler, Milton. ANTITRUST IN PERSPECTIVE; THE COMPLEMENTARY ROLES OF RULE AND DISCRETION. New York: Columbia University Press, 1957. 151 p.
  "Despite the historical implication of its title, the study is a valuable and sober appraisal of the current status of our coun-try's antitrust 'law.' Pitched to the highest level and fully documented, it presents and evaluates principles and points of view, and culminates in an analysis of the current trend marked by the Supreme Court's decision in United States v. E.I.DuPont de Nemours & Co., 353 U.S. 586 (1957)." George D. Horn-stein, 15 N.Y. County Lawyers' Association Bar Bulletin 168.

Handler, Milton assisted by Greenberg, Joshua F. CASES AND OTHER MA-TERIALS ON TRADE REGULATION. 3rd ed. (University Casebook Series) Brooklyn: Foundation Press, 1960. 1170 p.
  A casebook intended primarily for a teaching tool. Through a compilation of cases, the editor tells a story.

Hardwicke, Robert E. ANTITRUST LAWS, ET AL. v. UNIT OPERATION OF OIL OR GAS POOLS. Rev. ed. Dallas: Society of Petroleum Engineers, 1961. 352 p.
  Study grew out of a proposed chapter on legal problems in a volume on petroleum conservation. It discusses unit operation as so necessary to oil and gas conservation as to make the anti-trust laws inapplicable to this special situation.

Harms, John. OUR FLOUNDERING FAIR TRADE; AN INQUIRY AND CASE STUDY. New York: Exposition Press, 1956. 141 p.

Hauser, Rita E. and Hauser, Gustave M. A GUIDE TO DOING BUSINESS IN THE EUROPEAN COMMON MARKET, FRANCE AND BELGIUM. New York: Oceana, 1960. 271 p.

Intended to provide a general economic and juridical orientation for those planning to establish business operations within any of the Common Market countries. Provides a basic general introduction designed to acquaint the reader with the origin, context, and function of the Common Market, and with the fundamental framework in which business is conducted within the Common Market countries.

THE HAWAII ANTITRUST ACT. Honolulu: University of Hawaii, 1961. 68 p.

Herling, John. THE GREAT PRICE CONSPIRACY: THE STORY OF THE ANTITRUST VIOLATIONS IN THE ELECTRICAL INDUSTRY. Washington, D.C.: Robert B. Luce, 1962. 366 p.
An attempt to set forth the record of the story of the electrical industry's violations of the antitrust laws. Based on the study of official and company documents; first hand observations of the companies in action; travels around the country; interviews and conversations with participants, lawyers, businessmen, educators and the author's newspaper colleagues in Washington and other places.

Hidy, Ralph W. and Hidy, Muriel E. PIONEERING IN BIG BUSINESS, 1882-1911. HISTORY OF STANDARD OIL COMPANY (NEW JERSEY). New York: Harper, 1955. 839 p.
A biography of the Standard Oil combination, not the Standard Oil Company (New Jersey) alone. The break-up of a combination through the application of the antitrust laws ends this history.

Hoffman, M.A. and Winard, A.I., eds. ANTITRUST LAW AND TECHNIQUES. Albany: Matthew Bender, 1963. 3 vols.
A collection of landmark papers on the antitrust laws. List of contributors includes outstanding authorities in the field of antitrust.

Honig, Frederick, et al. CARTEL LAW OF THE EUROPEAN ECONOMIC COMMUNITY. London: Butterworths, 1963. 183 p.
The authors have tried to explain the law as it stands on May 1, 1963, given the fact that the United Kingdom is outside the Community, and also as it would be if the United Kingdom should ever become a member in the future.

Howard, Marshall C. LEGAL ASPECTS OF MARKETING. New York: McGraw-Hill, 1964. 173 p.
Discusses legal aspects of marketing with which the businessman must be familiar. Among the topics taken up are pricing, controlling distribution, advertising and labeling, and unfair trade practices. Written by an economist.

Hurst, James W. LAW AND THE CONDITIONS OF FREEDOM IN THE NINETEENTH-CENTURY UNITED STATES. Madison: University of Wisconsin Press, 1956. 139 p.
Text of a series of lectures delivered at Northwestern University School of Law in March 1955. The essays report work in prog-

ress under a long-term program of research in the history of
the interplay of law and other social institutions in the growth
of the United States. Antitrust laws as a government policy are
discussed, along with other factors.

International Bar Association. EDINBURGH CONFERENCE, 1962. Essen (Germany): Hans-Soldan-Stiftung.
Series of papers on antitrust problems in connection with dealings
with Common Market countries.

INTERNATIONAL CONFERENCE ON CONTROL OF RESTRICTIVE BUSINESS
PRACTICES, CHICAGO 1958 PROCEEDINGS. (Graduate School of Business,
University of Chicago, Studies in Business) Glencoe, Ill.: Free Press, 1960.
380 p.
Concerned with restrictive business practices conducted on an
international scale under private auspices.

Lectures and statements on restrictive trade practices of the United
Kingdom, The Netherlands, Norway, Germany, Austria, Belgium,
Canada, Denmark, France, Ireland, Japan, and Sweden. Also
contains summaries of discussions at closed sessions of government
policy toward restrictive business practices by members of the
government group and of the private group attending the conference. Conference was attended by representatives of sixteen
countries. Government officials were invited in an individual
and not an official capacity. Others attending included businessmen, economists, and lawyers.

Isaacs, Asher and Slesinger, Reuben E. BUSINESS, GOVERNMENT AND
PUBLIC POLICY. Princeton, N.J.: Van Nostrand, 1964. 461 p.
Designed for use in a college course, and includes fundamental
economic material. Major attention is paid to the antitrust
field. However, other areas such as labor, transportation, public utilities, small business, and agriculture are taken up to
illustrate the increasing role of government in the economy.
The influence of government on the national scene is treated
first, followed by a treatment of state and local, and the international governmental regulations and relationships.

Jackson, Elmo L. THE PRICING OF CIGARETTE TOBACCOS. Gainesville,
Florida: University of Florida Press, 1955. 239 p.
A study of the process of price development in the flue-cured
and burley auction markets.

A sequel to Professor William H. Nicholl's major study of price
policies in the cigarette industry. This study makes a further
examination of tobacco-leaf pricing.

Johnson, Arthur M. THE DEVELOPMENT OF AMERICAN PETROLEUM PIPE
LINES: A STUDY OF ENTERPRISE AND PUBLIC POLICY, 1869-1906. Ithaca,
N.Y.: Cornell University Press, 1955. 307 p.
Traces relationship of private enterprise to public policy in connection with the pipe lines and their relations to other branches
of the petroleum industry.

Johnson, Arthur M. GOVERNMENT AND BUSINESS RELATIONS. Columbus, Ohio: Merrill, 1965. 384 p.
> For college students.

Johnson, Arthur M. GOVERNMENT-BUSINESS RELATIONS, A PRAGMATIC APPROACH TO THE AMERICAN EXPERIENCE. Columbus, Ohio: Merrill, 1965. 446 p.

Joskow, Jules and Stelzer, Irwin M. THE CONSUMER AND ANTITRUST. (Consumer Problem Series, No. 4) Greeley, Colo.: Council on Consumer Information, 1957. 31 p.

Judicial Conference of the United States. HANDBOOK OF RECOMMENDED PROCEDURES FOR THE TRIAL OF PROTRACTED CASES. Report of the Judicial Conference Study Group on Procedure in Protracted Litigation. Washington, D.C.: March 1960.
> A report adopted by the Judicial Conference of the United States in March 1960. A study of the pretrial organization and trial of long and complicated civil and criminal litigation in the United States district courts. It represents the culmination of three years of intensive investigation and deliberation, and a careful marshalling of experience by a study group consisting of a special panel of federal judges commissioned by Chief Justice Earl Warren. It is a collection of procedures which are "recommended" because they are deemed worthy of consideration by all. Primarily it is a compendium of the ideas and suggestions expressed by experienced judges and trial counsel at the Seminars on Protracted Cases held at the New York University Law Center in 1957 and at the University of Stanford School of Law in 1958.

Kamerman, Michael. RESALE PRICE MAINTENANCE--AN EXAMPLE OF VERTICAL MARKET COORDINATION. (Graduate Economics Seminar Publication, No. 15) Syracuse: Department of Economics, Syracuse University, 1955. 20 p.
> A paper delivered before the Graduate Economics Seminar. An analysis whose purpose is to develop, by means of a study of market structures, a method of studying the presence and conditions of resale price maintenance in the market. Provides an economic rationale for it.

Kaplan, A.D.H. BIG ENTERPRISE IN A COMPETITIVE SYSTEM. Rev. ed. Washington, D.C.: Brookings Institution, 1964. 240 p.
> The purpose of the first edition of this book, published in 1954, was to contribute to a more realistic understanding of the position and performance of big business in the American economy. The study pointed to the need to revise a number of traditional conceptions of the way in which large firms operate and the way competition works.
>
> This revised edition takes a second look at the problem in the light of developments during the past decade and brings the study up to date.

Kaplan, Abraham D.H., et al. PRICING IN BIG BUSINESS: A CASE APPROACH. Washington, D.C.: Brookings Institution, 1958. 344 p.

Deals with price policy and pricing practices. Based on a series
of interviews with top management of a representative group of
large-scale enterprises in the fields of primary production, manufacturing and distribution. The survey was conducted primarily
for the purpose of interpreting the general role of big business
in the American economy, and pricing was considered within the
context of comprehensive company policy.

Kaysen, Carl and Turner, Donald F. ANTITRUST POLICY: AN ECONOMIC
AND LEGAL ANALYSIS. (Harvard University Series on Competition in American Industry, No. 7) Cambridge: Harvard University Press, 1959. 345 p.
This study undertakes a thorough reassessment of antitrust policy
and offers a number of suggestions for improvement. One of its
most controversial proposals is unreasonable market power as a
test of antitrust violation.

Kaysen, Carl. UNITED STATES v. UNITED SHOE MACHINERY CORPORA-
TION; AN ECONOMIC ANALYSIS OF AN ANTI-TRUST CASE. (Harvard
Economic Studies, v. 99) Cambridge: Harvard University Press, 1956. 404 p.
All but three chapters are the memoranda prepared for the court
by the author who was clerk to Judge Wyzanski, before whom
the trial was conducted.

Kefauver, Estes (with the assistance of Till, Irene) IN A FEW HANDS--MO-
NOPOLY POWER IN AMERICA. New York: Pantheon Books, 1965.
Based on hearings on administered prices held by the Senate
Subcommittee on Antitrust and Monopoly from 1956 to 1963.
Investigations covered drug, automobile, steel and bread in-
dustries.

Kintner, Earl W. AN ANTITRUST PRIMER. A GUIDE TO ANTITRUST AND
TRADE REGULATION LAWS FOR BUSINESSMEN. New York: Macmillan,
1964. 316 p.
Intended to help the businessman become familiar with the antitrust and trade regulation laws. The author, formerly chairman
and general counsel of the Federal Trade Commission, tells why
these laws were enacted, what they provide, who enforces
them, and how they are enforced. Special treatment is given
to deceptive advertising.

Kirsch, William. MONOPOLY AND SOCIAL CONTROL. Washington, D.C.:
Public Affairs Press, 1952. 158 p.

Knauth, Oswald. BUSINESS PRACTICES, TRADE POSITION AND COMPETI-
TION. New York: Columbia University Press, 1956. 181 p.
A history of the development of business practices and an eco-
nomic theory of them.

Concerned with that portion of the economy falling under the
general heading of mass production and distribution, continuous
flow of goods and dynamic change, which composes about two-
thirds of our economy. The remaining one-third is operated by
the government and small business.

Koontz, Harold and Gable, Richard W.   PUBLIC CONTROL OF ECONOMIC
ENTERPRISE. New York: McGraw-Hill, 1956. 851 p.
> Designed to describe and analyze the field of public control of
> economic enterprise in the United States. The word "control" is
> interpreted to apply, in addition to specific regulation of busi-
> ness, to the intervention of government into economic affairs
> through aids and ownership and through broader fiscal monetary
> controls designed to influence the entire economy. Special em-
> phasis has been given to transportation and public utilities since
> they have furnished much which has become a pattern for posi-
> tive control when extended to other businesses. Emphasis is
> also placed on programs of control to maintain competition.

Kreps, T.   AN EVALUATION OF ANTITRUST POLICY; ITS RELATION TO
ECONOMIC GROWTH, FULL EMPLOYMENT AND PRICES. Washington,
D.C.: Government Printing Office, 1960. 49 p.

Krislov, Samuel and Musolf, L. D., eds.   THE POLITICS OF REGULATION; A
READER. Boston: Houghton-Mifflin, 1964. 261 p.

Kronstein, Heinrich D., et al.   MODERN AMERICAN ANTITRUST LAW: A
GUIDE TO ITS DOMESTIC AND FOREIGN APPLICATION. New York:
Oceana, 1958. 319 p.
> Divided into ten chapters, each dealing with a major antitrust
> problem and subdivided as seemed appropriate to clarify the
> subject. For those who desire to go beyond a brief orientation,
> as well as to compare materials on the more settled areas of
> the law, the book is designed to be a ready and reliable,
> though selective, reference tool.

Kronstein, Heinrich D.   REGULATION OF TRADE, A CASE AND TEXTBOOK.
New York: Fallon, 1953. 1188 p.

Labor Research Association.   MONOPOLY TODAY. New York: International
Publishers, 1950. 128 p.
> Draws mainly on government documents to illustrate the present
> workings of monopoly in the United States during World War II
> and the subsequent period of the cold war.

Lamb, George P. and Kittelle, Sumner S.   TRADE ASSOCIATION LAW AND
PRACTICE. (The Trade Regulation Series) Boston: Little, Brown, 1956.
284 p.
> "In subject matter, the coverage is broad, and no conventional
> trade association activity is neglected: Statistical Reporting;
> Price Activities (including a sensitive awareness of the problem
> of delivered prices and the use of freight books); Cost Account-
> ing; Product Standardization and Simplification; Credit Activities;
> Joint Research, Invention, and Patenting; and the so-called
> elimination of trade abuses are each thoroughly delineated. In
> addition, there is a useful chapter on the Webb-Pomerene Act,
> and a discerning discussion of relations between industry and the
> Federal Government including the specifics of 'lobbying' and of
> industry advisory committees." H. Thomas Austern, 56 Mich.
> L.R. 149.

Landau, Henry, ed. DOING BUSINESS ABROAD. New York: Practising
Law Institute, 1962. 2 vols.
> These volumes are an outgrowth of a two-day forum conducted
> by the Practising Law Institute. However, it is not a mere
> reprint of papers read at the forum. The speakers have included
> in their articles a vast amount of additional material, including
> a discussion of developments during recent months. In addition,
> helpful articles are included which did not form part of the
> Forum.
>
> The purpose of this work is to present the many areas of law
> and business which must be understood by legal advisers of busi-
> nessmen engaged in or contemplating foreign business opera-
> tion.

Lane, Robert E. THE REGULATION OF BUSINESSMEN. (Yale Studies in
Political Science, Vol. 1) New Haven: Yale University Press, 1954. 144 p.
> Main focus of book is upon the problems which emerge from
> Sherman Antitrust Act, Federal Trade Commission Act, Clayton
> Act, National Labor Relations Act, Robinson-Patman Act, Fair
> Trade (Miller-Tydings) Act, Fair Labor Standards Act, and Labor
> Management Relations Act.

Lanzillotti, Robert F. THE HARD-SURFACE FLOOR COVERING INDUSTRY:
A CASE STUDY OF MARKET STRUCTURE AND COMPETITION IN OLIGO-
POLY. Pullman, Washington: State College of Washington Press, 1955.
204 p.

Latham, Earl. THE GROUP BASIS OF POLITICS: A STUDY IN BASING-
POINT LEGISLATION. Ithaca, N.Y.: Published for Amherst College by
Cornell University Press, 1952. 244 p.
> This book is a study of the struggle in the 80th and 81st Con-
> gresses to enact legislation dealing with the basing-point system
> of quoting delivered prices which has been widely practiced in
> industries producing fungible goods, bulky in character, and
> normally delivered by railroad.

Learned, Edmund P. and Ellsworth, Catherine C. GASOLINE PRICING IN
OHIO. Boston: Graduate School of Business Administration, Harvard University, 1959. 258 p.
> Even though the data and analyses are based on the Ohio gaso-
> line market, the findings of the research have much broader
> relevance not only to marketers of gasoline in other states but
> to business managers generally and to students of pricing and
> other competitive practices in universities and regulatory agen-
> cies.

Leftwich, Richard H. THE PRICE SYSTEM AND RESOURCE ALLOCATION.
Rev. ed. New York: Holt, Rinehart, 1960. 381 p.
> Contains chapters on Pricing and Output under Pure Competition,
> Pricing and Output under Pure Monopoly, Pricing and Output
> under Oligopoly, Price and Output under Monopolistic Competi-
> tion, Pricing and Employment of Resources: Pure Competition,
> and Pricing and Employment of Resources: Monopoly and Monop-
> sony.

LEGAL ASPECTS OF COMPETITIVE BUSINESS PRACTICES. Berkeley: University of California Extension, Department of Continuing Education of the Bar, 1961.

Levin, Harvey J. BUSINESS ORGANIZATION AND PUBLIC POLICY: A BOOK OF READINGS. New York: Rinehart, 1958. 550 p.

Levin, Harvey J. BROADCAST REGULATION AND JOINT OWNERSHIP OF MEDIA. New York: New York University Press, 1960. 219 p.

Lilienthal, David E. BIG BUSINESS: A NEW ERA. New York: Harper, 1953. 209 p.
> Author's Note states: "In this book I write primarily of Bigness in business. But what I have in the back of my mind is more than the need for realism, honest emotion and sensible public policy about Big Business. We are ready for a new frame of mind about our newborn industrial civilization and its potentialities for the development of the individual personality. The time is right. There is the feel of change in the wind."

Lindahl, Martin L. and Carter, William A. CORPORATE CONCENTRATION AND PUBLIC POLICY. 3rd ed. Englewood Cliffs, N.J.: Prentice-Hall, 1959. 698 p.
> Emphasis in this revision, as in earlier editions, is upon materials relating to the modern large corporation, concentration of economic power in American industry, and the public policy of maintaining competition. Bringing these materials up to date required an expanded treatment of the interpretation and application of the Sherman Act, the Antimerger Act of 1950, and the Robinson-Patman Act.

Little, Arthur D., Inc. MERGERS AND ACQUISITIONS: PLANNING AND ACTION. 2nd ed. New York: Financial Executives Research Foundation, 1963. 229 p.
> A research study and report prepared for the foundation.

Loescher, Samuel M. IMPERFECT COLLUSION IN THE CEMENT INDUSTRY. (Harvard University Series on Competition in American Industry, No. 4) Cambridge: Harvard University Press, 1959. 331 p.
> This examination of economic developments in the American cement industry centers around the basing-point pricing system, which the author characterizes as imperfect, but effective, collusion. Drawn in large part from the massive economic record of the 1948 Cement case, the findings are applied to an introductory theory of geographical formula pricing.

Lyons, Barrow. TOMORROW'S BIRTHRIGHT: A POLITICAL AND ECONOMIC INTERPRETATION OF OUR NATURAL RESOURCES. New York: Funk & Wagnall, 1955. 424 p.

MacIntyre, Malcolm A. COMPETITIVE PRIVATE ENTERPRISE UNDER GOVERNMENT REGULATION. (Charles C. Moskovitz Lectures, No. 3) New York: New York University Press, 1964. 61 p.
> The number and complexity of the problems facing the airline industry in the United States today receive expert attention in this volume.

McAllister, Harry E. THE ELASTICITY OF DEMAND FOR GASOLINE IN THE STATE OF WASHINGTON. Pullman, Washington: State College of Washington, 1956. 80 p.

McCarthy, George D. ACQUISITIONS AND MERGERS. New York: Ronald, 1963. 353 p.
> The author is a partner in Price, Waterhouse & Co., accountants. His book is intended to offer a comprehensive guide and useful reference work to show the factors to be considered, and the steps undertaken in effecting corporate acquisitions and mergers. Among the topics discussed are: types of business combinations; financial and accounting information needed before effecting the deal; management, marketing and operating information needed before effecting the deal; how to value a company; how to account for a "purchase" or a "pooling of interests"; financial and other provisions of business combination agreements; federal tax aspects; SEC filing requirements; financial data required in SEC filings; stock exchange listing requirements.

McKie, James W. TIN CANS AND TIN PLATE: A STUDY OF COMPETITION IN TWO RELATED MARKETS. (Harvard Series on Competition in American Industry, No. 5) Cambridge: Harvard University Press, 1959. 321 p.

Machlup, Fritz. THE ECONOMICS OF SELLERS' COMPETITION, MODEL ANALYSIS OF SELLERS' CONDUCT. Baltimore: Johns Hopkins Press, 1952. 602 p.
> Confined to the economic theory of competition in selling. The author's book on the political economy of monopoly is a companion volume.

Machlup, Fritz. THE POLITICAL ECONOMY OF MONOPOLY, BUSINESS, LABOR AND GOVERNMENT POLICIES. Baltimore: Johns Hopkins Press, 1952. 560 p.
> Provides useful background knowledge for the student of the economics of competition and monopoly, while its companion volume, The Economics of Sellers' Competition, provides the necessary theoretical analysis.

Mansfield, Edwin, ed. MONOPOLY POWER AND ECONOMIC PERFORMANCE: PROBLEM OF INDUSTRIAL CONCENTRATION. New York: W.W. Norton, 1964. 174 p.
> Book consists of a group of essays divided into three parts: Part I. Market Structure, Resource Allocation, and Economic Progress; Part II. Industrial Concentration, Collusion, and the Social Responsibility of Big Business (includes the steel price controversy of 1962); Part III. The Antitrust Laws: Provisions, Effectiveness and Standards.

Martin, David D. MERGERS AND THE CLAYTON ACT. Berkeley: University of California Press, 1959. 351 p.
> The purpose of this study is to examine the reasons for the passage by Congress of the original and the amended Section 7 of the Clayton Act, and to analyze the administration of the section and the implications of its amendment. Some observations

are offered on the basic economic issues in the corporate merger policy of the United States.

Marx, Daniel, Jr. INTERNATIONAL SHIPPING CARTELS. Princeton: Princeton University Press, 1953. 323 p.

Mason, Edward S., ed. THE CORPORATION IN MODERN SOCIETY. Cambridge: Harvard University Press, 1960. 335 p.
> A collection of fourteen papers by such authorities as Eugene V. Rostow, Kingman Brewster, Jr., Neil W. Chamberlain and others analyzing the American corporate system.

Mason, Edward S. ECONOMIC CONCENTRATION AND THE MONOPOLY PROBLEM. (Harvard Economic Studies, v. 100) Cambridge: Harvard University Press, 1957. 411 p.
> Divided into four parts as follows: Part I. The Large Firm and the Structure of Industrial Market; Part II. Wage-Price Problems; Part III. Raw Materials, Security, and Economic Growth; Part IV. Antitrust Policy.

Massel, Mark S. COMPETITION AND MONOPOLY: LEGAL AND ECONOMIC ISSUES. Washington, D.C.: Brookings Institution, 1962. 477 p.
> "From the standpoint of content, the study is well organized and effectively presented. After discussing the confusion of goals and policy dilemmas involved in the regulation of competition, resulting in inconsistencies and interplay of countervailing forces, the author proceeds to a brief summary of the role of government. The discussion deals with both federal and state governmental activities, not only in the area of the antitrust law strictly speaking, but also in related areas such as interstate trade barriers, government purchasing activities, and the use of import and export regulations to further competition or, as a protectionist device, to promote forms of provincial monopoly." William H. Painter, 40 U. of Detroit L.J. 167.

Mathes, William C. and Devitt, Edward J. FEDERAL JURY PRACTICE AND INSTRUCTIONS, CIVIL AND CRIMINAL. St. Paul: West, 1965. 724 p.
> Chapter 19 contains sample instructions for federal criminal antitrust cases involving conspiracy and contracts in restraint of trade. Chapter 80 contains instructions for federal civil antitrust cases--"private" actions for treble damages. There are notes to each set of instructions, containing extensive citations to cases involving the points covered by the instructions.

Maurer, Herrymon. GREAT ENTERPRISE: GROWTH AND BEHAVIOR OF THE BIG CORPORATION. New York: Macmillan, 1955. 303 p.
> The aim of the book is to suggest what the large corporation is, and where it may be going.

Mayall, Kenneth L. INTERNATIONAL CARTELS: ECONOMIC AND POLITICAL ASPECTS. Rutland, Vt.: C.E. Tuttle Co., 1951. 173 p.
> In the present book the author ably defends that which he refers

to, in his own words, as the brazen support of an untenable thesis, but stimulating, nonetheless, because it brings into sharp focus the virtues and vices of international restrictive schemes, both at private and governmental level, based upon economic realism as opposed to economic idealism.

Means, Gardiner C. THE CORPORATE REVOLUTION IN AMERICA; ECONOMIC REALITY vs. ECONOMIC THEORY. New York: Crowell-Collier, 1962. 191 p.
This book contains a collection of essays on the subject of big business and administered prices.

Means, Gardiner C. PRICING POWER & THE PUBLIC INTEREST, A STUDY BASED ON STEEL. New York: Harper, 1962. 359 p.
This book brings together two concepts, that of separation of ownership and control and that of administered prices. Steel-pricing has been chosen as the basis for analyzing pricing power, partly because of the economic importance of the industry and partly because of the availability of data and argument in the 1957-1959 Senate Committee Hearings on Administered Prices; and perhaps most importantly because the large rise in steel prices after 1953 sharpened the issues of public policy.

Miller, John P. ed. COMPETITION, CARTELS AND THEIR REGULATION. (Studies in Industrial Economics, No. 4) Amsterdam: North-Holland Publishing Co., 1962. 428 p.
This work consists of articles which explore the current state of knowledge and the experience of various countries in their efforts to promote economic development, freedom and opportunity. The effect of government policy as to restrictive practice, in promoting or retarding economic growth, is considered. The experiences of Great Britain, Germany, and the United States are examined.

Morton, Herbert C. LIVING WITH THE ANTITRUST LAWS. Hanover, N.H.: Amos Tuck School of Business Administration, Dartmouth College, 1956. 16 p.

Mund, Vernon A. GOVERNMENT AND BUSINESS. 4th ed. New York: Harper & Row, 1965. 385 p.
A standard text on public policy and business. Examines the latest landmark court cases and commission applications of the laws regulating business. Explains how federal and state antitrust laws affect general business and the "regulated" industries. This work also illustrates the importance of economics and the expanding role of the economist in shaping public policy. Industrial organization, market structure, and present-day business practices, such as reciprocity, dual distribution, and refusal to sell, are discussed.

National Association of Attorneys General Antitrust Committee. HANDBOOK FOR STATE PROCUREMENT OFFICIALS ON IMPEDIMENTS TO COMPETITIVE BIDDING--HOW TO DETECT AND COMBAT THEM. Chicago: Council of State Governments, 1963. 38 p.

National Association of Manufacturers of the United States of America, Law Department. DIGEST ANALYSIS OF THE REPORT OF THE ATTORNEY GEN-ERAL'S NATIONAL COMMITTEE TO STUDY THE ANTITRUST LAWS. Washington: 1955. 36 p.

National Association of Manufacturers. THE FTC'S DEFENSE OF ITS RESEARCH AND NAM'S REPLY. (Economic policy division series No. 49.) New York: 1952. 71 p.

> Corwin D. Edwards, Director of the Bureau of Industrial Econom-ics of the Federal Trade Commission, has prepared a memorandum defending certain research studies published by that agency against criticisms contained in a NAM pamphlet.

National Association of Manufacturers. STUDIES ON CONCENTRATION. THE FEDERAL TRADE COMMISSION VERSUS THE FACTS. Prepared by George C. Hagedorn, research associate, Research Department, National Association of Manufacturers. New York: 1951. 40 p.

> An appraisal of three Federal Trade Commission studies: (1) Concentration of Productive Facilities; (2) The Divergence between Plant and Company Concentration; and (3) Interlocking Director-ates.

National Bureau Committee for Economic Research. BUSINESS CONCENTRA-TION AND PRICE POLICY, A CONFERENCE OF THE UNIVERSITIES. (National Bureau of Economic Research Special Conference, Series No. 5.) Princeton: Princeton University Press, 1955. 514 p.

> This conference was held at Princeton in June 1952. The papers and discussions have been revised since delivered. It deals with manufacturing industries almost exclusively.

National Industrial Conference Board. ECONOMIC CONCENTRATION MEA-SURES: USES AND ABUSES; A SESSION OF THE 41ST ANNUAL MEETING OF THE CONFERENCE BOARD HELD AT NEW YORK CITY May 17, 1957. AND A PAPER BY BETTY BOCK. (Studies in Business Economics, No. 57) New York: 1957. 55 p.

> Includes a discussion of the report about to be published at the time by the Antitrust Subcommittee of the Senate Committee on the Judiciary, on economic concentration, based on Bureau of the Census data on manufactures. The session was broadened to take in the significance and limitations of existing measures of economic concentration. Two economists spoke on the technical problems of constructing measures of concentration and the policy problems emerging therefrom. Another participant discussed some of the practical problems facing businesses that seek to expand through mergers.

National Industrial Conference Board. ADMINISTERED PRICING: ECONOM-IC AND LEGAL ISSUES. (The Conference Recorder). New York: 1958. 55 p.

Contains a series of valuable commentaries on "administered pricing," prepared in connection with the conference board's 42nd annual meeting in May, 1958. Among the topics discussed are: definition of administered prices by economists and uses of the concept in the study of problems of competition and economic growth; pricing problems in basic growth industries; behavior of prices in recession periods; and the relevance of the administered pricing concept to the antitrust laws.

National Industrial Conference Board. ANTITRUST IN AN EXPANDING ECONOMY. Transcript of a special one-day conference held May 16, 1962. New York: 1962. 102 p.
Speakers at the meetings addressed themselves to both the broad principles and practical operating problems involved in this increasingly complex and sensitive area of contact between government and business.

National Industrial Conference Board. ANTITRUST PROBLEMS OF EXPANDING BUSINESS ABROAD. New York: 1965. 31 p.
Addresses presented at a workshop held during the fourth conference on Antitrust in an Expanding Economy, March 4, 1965.

National Industrial Conference Board. THE CLIMATE OF ANTITRUST. Second Conference of Antitrust in an Expanding Economy. Transcript of special conference March 7, 1963. New York: 1963. 87 p.
These addresses are concerned with a broad analysis of the basic antitrust issues of 1963, as indicated by recent court decisions, and with the problems companies face in establishing and maintaining programs for effective compliance with antitrust laws and interpretations.

National Industrial Conference Board. THE "FAIR TRADE" QUESTION, prepared by the conference forum. (Studies in Business Economics No. 48.) New York: 1955. 112 p.
Considers the question of whether price competition in distribution should be carried out only at the manufacturing level, or whether there should be vigorous competition among retailers as well. Problem of loss-leader selling (when an article is sold in retail trade below cost to attract buyers for other merchandise) is explored. Also discusses advantages of freedom to raise or lower prices at all levels of the economy including retail distribution.

National Industrial Conference Board. FOREIGN LICENSING AGREEMENTS I. EVALUATION AND PLANNING. (Studies in Business Policy, No. 86.) New York: 1958.
Includes chapter entitled "Antitrust Considerations in Licensing." Topics covered include relevant legislation, the issue of jurisdiction, illegal or questionable practices, exclusive or non-exclusive rights, practical safeguards, production feasibility and costs, and sources of information and advice.

National Industrial Conference Board. THE IMPACT OF ANTITRUST ON ECONOMIC GROWTH. New York: 1964. 55 p.

A transcript of the Third Conference on Antitrust in an Expanding Economy, held March 5, 1964. The papers presented are: "Company Issues," by John J. Scott, General Counsel, Socony Mobil Oil Company; "Market Issues"--a corporate counsel's view, by Lawrence S. Apsey, General Attorney, Celanese Corporation of America--an economists's view, by M.A. Adelman, Professor of Economics, Massachusetts Institute of Technology; "The National Issue," by Philip Elman, Commissioner, Federal Trade Commission; and "How Antitrust Affects One Company's Long Range Planning," by Lawrence Litchfield, Jr., Chairman of the Board and Director, Aluminum Company of America.

National Industrial Conference Board. THE IMPACT OF ANTITRUST ON ECONOMIC GROWTH. New York: 1965. 52 p.
> Papers presented at the fourth conference on Antitrust in an Expanding Economy, held March 4, 1965.

National Industrial Conference Board. PUBLIC POLICY TOWARD COMPETITION, NEW ANTITRUST DIRECTIONS. Monographs by Corwin D. Edwards, James A. Rahl and Frederick M. Rowe. New York: The Conference Recorder, 1962. 44 p.
> The key antitrust issues are today both economic and legal since they are directed to the effects of company size and company practices as these impinge on opportunities of other companies to compete. The present publication contains three penetrating commentaries on the antitrust laws as instruments of government policy for a competitive era.

National Wholesale Druggists' Association. THE BASIS AND DEVELOPMENT OF FAIR TRADE. 3rd ed. New York: 1955. 170 p.
> A compendium of the law and practice of fair trade, in operation in 45 of the [then] 48 states, Puerto Rico and Hawaii, including an interpretive analysis of court decisions on the fair trade laws, samples of the fair trade laws and other laws relating to fair distribution, and model fair trade contract forms suitable for use under the fair trade laws.

Neale, A.D. THE ANTITRUST LAWS OF THE UNITED STATES OF AMERICA. A STUDY OF COMPETITION ENFORCED BY LAW. (National Institute of Economic and Social Research, Economic and Social Studies XIX.) Cambridge, Eng.: University Press, 1960. 516 p.
> "The book ... is an astoundingly good survey of all of American antitrust lore, as an enumeration of its chapters will show. Origins and early history are set forth in an introduction. Price fixing, exclusionary practices market sharing, trade associations and basing point problems are treated in chapters I, II, and III. Monopolization, including the oligopoly and 'conscious parallelism' problems, are set forth in chapters IV through VI. Chapter VII deals with exclusive dealing and tying, and with mergers under the Clayton Act. Price discrimination (chapter VIII), patents (chapter IX), international cartels (chapter X), and resale-price maintenance (chapter XI), follow. Chapters XII and XIII deal, respectively, with questions of administration and remedies. The

book's two final chapters contain a thoughtful assessment of
United States antitrust policy, of its interplay with economic
analysis, and of its 'exportability' to other countries." Kurt L.
Hanslowe, 47 Cornell L.Q. 322.

Nelson, Ralph L. CONCENTRATION IN THE MANUFACTURING INDUSTRIES
OF THE UNITED STATES: MIDCENTURY REPORT. (Economic Census Studies,
No. 2.) New Haven: Yale University Press, 1963. 288 p.
This study presents measures of plant concentration as well as
company concentration. It presents a variety of concentration
measures which permit examination of a number of aspects of
the structure of industries. In addition, it presents historically
comparable measures of product concentration.

Nelson, Ralph L. MERGER MOVEMENTS IN AMERICAN INDUSTRY, 1895-
1956. (National Bureau of Economic Research. General Series, No. 66.)
Princeton: Princeton University Press. 1959. 177 p.
Not content with providing a definitive record of the most important merger movement in our history, the author has also
tested some of the leading explanations for the tidal wave of
mergers from 1898 to 1920. Three of these hypotheses--empha-
sizing the retardation of industrial growth at that time, the
sharpening of competition consequent on development of a national transportation system, and the growth of the securities
markets--receive special attention.

Neuner, Edward J. THE NATURAL GAS INDUSTRY: MONOPOLY AND
COMPETITION IN FIELD MARKETS. Norman: University of Oklahoma
Press, 1960. 302 p.
The object of this study is to provide factual and analytical
materials needed for a rational policy decision on federal regulation of natural gas production, and to offer a policy judgment
on the monopoly issue in natural gas production. This aim is
sought to be accomplished by an investigation of natural gas
field markets over the period of 1945-1953, during which time
the major postwar expansion of the industry took place.

New York State Bar Association. Section on Antitrust Law. HOW TO COM-
PLY WITH THE ANTITRUST LAWS, edited by Jerrold G. Van Cise and Charles
Wesley Dunn. Chicago: Commerce Clearing House, 1954. 402 p.
Selected papers delivered before the Section on Antitrust Law of
the New York State Bar Association, including the 1954 Anti-

trust Law Symposium.

New York State Bar Association. Section on Antitrust Law. Special Committee to Study the New York Antitrust Laws. Report. Albany: 1957. 138 p.
Study of the New York State antitrust laws and their role in the federal system.

New York State Bar Association. Special Committee of the Section on Anti-Trust Law. LETTER OF TRANSMITTAL AND MEMORANDUM FOR THE PRESIDENT'S COMMITTEE ON BUSINESS AND GOVERNMENT RELATIONS. New York: 1950. 64 p.

Newman, Philip C. PUBLIC CONTROL OF BUSINESS. AN INTERNATIONAL APPROACH. New York: Praeger, 1955. 500 p.
The second volume of a two volume set, this book contains the materials and cases accumulated in preparing a treatise on government control of business activities. Part A covers cartel agreements, based on the licensing of patents; Part B, cartel agreements other than patent licensing; Part C, international commodity agreements; Part D, national laws on monopolies and combinations; Part E, the judicial interpretation of anti-monopoly legislation; Part F, consent judgments and other enforcement techniques; and Part G, international proposals to deal with the monopoly problem.

Part A is concerned with the private market control agreements based on patents and contracts between two giant companies, usually of different nationalities. Part B sets out types of agreements where there are a large number of cartel participants, both private and governmental. Part C sets out agreements as to international commodities by governments, generally in the field of agriculture. The other parts into which the book is divided are self-explanatory.

Norbye, O.D.K. MISSION REPORT ON RESTRICTIVE BUSINESS PRACTICES IN THE UNITED STATES. Paris: European Productivity Agency of the Organisation for European Economic Co-operation, 1959. 142 p.

Nordhaus, R.C. and Jurow, E.F. PATENT ANTITRUST LAW. Chicago: Jural, 1961. 460 p.
Since the patent laws, at least in a broad sense, authorize the granting of limited monopolies, while the antitrust laws are opposed to the development of monopolies, there is the ever present problem of how these laws can and should be reconciled. It is the resolution of this apparent, if not real, conflict with which this book is primarily concerned.

Northwestern University School of Law. CONFERENCE ON THE ANTITRUST LAWS AND THE ATTORNEY GENERAL'S COMMITTEE REPORT, A SYMPOSIUM (Trade Regulation Series No. 2.) New York: Federal Legal Publications, 1955. 268 p.
Proceedings held under the auspices of the Northwestern University Law School and the Committee on Antitrust Law of the Chicago Bar Association, May 10-11, 1955, in Chicago. Edited by James A. Rahl and Earle Warren Zaidins.

Nutter, G. Warren. THE EXTENT OF ENTERPRISE MONOPOLY IN THE
UNITED STATES, 1899-1939; a quantitative study of some aspects of monopoly.
Chicago: University of Chicago Press, 1951. 169 p.
> The author has explored existing studies and existing data and
> attempted to measure the extent and growth of monopoly in the
> United States. He contends that there is no basis for the im-
> pression that there has been a significant increase in monopoly
> in this country since about 1900, and that the effectively mono-
> polistic industries account for about a fifth of the national in-
> come. He concludes that while the problem is real, it is
> manageable.

Oberdorfer, Conrad W., et al. COMMON MARKET CARTEL LAW. New
York: Commerce Clearing House, 1963. 225 p.
> A commentary on articles 85 and 86 of the EEC treaty and regu-
> lations Nos. 17, 27 and 26, the antitrust provisions. A transla-
> tion of Recht und Wirtschaft.

Oppenheim, S. Chesterfield. FEDERAL ANTITRUST LAWS, CASES AND
COMMENTS. 2nd ed. (American Casebook Series.) St. Paul: West, 1959.
1188 p. 1964 Supplement, 538 p.
> Coverage is focused upon the case law under the Sherman Act
> of 1890, as amended, and the supplementary Federal Trade Com-
> mission and Clayton Acts, as amended. Text material in the
> form of notes, comments, and reprints of most of the Report of
> the Attorney General's National Committee to Study the Anti-
> trust Laws and a few other documents provide material to facili-
> tate study of subject matter not covered in the opinions of the
> courts.

Oppenheim, S. Chesterfield. UNFAIR TRADE PRACTICES, CASES AND COM-
MENTS. 2nd ed. St. Paul: West, 1965. 783 p.
> Constructed as a companion volume to the author's Federal Anti-
> trust Laws casebook. The following topics are covered: privilege
> to compete; trademarks, trade names, and imitation of appear-
> ance and dress of product; appropriation of values created by
> another; deceptive advertising--common law, state regulation,
> and remedy of a competitor; disparagement of product, title,
> and business methods; Federal Trade Commission regulation of
> unfair methods of competition, and unfair or deceptive acts or
> practices; resale price maintenance under state Fair Trade laws;
> state statutes prohibiting sales below cost; price and service dis-
> crimination under the Robinson-Patman Act; and interference
> with contractual relationships.

Organisation for Economic Co-operation and Development. GUIDE TO LEGIS-
LATION ON RESTRICTIVE BUSINESS PRACTICES, EUROPE AND NORTH
AMERICA. Paris: 4 vols. Looseleaf.
> Covers the following: legislation on restrictive business
> practices in force in participating countries and inter-
> national legislation applying to several states, with a brief
> introduction on the historical background and underlying basic
> principles, and an outline of the structure of such legislation; explan-

atory notes on the legislation; and a selection of administrative and court decisions. Published in the two official languages of the OECD, English and French.

Organisation for Economic Co-operation and Development. REGISTER OF RESEARCH ON RESTRICTIVE BUSINESS PRACTICES. Preliminary edition. Paris: Committee of Experts on Restrictive Business Practices, June 29, 1962. 301 p. (Restricted).

The general aim of this register is to provide a guide to research on particular aspects of restrictive business practices undertaken in the various OECD countries.

Organisation for Economic Co-operation and Development. RESTRICTIVE BUSINESS PRACTICES, COMPARATIVE SUMMARY OF LEGISLATION IN EUROPE AND NORTH AMERICA. Paris: 1964. 134 p.

This summary follows the same aims as the Guide to Legislation on Restrictive Business Practices. Provides information in concise form on the attitude adopted by various legal systems with regard to seventeen main items selected from the field of restrictive business practices, set out in table form. This information is accompanied by references to laws and regulations, to decisions of the courts, and also to the Guide to Legislation on Restrictive Business Practices. Intended as a working document providing easy and rapid comparison between the various attitudes adopted by member countries and international organizations towards restrictive business practices.

Oxenfeldt, Alfred R., et al. INSIGHTS INTO PRICING, FROM OPERATIONS RESEARCH AND BEHAVIORAL SCIENCE. Belmont, California: Wadsworth, 1961. 124 p.

Oxenfeldt, Alfred R. INDUSTRIAL PRICING AND MARKET PRACTICES. New York: Prentice-Hall, 1951. 602 p.

Concerned with the pricing of industrial products. Both price theory and pricing practices are discussed in an effort to present a full and accurate, yet fairly general, explanation of price behavior.

Palamountain, J.R., Jr. THE POLICIES OF DISTRIBUTION. Cambridge: Harvard University Press, 1955. 250 p.

Papandreou, Andreas G. and Wheeler, John T. COMPETITION AND ITS REGULATION. New York: Prentice-Hall, 1954. 504 p.

Intended to bridge economic analysis, institutional description and legal interpretation. Book One, on "Competition," is devoted to a systematic formulation of the analytical equipment which is necessary for an understanding of the problems of regulation of competitive behavior. Book Two, on "Regulation of Competition," is devoted to an evolutionary analysis of our antitrust law. The major novel feature is the use of game theoretical concepts and the evaluation of public policy in terms of criteria based on strategy or behavior types.

The authors are economists on the faculty of the University of Minnesota.

Patman, Wright. COMPLETE GUIDE TO THE ROBINSON-PATMAN ACT.
Englewood Cliffs, N.J.: Prentice-Hall, 1963. 401 p.
> While this volume was prepared with a view to making it useful
> to members of the legal and accounting professions, thought and
> effort was devoted also to making it a helpful tool for business-
> men who need at hand a ready explanation of the Robinson-
> Patman Act, and how to comply with its provisions.

Peck, Merton J. COMPETITION IN THE ALUMINUM INDUSTRY, 1945-1958.
Cambridge: Harvard University Press, 1961. 227 p.
> Intended to fill the gap as to the economic results that the anti-
> trust opinions of Judges Hand and Knox, affecting the aluminum
> industry, helped bring about. Describes the nature of competi-
> tion in the postwar aluminum industry. Argues that the "infor-
> mal antitrust" represented by non-judicial action, has had a
> greater economic effect than have the decisions of the courts.
> This "informal antitrust" consists of acts of administrative agen-
> cies and investigations by Congressional committees. The study
> is limited to the years 1945 to 1958.

Pegrum, Dudley F. PUBLIC REGULATION OF BUSINESS. Rev. ed. Homewood, Illinois: Irwin, 1965. 766 p.
> Part IV entitled "The Antitrust Laws" covers: (a) The Legal
> Foundation of Regulation; (b) Antitrust Legislation; (c) Agencies
> for Enforcing the Antitrust Law; (d) Mergers and Consolidations
> under the Sherman Act; (e) Agreements Restricting Competition;
> (f) Enforcement by the Federal Trade Commission; (g) Patents
> and the Antitrust Laws; (h) International Combinations; and (i)
> Can the Antitrust Laws Succeed?

Phillips, Almarin. PERSPECTIVES ON ANTITRUST POLICY. Princeton:
Princeton University Press, 1965. 454 p.
> A collection of 17 essays, presented as papers at a seminar on
> antitrust policy at the University of Virginia in 1963.
>
> Chapters 4 through 14 deal with topics such as conscious parallel-
> ism, administered prices, the merger provision of the Clayton
> Act, bank mergers, and competition in transportation.

Phillips, Almarin. MARKET STRUCTURE, ORGANIZATION AND PERFOR-
MANCE. AN ESSAY ON PRICE-FIXING AND COMBINATIONS IN RE-
STRAINT OF TRADE. Cambridge: Harvard University Press, 1962. 257 p.
> Part One includes a chapter on the theory of interfirm organization.
> (This theory is based on the assumption that competition, as it ap-
> pears in the real world, takes the form of interdependent rivalry.)
> Part Two considers "Conscious Parallelism and the Informal Organi-
> zation of Oligopoly," (Ch. III); "Exempted Industries: Sanctioned
> Organizational Formality" (Ch. IV.); and such cases as United
> States v. Addyston Pipe and Steel Co., the Appalachian Coals

case, the Hardwood Cases, the Trenton Potteries Case, and the Plate Glass Mirror Case. Final chapters cover the development of the per se rule and policy conclusions.

Phillips, Charles F., Jr. COMPETITION IN THE SYNTHETIC RUBBER INDUSTRY. Chapel Hill: University of North Carolina Press, 1963. 281 p.

Phillips, Joseph D. LITTLE BUSINESS IN THE AMERICAN ECONOMY. (Illinois Studies in the Social Sciences, Vol. 42.) Urbana: University of Illinois Press, 1958. 135 p.
> This book describes and analyzes the mass of truly small business firms in commerce and industry, nearly half of them with no paid employees. The author considers how independent they are; how important they are in the aggregate, quantitatively; what their prospects are; and what issues of public policy they create.

Pollzien, Gotz M. and Bronfen, George B. eds. INTERNATIONAL LICENSING AGREEMENTS. Indianapolis: Bobbs-Merrill, 1965. 426 p.
> Covers 22 countries. Includes brief coverage of antitrust or cartel laws of countries in which they exist. Part three is entitled "Licensing Agreements under the Antitrust Rules of the Common Market."

Proxmire, William. CAN SMALL BUSINESS SURVIVE? New York: Regnery, 1965. 225 p.
> The author, who is chairman of the Small Business Subcommittee of the Senate Committee on Banking and Currency, advocates more stringent antitrust laws with regard to mergers.

Purdy, Harry, et al. CORPORATE CONCENTRATION AND PUBLIC POLICY. (Prentice-Hall Economic Series.) 2nd ed. New York: Prentice-Hall, 1950. 729 p.
> Devoted to the problems and public policies arising from the concentration of economic power in the United States. Confined to monopoly and monopolistic competition in the general field of industry.

Quinn, Theodore K. GIANT BUSINESS: THREAT TO DEMOCRACY. THE AUTOBIOGRAPHY OF AN INSIDER. New York: Exposition Press, 1953. 321 p.
> The author, through his autobiography, sets out his views that unless the trend toward bigger and bigger corporations can be controlled and restrained, the country must expect more socialism. It is his view that public interest demands regulation of the giants and their concentrated economic power over the nation.

Quinn, Theodore K. GIANT CORPORATIONS; CHALLENGE TO FREEDOM; THE AMERICAN ECONOMIC REVOLUTION. New York: Exposition, 1956. 198 p.

Quinn, Theodore K. UNCONSCIOUS PUBLIC ENEMIES. Foreword by Estes Kefauver. New York: Citadel, 1962. 253 p.
> Theodore K. Quinn, a former vice president of General Electric Company, presents the case against monopoly, autocratic giant

corporations, price-fixing, profiteering, and many other anti-social activities which too often characterize Big Business in the United States. He holds that these evils have impeded the United States in its efforts to win support among the peoples of the world in its competition with the Communist way of life.

Redford, Emmette S. AMERICAN GOVERNMENT AND THE ECONOMY. New York: Macmillan, 1965. approx. 672 p.

A survey of the role of the government in our economic system, paying particular attention to the historical development of this role. Chapters are concerned with the antitrust laws; regulation and promotion of industries; and the system of administrative regulation.

Restrictive Practices Commission. PRICING PRACTICES IN THE PENCIL IN-DUSTRY. (RTPC No. 31 Series 1959.) Ottawa, Canada: 1964. 56 p.

A report on an inquiry under the Combines Investigation Act concerning the manufacture, distribution, and sale of pencils.

Richmond, Samuel B. REGULATION AND COMPETITION IN AIR TRANSPOR-TATION. New York: Columbia University Press, 1961. 309 p.

Concerned with the question of how to ascertain and realize the proper amount of competition in air transportation. Some problems considered are: what is competition; what is the proper amount of competition; which should be the competing carriers; can competition and regulatory policing be substituted for one another; how can regulation and competition be blended; what control mechanisms or courses of action are available to the Civil Aeronautics Board for its regulation of competition; and what has the Board tried to do.

Robinson, Joan. THE ECONOMICS OF IMPERFECT COMPETITION. London: Macmillan; New York: St. Martin's, 1961. 352 p.

This work was first published in 1933 and has since been reprinted numerous times, 1961 being the latest. The author tries to carry out the idea that the whole theory of value should be treated in terms of monopoly analysis.

The book has two major parts: monopoly--the principles of selling; and monopsony--the principles of buying. The topics treated under these parts are: monopoly equilibrium; competitive equilibrium; comparison of monopoly and competitive output; price discrimination; monopsony; demand as a factor of produc-tion; comparison of monopoly and competitive demand for labor; exploitation; and the world of monopolies.

Rowe, Frederick M. PRICE DISCRIMINATION UNDER THE ROBINSON-PAT-MAN ACT. (The Trade Regulation Series.) Boston: Little, Brown, 1962. 675 p. 1964 supplement, 185 p.

The plan and organization of this volume seek to facilitate an analytical and policy-oriented approach by the practitioner, rather than to supply pat but illusory answers, or to profess legal certainty where none exists. Rather, to the extent statu-tory interpretation remains in doubt, the contents of this book recognize the Supreme Court's <u>Automatic Canteen</u> formulation of 1953: to "reconcile" the vague provisions of the Robinson–Patman Act with "broader antitrust policies," in order to avert a price uniformity and rigidity in open conflict with the purposes of other antitrust legislation.

"Book provides not only an excellent guide through the intricacies of the Robinson–Patman Act, and the best available summary of the act's legislative history, but also an able critique of the law." Corwin D. Edwards, 111 U. of Pa. L.R. 258.

Rozwenc, Edwin C., ed. ROOSEVELT, WILSON AND THE TRUSTS. (Problems in American civilization; readings selected by the Department of American Studies, Amherst College) Boston: Heath, 1950. 115 p.
Readings chosen to help the reader form a judgment on the question of whether the government should try to create a regulatory commission powerful enough to control big corporations, or whether the government should try to prevent monopoly by creating a body of laws for the economy.

Rohlfing, Charles C., et al. BUSINESS AND GOVERNMENT. 6th ed. Brooklyn: Foundation, 1953. 866 p.
Designed for student use in "Business and Government" college courses.

Sage, George H. BASING–POINT PRICING SYSTEMS UNDER THE FEDERAL ANTITRUST LAWS; A LEGAL, BUSINESS, AND ECONOMIC ANALYSIS. St. Louis: Thomas Law Book, 1951. 381 p.
Devoted to the subject of legal problems of legality of basing-point pricing systems under the Federal Antitrust Laws. Purpose is to indicate and discuss the principal legal problems of legality present in any industrial or business situation in which a basing-point pricing system is being observed by a manufacturer group or an individual manufacturer.

Business and economic aspects are set forth and correlated with the legal problems.

Sawyer, Albert E. BUSINESS ASPECTS OF PRICING UNDER THE ROBINSON–PATMAN ACT. (The Trade Regulation Series.) Boston: Little, Brown, 1963. 514 p.
Aims to serve the broad needs of members of the bar in approaching the complex legal and business problems which must be dealt with in determining the limitations upon price differentials imposed by the Robinson–Patman Amendment to the Clayton Act.

Scharf, Charles A. TECHNIQUES FOR BUYING, SELLING, AND MERGING BUSINESSES. Englewood Cliffs, N.J.: Prentice-Hall, 1964. 258 p.
"Notwithstanding antitrust, New York attorney Scharf provides a how-to on selling and buying businesses, usually to or from other businesses. The book describes steps in the acquisition process from beginning to end: Planning to buy or sell, choosing a buyer or seller, setting the price, negotiating the contract, and closing the deal. Also noted are typical tax, accounting, and legal problems, including the antitrust problem, which could

come up along the way." Mary Jean Bennett, Wall Street
Journal. Sept. 11, 1964.

Schmidt, Heinz. CARTELS AND TRUSTS, THEIR ORIGIN, DEVELOPMENT
AND PRESENT DAY SIGNIFICANCE: AN ECONOMIC STUDY. Translated by
Fay Castles. Copenhagen: International Union of Food and Drink Workers'
Association, 1950. 137 p.

Schwartz, Louis B. FREE ENTERPRISE AND ECONOMIC ORGANIZATION;
LEGAL AND RELATED MATERIALS. (University Casebook Series) 2nd ed.
Brooklyn, N.Y.: Foundation Press, 1959. 1065 p.
> The common theme of all the branches of law dealt with in
> this book is the necessity of reconciling individual economic
> freedom with a variety of demands for private or official re-
> straint of freedom.

Shubik, Martin. STRATEGY AND MARKET STRUCTURE; COMPETITION,
OLIGOPOLY, AND THE THEORY OF GAMES. New York: John Wiley,
1959. 387 p.
> The primary purpose of this book is to develop a unified approach
> to the various theories of competition and markets. Primarily
> designed for economists, but parts are of interest to others.
> Expounds the "game theory."

Simmons, Andre. THE SHERMAN ANTITRUST ACT AND FOREIGN TRADE.
(University of Florida Monographs. Social Sciences, No. 16.) Gainesville:
University of Florida Press, 1962, c. 1963. 73 p.

Simon, William. GEOGRAPHIC PRICING PRACTICES; BASING-POINT SELL-
ING. Chicago: Callaghan, 1950. 381 p.
> The author's primary purpose is to compile available thinking on
> the subject.

Smith, G. Ralph and Smith, Hilda. AN ECONOMIC APPRAISAL OF RESALE
PRICE MAINTENANCE. (Study No. 202, Committee on Research, School of
Business Administration.) New Orleans: Loyola University, 1957. 138 p.
> Reviews and evaluates the economic effects of resale price
> maintenance on our competitive economy. Stresses the applica-
> tion of economic theory on this pricing practice. Does not
> include sales-below-cost, or unfair practices legislation.

Smith, Howard R. GOVERNMENT AND BUSINESS. New York: Ronald,
1958. 802 p.
> Emphasizes the underlying context within which economic policy
> is formulated rather than merely particular policies set in mo-
> tion. A modified historical approach is used. The author is
> Professor of Economics at the University of Georgia.

Southwestern Legal Foundation. PROCEEDINGS OF THE 1958 INSTITUTE ON
ANTITRUST LAWS. New York: Matthew Bender, 1958. 394 p.
> Consists of papers presented at the institute held in Dallas,
> Texas in April 1958. Topics covered are: marketing and the
> Robinson-Patman Act; similarity of prices with those of competi-
> tors; enforcement policy of the United States Department of
> Justice; antitrust problems under price war conditions; three D's

of antitrust enforcement; impact of duPont decision--section 7
of Clayton Act; recent developments in patent cross-licensing;
mergers and the new section 7; effect of foreign antitrust laws
on United States business; quantity discounts; Federal Trade
Commission--recent developments in unfair trade practices; and
copyrights and some antitrust problems.

State Bar of California. Committee on Continuing Education of the Bar.
LEGAL ASPECTS OF COMPETITIVE BUSINESS PRACTICES. Berkeley: 1961.
500 p.

A collection of papers on the following topics: how to acquire
or lose a trademark; trademark infringement action as a protective
means; copying a competitor; competition from an ex-employee;
civil and administrative limitations on selling and advertising;
civil liability based on selling and advertising; what competitors
can say about each other or their products; prices, premiums,
and lotteries; treble damages and attorneys' fees in antitrust
cases; and tax aspects of trademarks, litigation expenses, and
damages.

State Bar of California. Committee on Continuing Education of the Bar.
LEGAL ASPECTS OF DOING BUSINESS UNDER THE ANTITRUST LAWS.
Sponsored by the State Bar of California through University Extension, University of California. (California Specialty Handbook No. 2.) Berkeley: 1959.
185 p.

Presents, in very general terms, the framework of antitrust law.
No attempt is made to create a definitive source-book from
which all antitrust questions can be answered. The objective has
rather been to offer, in the form of concrete factual situations,
a view of areas of business activities within which the antitrust
laws may have a bearing, and the considerations and policies
involved in the solution of problems usually met by the practitioner in both federal and California areas.

Stein, Eric, ed. AMERICAN ENTERPRISE IN THE EUROPEAN COMMON
MARKET; A LEGAL PROFILE. Ann Arbor: University of Michigan Press,
1960. 2 vols.
Chapter X covers the cartel laws of the European Economic
Community.

Steiner, George A. GOVERNMENT'S ROLE IN ECONOMIC LIFE. New
York: McGraw-Hill, 1953. 415 p.
Prepared primarily for the author's students, but also for the
average person who thinks seriously about government's economic
actions and their relations to private economic life. Provides
background for the consideration of the proper role of government in the economic life of today.

Stelzer, Irwin M., ed. SELECTED ANTITRUST CASES; LANDMARK DECISIONS
IN FEDERAL ANTITRUST. Rev. ed. Homewood, Ill.: R.D. Irwin, 1961.
252 p.

Stickells, Austin T. LEGAL CONTROL OF BUSINESS PRACTICE. Mount
Kisco, New York: Baker, Voorhis, 1965. 843 p.

Presents existing federal law governing competition, covering common law as background. Chapter headings are: common law; federal regulation of competition--statutes; Sherman Anti-Trust Act; monopoly; trade associations; conscious parallelism-- uniform business behavior; delivered pricing; distribution-contracts; resale price maintenance--fair trade laws; mergers; intercorporate conspiracy; price discrimination--Robinson-Patman Act; patents and copyrights; false advertising--Federal Trade Commission Act; Federal Food, Drug and Cosmetic Act; Wool Products Labeling Act; Flammable Fabrics Act; enforcement of the antitrust laws.

Stigler, George J. THE THEORY OF PRICE. Rev. ed. New York: Macmillan, 1952. 310 p.
A general rewriting of a volume which was first published in 1942, with the addition of chapters on distribution of income by size, and on general equilibrium.

This work is concerned primarily with the analysis of the role of the price system in the enterprise type of economy. The author has sought to emphasize the relationship between theory and empirical evidence--how the theory is tested by the evidence and how evidence instructs on the forms of relationships.

Stigler, George J. and Boulding, Kenneth E. READINGS IN PRICE THEORY. Chicago: Irwin, 1952. 568 p.
Readings selected by a committee of the American Economic Association. Concentrates on the mechanics of the pricing process rather than on its evaluation. Excludes articles which are more in the nature of applied economics and concentrates on those of general theoretical interest. Takes a comprehensive view of the economic literature of the past 40 years.

Stocking, George W. BASING POINT PRICING AND REGIONAL DEVELOPMENT. A CASE STUDY OF THE IRON AND STEEL INDUSTRY. Chapel Hill, N.C.: University of North Carolina Press, 1954. 274 p.
Begun as a study of the significance to the South of basing-point pricing in the iron and steel industry. Expanded to analyze the industry's structure and its pricing practices. A case study in industrial structure, pricing practices and economic welfare. For the most part, it stops with 1939.

Stocking, George W. and Watkins, Myron W. MONOPOLY AND FREE ENTERPRISE. New York: Twentieth Century Fund, 1951. 596 p.
Focuses primarily on the relation of business organization to the structure and behavior of markets--how enterprise can be fostered and freedom of choice preserved without sacrificing efficiency or tolerating inequity. Much of the analysis of this study is based on patterns of industrial organization and business conduct prevailing before World War II.

Stocking, George W. WORKABLE COMPETITION AND ANTITRUST POLICY. Nashville: Vanderbilt University Press, 1961. 451 p.

"It is the adequacy of our present approach to antitrust problems with which Professor Stocking is mainly concerned. The central focus of his book, as its title suggests, is upon the interplay between the concept of 'workable competition' and antitrust policy." Kurt L. Hanslowe, 47 Cornell L.Q. 322.

Summer Institute on International and Comparative Law, University of Michigan, 1953. LECTURES ON FEDERAL ANTITRUST LAWS, delivered at University of Michigan Law School, June 17-19, 1953. Ann Arbor: University of Michigan Law School, 1954. 321 p.

The papers delivered at the 1953 Institute deal chiefly with current problems and policy questions under three major federal antitrust laws: the Sherman act; the Federal Trade Commission Act, and the Clayton Act, including the Robinson-Patman Amendment. These statutes affect the daily operations of all sizes and types of American business. Judicial interpretations and the administration and enforcement of these laws involve both legal and economic criteria, and tests of competition and monopoly. The institute provided a forum for authoritative analysis of these aspects in order to create a better understanding of the antitrust laws as one of the most important segments of national public policy affecting the relation of government to private business enterprise.

Sutton, Francis X., et al. THE AMERICAN BUSINESS CREED. Cambridge: Harvard University Press, 1956. 414 p.

An examination of the ideology of American business, as revealed in the public statements of business leaders, the institutional advertisements of large corporations, the literature of such business associations as the United States Chamber of Commerce, the Committee for Economic Development, and the National Association of Manufacturers. Much of the material is drawn from the period 1948-49.

Suviranta, Bruno, THE VIABILITY OF THE COMPETITIVE MARKET. (National Bank of Egypt Fiftieth Anniversary Commemoration Lectures.) Cairo: National Bank of Egypt, 1956. 28 p.

A lecture which takes up the long predominance of the classical theory of a competitive market, its sudden decline during the present century, and the revival of the theory of a competitive market, as experienced in recent years. The author is Professor of Economics at Helsinki University.

Taggart, Herbert F. COST JUSTIFICATION. (Michigan Business Studies, v. XIV, No. 3.) Ann Arbor: Bureau of Business Research, School of Business Administration, University of Michigan, 1959. 588 p.

The purpose of this volume is to array all of the recorded instances in which respondents to Federal Trade Commission complaints or defendants in treble damage suits have attempted to defend their pricing practices by presenting information about their costs.

Thompson, George C., and Brady, Gerald P. ANTITRUST FUNDAMENTALS. (Law in a Business Environment Series.) Belmont, Calif.: Wadsworth, 1964.

182 p.

> Provides basic introductory materials in the antitrust field. The landmark cases are edited down to workable size and interwoven with the text.

Thorelli, Hans B. THE FEDERAL ANTITRUST POLICY. Baltimore: Johns Hopkins, 1955. 658 p.

> In three chapters on the background of the Sherman Act, the author traces not only its origins in American common law and the English law of trade restraint, but also its roots in industrial evolution, constitutional theory, social conflict, and political and economic ideology. In a chapter on the passage of the Sherman Act, he supplies an account of the play of ideas which produced the law. In subsequent chapters he treats the interaction between economic and political trends, administrative policy, and court decisions prior to the establishment of the Antitrust Division of the Bureau of Corporations in 1903.

Timberlake, E. Compton. FEDERAL TREBLE DAMAGE ANTITRUST ACTIONS. Mundelein, Ill.: Callaghan, 1965. 404 p.

> Designed to assist those concerned with private actions under the antitrust laws. It discusses and attempts to delineate many of the intriguing problems which are commonly encountered in such cases.

> Volume includes chapters on plaintiff's standing to sue; jurisdiction, venue and process; the complaint and motions related thereto; preliminary injunctions; the statute of limitations; defense that plaintiff has violated the antitrust laws and defense of release; discovery; final pre-trial conferences; summary judgment; public injury in private Sherman Act cases; use of judgment from prior government action; legal injury; proof of the amount of damages; unitary verdicts in multiple defendant private antitrust actions; and attorney's fees and costs.

Toulmin, Harry A., Jr. A TREATISE ON THE ANTI-TRUST LAWS OF THE UNITED STATES AND INCLUDING ALL RELATED TRADE REGULATORY LAWS. Cincinnati: Anderson, 1949, with 1966 pocket supplements. 7 vols.

> Volumes 1, 2 and 3 cover the statutes and their legislative history; volumes 4 and 5 cover the application of the anti-trust laws; and volumes 6 and 7 deal with enforcement of the anti-trust laws.

> Written from the point of view of the trial lawyer specializing in the field of anti-trust and regulatory laws of business, particularly in the federal courts.

Travis, William P. THE THEORY OF TRADE AND PROTECTION. (Harvard Economic Studies, vol. 121.) Cambridge: Harvard University Press, 1964. 296 p.

> Discusses trade theory and analyzes the effects of restrictionist policies on a country's trade and production structure, allocation of resources, and general economic efficiency.

Tun, Thin. THE THEORY OF MARKETS, Cambridge: Harvard University Press
1960. 120 p.
> Intended for readers who have already been initiated into the
> theories of markets. A general study of pricing in three different
> markets: perfect competition; perfect monopoly; and imperfect
> competition. The main part of the book is concerned with
> oligopoly.

Universities National Bureau Committee for Economic Research. BUSINESS
CONCENTRATION AND PRICE POLICY. Princeton, N.J.: Princeton University Press, 1955. 511 p.
> A report of the National Bureau of Economic Research. Revised
> papers and discussions of the Conference on Business Concentra-
> tion and Price Policy held at Princeton University, June 17–19,
> 1952.

Van Cise, Jerrold G. THE FEDERAL ANTITRUST LAWS. Washington, D.C.:
American Enterprise Association, 1962. 86 p.
> The primary object of this study is to describe and explain the
> antitrust laws to non-lawyers, and through a better understand-
> ing of their intent and operation, to help the layman who must
> cope with this legislation. Deals with the major provisions of
> the antitrust laws, the purposes of Congress in enacting them,
> their interpretation and application by the courts, their enforce-
> ment and observance, and their effects upon the economy and
> society.

Van Cise, Jerrold G. UNDERSTANDING THE ANTITRUST LAWS. New York:
Practising Law Institute, 1966. 382 p.
> The objective of this monograph is to provide the general prac-
> titioner approaching this field of law for the first time with
> an initial over-all impression of the antitrust laws.

Waer, David K. COMMON MARKET ANTITRUST: A GUIDE TO THE LAW,
PROCEDURE AND LITERATURE. The Hague: Nijhoff, 1964. 67 p. 1965
supplement, 28 p.
> Literature, sources of law, and the procedure relating to Common
> Market antitrust problems. The first chapter outlines the set-up
> of the European Economic Community.

Wallace, Donald H. ECONOMIC CONTROLS AND DEFENSE. New York:
Twentieth Century Fund, 1953. 260 p.
> Deals principally with fundamental problems raised by use of
> direct controls in a long defense period. Treats the use of
> direct controls over materials, manpower, prices, and wages.
> A chapter, Basic Problems and Policies, by J. M. Clark, Chair-
> man of the Twentieth Century Fund Committee on Economic
> Stabilization, analyzes the basic problems with which the report
> is concerned, and sets forth the policies he believes are called
> for to meet them.

Walton, Clarence C. and Cleveland, Frederick W., Jr. CORPORATIONS
ON TRIAL: THE ELECTRIC CASES. Belmont, Calif.: Wadsworth, 1964.
138 p.

An account of the price-fixing charges made against major
electrical manufacturers. Useful features include a table listing federal antitrust cases in which major electrical manufacturers were defendants, a table listing electrical case indictments,
a glossary of technical terms, and a glossary of names.

Weiler, Emanuel. THE AMERICAN ECONOMIC SYSTEM: AN ANALYTICAL
APPROACH TO PUBLIC POLICY. New York: Macmillan, 1957. 623 p.
Designed for the student. The objective has been to
relate economic theory, economic institutions, and economic
facts to the public policy issues facing the nation. Emphasis
has been placed on the change and growth of the economy.

Wernette, John P. GOVERNMENT AND BUSINESS. New York: Macmillan,
1964. 534 p.
Deals with the proper roles of government and private sectors in
dealing with the fundamental domestic problem of how to use
material well-being as the foundation on which to build the
good society. Topics taken up are the structure of the government, government finance, economic growth, inflation, monopoly, regulation of public service industries, labor, the farm
problem, conservation of natural resources, government ownership of businesses, electric power and atomic energy, and international trade and development.

Weston, John F. THE ROLE OF MERGERS IN THE GROWTH OF LARGE
FIRMS. (Publications of the Bureau of Business and Economic Research,
University of California.) Berkeley: University of California Press, 1953.
159 p.
The extent of oligopoly in the American economy, its causes,
its economic and social consequences, and the formulation of
public policy for dealing with it are subjects of much current
interest. This study treats an important aspect of the historical
origin of concentration. It seeks to provide additional factual
material for appraising alternative public policies toward oligopoly.

White, William R. TRADE REGULATION AND SECURITY DEVICES, (Pace
Business Law Series, Unit 7.) New York: Pace & Pace, 1962. 142 p.
A basic book for students. Deals with advertising and publicity,
prices, restraints of trade and monopolies, insurance, guaranty,
and suretyship. The final chapter presents cases and propositions
for general review.

Whitney, Simon N. ANTITRUST POLICIES; AMERICAN EXPERIENCE IN
TWENTY INDUSTRIES. New York: Twentieth Century Fund, 1958. 2 vols.
"This study, by the ex-Chief of the Twentieth Century Fund's
Research Department and present Chief Economist for the Federal
Trade Commission, examines the operation of the antitrust laws
in twenty major industries. The pattern followed is much the
same for each: a description of the industry structure, the antitrust litigation that has occurred and its effects, and an examination of the resulting competitive status. Each individual study

closes with a useful summary. Following the individual studies, there is an over-all evaluation by the author, a brief commentary report by the Fund's Committee on Antitrust Policy, and a series of invited comments by experts in the several fields covered." John C. Stedman, 107 University of Pennsylvania L.R. 887.

Wilcox, Clair. PUBLIC POLICIES TOWARD BUSINESS. Rev. ed. Homewood, Ill.: Richard D. Irwin, 1960. 921 p.

Designed as a text for college and university courses in economics and political science dealing with public policy toward business enterprise. Seeks to give equal emphasis to the economic and political aspects of the policies that it examines. Equal attention is given to the major types of public policy toward business activity: maintaining competition, supplementing competition, moderating competition, substituting regulation for competition, and substituting public for private enterprise.

Williams, C. Arthur, Jr. PRICE DISCRIMINATION IN PROPERTY AND LIABILITY INSURANCE. (Studies in Economics and Business.) Minneapolis: University of Minnesota Press, 1959. 100 p.

No adequate study of discrimination in property and liability insurance premiums has heretofore been available. Professor Williams has delved deeply into the subject and has analyzed in some detail the various facets of premium discrimination in these two fields. Specifically, the study is limited to advance-premium property and liability insurance sold by stock and mutual companies. In this monograph the author presents the highlights of his study, including a discussion of the several rating methods available, dividend structures, group insurance plans, and the practice of pricing in concert. A major contribution is an analysis of the state statutes regulating liability and property insurance and the administration of these statutes.

Wright, David McCord. GROWTH AND THE ECONOMY. New York: Scribners, 1964. 398 p.

This book "goes beyond providing a refresher course in college economics and comes up, in plain English, with workable and apparently universal economic principles which throw light on many of the big economic issues of the hour." Wall Street Journal, December 30, 1964.

Yamey, B. S. THE ECONOMICS OF RESALE PRICE MAINTENANCE. London: Pitman, 1954. 182 p.

Deals with three related subjects: the conditions in distributive markets before the coming of price maintenance; the nature and effects of price maintenance; and the changes which are likely to take place if price maintenance is abolished. The book is an amalgamation of history, analysis, and speculation. The second part of the book is devoted exclusively to the origins and subsequent development of price maintenance in selected branches of industry and trade.

Yamey, B.S. RESALE PRICE MAINTENANCE AND SHOPPERS' CHOICE.
(Hobart Paper No. 1) London: Institute of Economic Affairs, 1960. 48 p.
The author reviews public policy on resale price maintenance,
discussing its consequences for the British consumer. He suggests
that it inflates costs and prices, restricts choice, and obstructs
technical progress in retailing.

GOVERNMENT PUBLICATIONS

ANNUAL REPORT OF THE ATTORNEY GENERAL OF THE UNITED STATES.
Washington, D.C.: Department of Justice.
Includes "Report of the Assistant Attorney General in Charge of
the Antitrust Division."

Department of Justice. FEDERAL ANTITRUST DECISIONS. Adjudicated Cases
and Opinions of Attorneys General Arising Under or Involving the Federal
Antitrust Laws and Related Acts. 1890-1931. Washington, D.C.: Government Printing Office, 1907-1935. 12 vols.

Federal Trade Commission. ANNUAL REPORT. Washington, D.C.: Government Printing Office, 1915-
Covers the activities and accomplishments of the Commission for
each fiscal year ending in June.

Federal Trade Commission. DECISIONS. Washington, D.C.: Government
Printing Office, 1915-   , vol. 1- .
Findings, orders, and stipulations. (In 1961, stipulations were
superseded by a new consent order procedure.)

Federal Trade Commission. ORGANIZATION, PROCEDURES, RULES OF
PRACTICE, AND STATUTES. August, 1963. Washington, D.C.: Government
Printing Office, 1963. 230 p.

Federal Trade Commission. QUARTERLY FINANCIAL REPORT FOR MANUFAC-
TURING CORPORATIONS. (Published jointly with the Securities and Exchange
Commission.) Washington, D.C.: Government Printing Office, 1947-
Since 1947, the Federal Trade Commission has summarized for
each calendar quarter uniform, confidential financial statements
collected from a probability sample of all enterprises classified
as manufacturers, except newspapers which are required to file
U.S. Corporation Income Tax Form 1120.

Federal Trade Commission. REPORT OF THE FEDERAL TRADE COMMISSION
ON RATES OF RETURN FOR IDENTICAL COMPANIES IN SELECTED MANU-
FACTURING INDUSTRIES 1954-1963. Washington, D.C.: 52 p.
This report is a continuation of a series of reports comparing
rates of return for identical companies in selected manufacturing
industries. Part A covers rates of return on stockholders' investment for 363 identical companies in 23 selected manufacturing
industries, 1954-1963. Part B covers rates of return of the 12
largest companies in 38 industries, 1962 and 1963. Includes
tables and charts.

Federal Trade Commission. STATUTES AND COURT DECISIONS. Washington, D.C.: Government Printing Office, 1914-   , vol. 1-
> Includes the statutes administered by the Commission and the court decisions construing them.

NEWS RELEASE. Washington, D.C.: Federal Trade Commission. Frequent mailings.
> Summarizes all activities of the Commission including complaints, notices of hearings, initial decisions of hearing examiners, cease and desist orders, consent orders, orders dismissing Federal Trade Commission charges, answers of the respondent, final orders, rules, investigations, and items on personnel. Includes a weekly calendar of proceedings before the Commission which lists arguments and hearings on formal complaints to be held during the ensuing week with the names of the respondents and a short description of the alleged violations. Since August 7, 1964, Advisory Opinion Digests have been included. In November of 1965, releases covering Summaries of Matters Closed by FTC, based on "Assurances of Voluntary Compliance" were added.

NEWS SUMMARY. Washington, D.C.: Federal Trade Commission. Weekly.
> A cumulative list of the Commission's activities previously digested in the News Release.

RELEASES. Washington, D.C.: Department of Justice. Frequent mailings.
> The majority of these press releases are concerned with alleged antitrust violations.

TRADE PRACTICE RULES. Washington, D.C.: Federal Trade Commission.
> Pamphlet copies of rules promulgated for various industries.

U.S. Congress. BILLS AND DEBATES RELATING TO TRUSTS. (50th Congress to 63rd Congress.) Washington, D.C.: Government Printing Office, 3 vols.
> These volumes are an excellent source for a legislative history of the Sherman Act and for background on the Clayton Act, passed in 1914.

LANDMARK INVESTIGATIONS

One of the most important investigations in recent years was that undertaken by the Attorney General's National Committee to Study the Antitrust Laws. The report of this committee, a description of which follows, is a basic reference tool for the lawyer or student engaged in antitrust research.

REPORT OF THE ATTORNEY GENERAL'S NATIONAL COMMITTEE TO STUDY THE ANTITRUST LAWS. Washington, D.C.: Government Printing Office, March 31, 1955. 393 p.
> On June 26, 1953, Attorney General Herbert Brownell, Jr., announced his intention to establish a National Committee to Study the Antitrust Laws. At the same time, the President of the United States expressed the hope that this group would "provide an important instrument to prepare the way for modernizing and strengthening our laws to preserve American free enterprise against monopoly and unfair competition."
>
> Antitrust problems were divided into major areas for study purposes. These included Sections 1 and 2 of the Sherman Act

generally, foreign commerce, distribution, mergers, patents, exemptions, economic indicia of competition and monopoly, and antitrust administration and enforcement. The Committee members were aided by Antitrust Division and Federal Trade Commission legal and economic staff members specializing in particular antitrust areas, as well as by conferees chosen for their special qualifications. In addition, views were received from the Departments of State, Commerce, Defense and Labor, the Foreign Operations Administration, and outside parties.

In the late thirties, following the great depression, the condition of the economy was such that a general investigation of all phases of national industry, including the antitrust laws, was indicated. The Temporary National Economic Committee undertook this monumental task. A description of the Committee, its hearings and monographs follows:

Temporary National Economic Committee. Congress of the United States. INVESTIGATION OF CONCENTRATION OF ECONOMIC POWER.

. . . Hearings before above committee pursuant to Public Resolution No. 113 (75th Cong., 3rd Sess.) Washington, D.C.: 1939–1941. 37 vols.

. . . Preliminary Report pursuant to Public Resolution No. 113 (75th Cong.) S. Doc. No. 95 (76th Cong., 1st Sess.) Washington, D.C.: Government Printing Office, 1939. 39 p.

. . . Monographs printed for the use of the above committee. Senate Committee Print (76th Cong., 3rd Sess.) Washington, D.C.: Government Printing Office, 1940–1941. 43 parts.

. . . Final Report of the Executive Secretary to the above committee, pursuant to Public Resolution No. 113 (75th Cong.) Senate Committee Print (77th Cong., 1st Sess.) Washington, D.C.: Government Printing Office, 1941. 435 p.

. . . Final Report and Recommendations pursuant to Public Resolution No. 113 (75th Cong.) Senate Document No. 35 (77th Cong., 1st Sess.) Washington, D.C.: Government Printing Office, 1941. 783 p.

. . . Description of Hearings and Monographs. Senate Committee Print (76th Cong., 3rd Sess.) Washington, D.C.: Government Printing Office, 1941. 32 p.

> The Temporary National Economic Committee was created by the Congress of the United States June 13, 1938, in response to a message from President Franklin D. Roosevelt setting forth the need for a thorough study of the concentration of economic power and its detrimental consequences.
>
> The TNEC, as it was known, held hearings at which testimony was taken to determine the status of competition and monopoly in American industry. Among the subjects and industries covered by the hearings were patents, life insurance, investment banking, monopolistic practices in industry, savings and invest-

ments, cartels; and the construction, petroleum, iron and steel, and the milk and poultry industries.

The 43 monographs by various government agencies and staff economists on certain topics assigned to them by the TNEC included such titles as: Price Behavior and Business Policy; Bureaucracy and Trusteeship in Large Corporations; Financial Characteristics of American Manufacturing Corporations; Antitrust in Action; Problems of Small Business; Trade Association Survey; Competition and Monopoly in American Industry; The Structure of Industry; the Distribution of Ownership in the 200 largest Nonfinancial Corporations; Survey of Shareholdings in 1,710 Corporations with Securities Listed on a National Securities Exchange; Patents and Free Enterprise; Economic Standards of Government Price Control; Control of Unfair Competitive Practices Through Trade Practice Conference Procedure of the Federal Trade Commission; Reports of the Federal Trade Commission; A Study of the Construction and Enforcement of the Federal Antitrust Laws; Price Discrimination in Steel; and the Basing Point Problem.

Among the questions considered by the Committee were the following: Are the obvious maladjustments of modern economy due wholly, or in part, to a decline in competition?

What is the effect upon competition, upon unemployment, and upon prosperity, of the substitution of organized commercial effort for individual commercial effort?

Is there any different rule for competition among corporations from the historic rule which governed competition among individuals? To what degree, in what areas, and by what agencies, has competition as an automatic regulating force been set aside?

What circumstances, agreements, and conditions govern price and production policies?

What justification is there for the allegation so frequently made that the antitrust laws are vague and inadequate, and what should be done to make them more definite?

What are the effects of concentration of economic power and of size upon commercial activity, trade, employment, and the distribution of income?

The TNEC had no legislative jurisdiction. Action on its recommendations and findings, through remedial and perfecting legislation, was the responsibility of the standing committees of the House and the Senate.

REPORTS AND STUDIES BY CONGRESSIONAL COMMITTEES, FEDERAL ADMINISTRATIVE AGENCIES AND DEPARTMENTS OF THE GOVERNMENT

Many valuable reports and studies are prepared each year by or for Congressional committees, federal administrative agencies and departments. The following is a selected list of those reports which are pertinent to the field of antitrust and trade regulation. Although many of the reports and investigations were preceded by lengthy hearings, the latter will not be included in this chapter. References to publications which list Congressional hearings will be found in the appendix.

Investigations of the Federal Trade Commission

Section 6 of the Federal Trade Commission Act empowers the Commission "to gather and compile information concerning, and to investigate from time to time, the organization, business, conduct, practices, and management of any corporation engaged in commerce."

A listing of these investigations can be found by consulting the following sources:

(1) The annual report of the commission for 1962, which cumulates an alphabetical list of all general investigations made since 1915, when it was established. Such pertinent information as the reason for, or the purpose of, the investigation, dates, the area covered, document number, and availability of the study is also included. Unpublished investigations for the use of other agencies are listed separately.

(2) The CCH Trade Regulation Reporter (See page 122) which contains a section devoted to Federal Trade Commission investigations and reports. Those that are past and available to the public are summarized. Details concerning pending investigations are supplied. The table of contents for the section is an alphabetical listing by subject matter.

Congressional Reports and Studies

U.S. Congress. Joint Economic Committee. AN EVALUATION OF ANTI-TRUST POLICY: ITS RELATION TO ECONOMIC GROWTH, FULL EMPLOY-MENT AND PRICES, by Theodore J. Kreps. Materials prepared in connection with the study of employment, growth, and price levels. (86th Cong., 2nd Sess.) Study Paper No. 22. Joint Committee Print. January 30, 1960. Washington, D.C.: Government Printing Office, 1960. 49 p.

> Paper covers meaning of antitrust policy; diversity of views concerning its impact; relation of antitrust policy to economic growth, "full" employment, and price levels. Appendix is entitled "Billionaire enterprises--Business versus Governmental, ranked according to size."

U.S. Congress. Joint Economic Committee. GOVERNMENT POLICY TOWARD COMPETITION AND PRIVATE PRICING by Myron W. Watkins, and Joel B. Dirlam. (Reprinted from "The Relationship of Prices to Economic Stability and Growth," compendium of papers submitted by panelists appearing before the Joint Economic Committee, March 31, 1958.) Washington, D.C.: Government Printing Office.

> The subject of this paper is the influence that governmental measures of various types have on the pricing by privately owned and privately operated business units.

U.S. Congress. Senate. Subcommittee on Antitrust and Monopoly of the Committee on the Judiciary. ADMINISTERED PRICES, ASPHALT ROOFING. Report of above subcommittee pursuant to S. Res. 231 (85th Cong., 2nd Sess.) Committee Print. December 15, 1958. Washington, D.C.: Government Printing Office, 1958. 56 p.

>   The hearings upon which this report is based centered on the development and operation of a complicated and arbitrary zone delivered pricing system and its effect upon new and small producers. The purpose was to determine whether this system was a mechanism for administering prices and whether the antitrust laws were effective under the circumstances.

U.S. Congress. Senate. Subcommittee on Antitrust and Monopoly of the Committee on the Judiciary. ADMINISTERED PRICES--AUTOMOBILES. Report of above subcommittee pursuant to S. Res. 231 (85th Cong., 2nd Sess.) Committee Print. November 1, 1958. Washington, D.C.: Government Printing Office, 1958. 314 p.

>   Chapters cover: trends and forms of economic concentration; nature of competition in the automobile industry; nonprice competition; costs, demand, and price policy; and antitrust implications. Concerned with dominance of General Motors in the automobile industry; also considers positions of Ford and Chrysler.

U.S. Congress. Senate. Subcommittee on Antitrust and Monopoly of the Committee on the Judiciary. ADMINISTERED PRICES--BREAD. Report of above subcommittee pursuant to S. Res. 238 (86th Cong., 2nd Sess.) Report No. 1923. August 27, 1960. Washington, D.C.: Government Printing Office, 1960. 301 p.

>   Covers alleged price discrimination in the sale of bread, including plant price discrimination and route price discrimimation. Chain grocery baking operations are investigated, as well as the level of concentration and the history of merger and acquisition in the wholesale baking industry. The final chapter deals with raising prices "to meet competition." Report contains many valuable tables, exhibits, and statistics on the industry.

U.S. Congress. Senate. Subcommittee on Antitrust and Monopoly of the Committee on the Judiciary. ADMINISTERED PRICES: A COMPENDIUM ON PUBLIC POLICY. Report of the above subcommittee pursuant to S. Res. 56 (88th Cong., 1st Sess.) Committee Print. Washington, D.C.: Government Printing Office, 1963. 276 p.

>   The document presents the views of 18 eminent legal and economic authorities relating to the question of appropriate public policy with regard to administered prices.

U.S. Congress. Senate. Subcommittee on Antitrust and Monopoly of the Committee on the Judiciary. ADMINISTERED PRICES--DRUGS. Report of the above subcommittee pursuant to S. Res. 52 (85th Cong., 1st Sess.) Report No. 448. June 27, 1961. Washington, D.C.: Government Printing Office, 1961. 373 p.

>   Divided into five parts, entitled: I. The reasonableness of price; II. The control of the market; III. Patents and research in drugs; IV. Advertising and promotion of drugs; and V. Generic names versus trade names.

U.S. Congress. Senate. Subcommittee on Antitrust and Monopoly of the Committee on the Judiciary. ADMINISTERED PRICES--STEEL. Report of above subcommittee pursuant to S. Res. 57 (85th Cong., 1st Sess.) Report No. 1387. March 13, 1958. Washington, D.C.: Government Printing Office, 1958. 204 p.

Prices which are "administratively set," "administratively maintained," and are insensitive to changes in the market; e.g., they are maintained when demand falls off through a curtailment in output, are the "administered prices" with which most of the historical literature on the subject is concerned; these are the prices with the potential for inducing economic distress; and these are the prices which were of concern to this subcommittee in its inquiry into "administered prices."

Administered prices in the iron and steel industry were selected for examination because of the importance of the industry, and because the steel industry had announced a rise in prices effective July 1, 1957.

U.S. Congress. Senate. Subcommittee on Antitrust and Monopoly of the Committee on the Judiciary. ANTITRUST DEVELOPMENTS IN THE EUROPEAN COMMON MARKET. Report of the above subcommittee pursuant to S. Res. 262 (88th Cong., 2nd Sess.) Committee Print. Washington, D.C.: Government Printing Office, 1964. 511 p.

Prepared by Professor Herman Schwartz, assistant counsel to the subcommittee. Deals with the Common Market antitrust developments, certain of the national antitrust laws, and finally the significance for American interests. The Common Market section discusses the current public and private attitudes toward competition and antitrust, and the official community policies with respect to competition and planning, including analyses of some legal and administrative problems. This section concludes with a tentative assessment of the impact, so far, of the antitrust activities of the Common Market. The second part of the report deals with approximately the same matters with respect to France, Germany, The Netherlands, and Belgium. The report concludes with a discussion of the future of antitrust in Europe, and of its significance for American public and private interests.

U.S. Congress. Senate. Subcommittee on Antitrust and Monopoly of the Committee on the Judiciary. BIGNESS AND CONCENTRATION OF ECONOMIC POWER--A CASE STUDY OF GENERAL MOTORS CORPORATION. Report of above subcommittee pursuant to S. Res. 61 (84th Cong., 1st. Sess., as extended). Report No. 1879. April 30, 1956. Washington, D.C.: Government Printing Office, 1956. 119 p.

One of the major phases of the subcommittee's comprehensive study and investigation of the antitrust laws relates to the complex problems connected with big business and economic concentration. The case study of General Motors Corp. was intended to illustrate these problems through a detailed factual analysis of the largest manufacturing corporation in the world which is the dominant producer in one of the most highly concentrated industries in the country.

U.S. Congress. Senate. Subcommittee on Antitrust and Monopoly of the Committee on the Judiciary. CASE STUDY OF INCIPIENT MONOPOLY IN MILK DISTRIBUTION. Report of above subcommittee pursuant to S. Res. 231 (85th Cong., 2nd Sess.) Committee Print. November 15, 1958. Washington, D.C.: Government Printing Office, 1958. 50 p:
> A study of the Adams dairy companies of Missouri. The origin, the system of operations, the entry into new markets of the Adams system, and possible antitrust implications are explored.

U.S. Congress. Senate. Subcommittee on Antitrust and Monopoly of the Committee on the Judiciary. CONCENTRATION IN AMERICAN INDUSTRY. Report of the above subcommittee pursuant to S. Res. 57 (85th Cong., 1st Sess.) Committee Print. Washington, D.C.: Government Printing Office, 1957. 756 p.
> Provides a comprehensive body of objective information on the degree of "concentration" in the manufacturing segment of the industrial economy of America. All information is from the Census of Manufactures for 1954, 1947, and 1935 and from the 1950 and 1951 Annual Survey of Manufactures.

U.S. Congress. Senate. Subcommittee on Antitrust and Monopoly of the Committee on the Judiciary. CONCENTRATION RATIOS IN MANUFACTURING INDUSTRY--1958. Report prepared by the Bureau of the Census for the above subcommittee. Part I and Part II. (87th Cong., 2nd Sess.) Committee Print. Washington, D.C.: Government Printing Office, 1962. 510 p.
> Consists of a presentation of concentration ratios for manufacturing based on the 1958 Census of Manufactures and other years.
> Through years of usage the term "concentration ratio" has come to mean the share of the total activity or resources of a given segment of the economy accounted for by its largest companies. In order to avoid disclosure of the operations of any individual firms, concentration ratios based on census data are presented in groups of four or more companies, that is, the four largest, the eighth largest, and so forth.
>
> In this, as in similar previous reports, no attempt is made to interpret the significance of the concentration figures. The ratios are not used as the basis for an analysis of either the causes or effects of concentration. The report consists merely of a presentation of the ratios themselves.

U.S. Congress. Senate. Subcommittee on Antitrust and Monopoly of the Committee on the Judiciary. CORPORATE MERGERS AND ACQUISITIONS. A staff study by the above subcommittee pursuant to S. Res. 170 (84th Cong., 2nd Sess. as extended by S. Res. 84, 85th Cong.) Report No. 132. March 4, 1957. Washington, D.C.: Government Printing Office, 1957. 74 p.
> Report covers: (a) legislative background of Merger Act; (b) developments since amendment of Section 7 of the act; (c) the subcommittee's study of the merger problem including testimony of economists, attorneys, businessmen, and government officials; (d) suggested improvements; and (e) conclusions as to policy objectives and proposals for consideration.

U.S. Congress. Senate. Subcommittee on Antitrust and Monopoly of the Committee on the Judiciary. FOREIGN TRADE CONFERENCES. Staff memorandum of the above subcommittee pursuant to S. Res. 61 (84th Cong., 1st Sess.) Committee Print. Washington, D.C.: Government Printing Office, 1955. 18 p.

> This memorandum is a resume of conferences held in London, Paris, and Rome with representatives of the American chambers of commerce and with representatives of business and government in each of the mentioned cities in order better to appraise the conditions under which American businessmen were required to operate with respect to their trade and investments.

U.S. Congress. Senate. Subcommittee on Antitrust and Monopoly of the Committee on the Judiciary. THE INSURANCE INDUSTRY--AVIATION, OCEAN MARINE, AND STATE REGULATION. Report of the above subcommittee pursuant to S. Res. 238 (86th Cong., 2nd Sess.) Report No. 1834. August 10, 1960. Washington, D.C.: Government Printing Office, 1960. 337 p.

> The U.S. Supreme Court on June 5, 1944, held that the business of insurance was within the regulatory power of Congress under the commerce clause and thus subject to the Sherman Antitrust Act. Thereafter, bills were introduced in Congress seeking a complete exemption of insurance from the federal antitrust laws. However, on March 9, 1945, the McCarran-Ferguson Act, or Public Law 15 as it became generally known in the industry, was enacted into law. It declared that the continued regulation and taxation of the business by the States is in the public interest.
>
> The present study was the first comprehensive effort by the Congress to re-examine the insurance industry, in the light of the McCarran-Ferguson Act, and to measure the effectiveness of the resulting State regulation.

U.S. Congress. Senate. Subcommittee on Antitrust and Monopoly of the Committee on the Judiciary. THE INSURANCE INDUSTRY-INSURANCE RATES, RATING ORGANIZATIONS AND STATE RATE REGULATION. Report of the above subcommittee pursuant to S. Res. 52 (87th Cong., 1st Sess.) Report No. 831. August 29, 1961. Washington, D.C.: Government Printing Office, 1961. 172 p.

> A principal objective of the subcommittee was to determine whether State insurance regulation had afforded sufficient opportunity to the free play of competitive forces consistent with sound insurance principles. Prime attention is given to the ratemaking process and the regulation thereof by the States.

U.S. Congress. Senate. Subcommittee on Antitrust and Monopoly of the Committee on the Judiciary. MONOPOLY IN THE POWER INDUSTRY. Interim report of the above subcommittee. (83rd Cong., 2nd Sess.) Committee Print. Washington, D.C.: Government Printing Office, 1955. 115 p.

> Detailed report on investigation of alleged monopoly abuses in the power industry. Covers such subjects as the revival of holding company evils; public relations, politics and corruption; and the Dixon-Yates contract.

U.S. Congress. Senate. Subcommittee on Antitrust and Monopoly of the Committee on the Judiciary. PETROLEUM, THE ANTITRUST LAWS AND GOVERNMENT POLICIES. Report of the above subcommittee pursuant to S. Res. 57 (85th Cong., 1st Sess.) Report No. 1147. August 27, 1957. Washington, D.C.: Government Printing Office, 1957. 164 p.

A report on competitive problems in the oil industry, including the Government-sponsored oil lift program which followed the stoppage of the Suez Canal, and the IPC pipeline.

U.S. Congress. Senate. Subcommittee on Antitrust and Monopoly of the Committee on the Judiciary. POWER POLICY DIXON-YATES CONTRACT. Staff report of above subcommittee pursuant to S. Res. 61, as extended by S. Res. 170 (84th Cong., 2nd Sess.) Committee Print. Washington, D.C.: Government Printing Office, 1956. 172 p.

The contract to furnish electric energy was between the Atomic Energy Commission and the Mississippi Valley Generating Co., a newly incorporated company created as a subsidiary of two private utility holding companies, headed by Messrs. Dixon and Yates. Report deals with evidence which brought about the collapse of the project.

U.S. Congress. Senate. Subcommittee on Antitrust and Monopoly of the Committee on the Judiciary. RAPID AMORTIZATION IN REGULATED INDUSTRIES. Report of above subcommittee pursuant to S. Res. 57 (85th Cong., 1st Sess.) Report No. 1380. March 12, 1958. Washington, D.C.: Government Printing Office, 1958. 134 p.

The report is based upon the record of hearings with respect to the use by electric utilities of tax amortization as a vehicle for the furtherance of monopolistic control.

U.S. Congress. Senate. Subcommittee on Antitrust and Monopoly of the Committee on the Judiciary. RESTRICTIVE BUSINESS PRACTICES. Conference of members and staff of the above subcommittee, with the European Productivity Agency Mission on Restrictive Business Practices and Restrictive Trade Practices Study Team of Japan, pursuant to S. Res. 57 and S. Res. 231 (85th Cong., 2nd Sess.) Committee Print. February 3, 1958. Washington, D.C.: Government Printing Office, 1958. 37 p.

First 24 pages are devoted to the proceedings of the conference. Appendix contains program and itinerary of the European Productivity Agency Mission to the United States (EPA Project No. 414); and program and itinerary of the Japanese Restrictive Business Practices Study Team (Restrictive Business Practices Study Project 88-8004).

U.S. Congress. Senate. Subcommittee on Antitrust and Monopoly of the Committee on the Judiciary. A STUDY OF THE ANTITRUST LAWS. ATTEMPTED MERGER OF PUGET SOUND POWER AND LIGHT CO. AND THE WASHINGTON WATER POWER CO. Staff report of above subcommittee pursuant to S. Res. 170 (84th Cong., 2nd Sess.) Committee Print. Washington, D.C.: Government Printing Office, 1956. 82 p.

Comprehensive report on attempt by a large public utility company to force a merger upon an unwilling neighboring company, and to absorb it.

U.S. Congress. Senate. Subcommittee on Antitrust and Monopoly of the Committee on the Judiciary. THE TELEVISION BROADCASTING INDUSTRY. Report of the above subcommittee pursuant to H. Res. 107. (85th Cong., 1st Sess.) Report No. 607. June 24, 1957. Washington, D.C.: Government Printing Office, 1957. 148 p.

The committee's study and hearings on broadcasting encompassed the following matters, among others: the development of television broadcasting; the present structure of the industry; the UHF problem; the economic and financial position of television networks; network practices; relationships between networks and stations; the manner in which the Federal Communications Commission and the Department of Justice have discharged their antitrust responsibility in important areas of broadcasting; regulation by the Federal Communications Commission of coaxial cable and microwave relay rates and of private intercity relay systems, and joint activities by broadcasters in music licensing.

U.S. Congress. Senate. Subcommittee on Antitrust and Monopoly of the Committee on the Judiciary. TRUTH IN PACKAGING. Report of the above subcommittee pursuant to S. Res. 262 (88th Cong., 2nd Sess.) Committee Print. August 4, 1964. Washington, D.C.: Government Printing Office, 1964. 111 p.

Concerned with S. 387, a bill on packaging and labeling practices, introduced by Senator Philip A. Hart on January 21, 1963. The need for S. 387, according to the report, arises chiefly from the fact that when marketing depends on prepackaging, the consumer cannot examine the product itself, nor can he readily compare products and their prices; and he cannot look to the seller and get an assurance from him as to the product. Thus handicapped, the buyer finds it more difficult, if not impossible, to judge accurately the prices of competing products, and to make a rational choice among them.

U.S. Congress. House. Antitrust Subcommittee (Subcommittee No. 5) of the Committee on the Judiciary. AIRLINES. Report of above subcommittee pursuant to H. Res. 107 (85th Cong., 1st Sess.) Report No. 1328. April 5, 1957. Washington, D.C.: Government Printing Office, 1957. 358 p.

Report covers the present structure of the industry, the Civil Aeronautics Board's structure and functions, the non-sked problem, the organization and functions of the Air Transport Association of America, and the International Air Transport Association, and the Pan American World Airways system.

U.S. Congress. House. Antitrust Subcommittee (Subcommittee No. 5) of the Committee on the Judiciary. THE ANTITRUST LAWS--A BASIS FOR ECONOMIC FREEDOM. A staff report to the above subcommittee pursuant to H. Res. 36 (88th Cong., 2nd Sess.) Washington, D.C.: Government Printing Office, 1965. 119 p.

Beginning with the text of the Sherman Act, passed by Congress in 1890, this Staff Report provides a comprehensive compendium of antitrust laws as of January 1, 1965. It includes all of the amendments of the existing laws, new laws which have been enacted, and laws which, while not specifically antitrust in substance, are related to the antitrust laws. For ease of reference,

these laws have been grouped under five general categories: Pro-
hibition and penalty; implementation and policy formation; exception and exemption; process and procedure; and related laws.

U.S. Congress. House. Antitrust Subcommittee (Subcommittee No. 5) of the
Committee on the Judiciary. ANTITRUST PROBLEMS IN THE EXPLOITATION
OF PATENTS. A staff report of the above subcommittee. (84th Cong., 2nd
Sess.) Committee Print. October 15, 1956. Washington, D.C.: Govern-
ment Printing Office, 1957. 25 p.

The report briefly describes the patent system, its relation to the
antitrust laws, the kinds of transactions involving patents which
have given rise to antitrust questions, and the criteria, principles
and remedies which the courts have brought to bear on the solution of those questions.

U.S. Congress. House. Antitrust Subcommittee (Subcommittee No. 5) of the
Committee on the Judiciary. BANK MERGERS AND CONCENTRATION OF
BANKING FACILITIES. A staff report to the above subcommittee. (82nd
Cong., 2nd Sess.) Committee Print. Washington, D.C.: Government Print-
ing Office, 1952. 71 p.

The continuing decline in the nation's banking population coupled
with the merger movement in the field of finance gave rise to
concern by the committee lest competition be severely restricted
or eliminated among banking facilities, or the credit resources of
the country be unduly concentrated within the vaults of a few
large financial institutions.

This report was undertaken to appraise accurately the present
structure of the banking system in the United States and to determine if remedial legislation with respect to bank mergers or other
aspects of banking concentration was necessary.

U.S. Congress. House. Antitrust Subcommittee (Subcommittee No. 5) of the
Committee on the Judiciary. BUSINESS ADVISORY COUNCIL FOR THE DE-
PARTMENT OF COMMERCE. Interim report of above subcommittee pursuant
to H. Res. 22 (84th Cong., 1st Sess.) Washington, D.C.: Government
Printing Office, 1955. 68 p.

The membership of the Business Advisory Council for the Department of Commerce consists of representatives from many different
industries. It is concerned with overall government policies
affecting business, including antitrust. The report covers the
membership, finances, proceedings, activities, and accessibility
of the records of the council.

U.S. Congress. House. Antitrust Subcommittee (Subcommittee No. 5) of the
Committee on the Judiciary. CONSENT DECREE PROGRAM OF THE DE-
PARTMENT OF JUSTICE. A report of the above subcommittee pursuant to
H. Res. 27 (86th Cong., 1st Sess.) January 30, 1959. Washington, D.C.:
Government Printing Office, 1959. 379 p.

An antitrust consent judgment, for purposes of this report, is an
order of the court agreed upon by representatives of the Attorney
General and of the defendant, without trial of the conduct chal-
lenged by the Attorney General, in proceedings instituted under
the Sherman Act, the Clayton Act, or related statutes. Normally,

the consent decree recites that it does not constitute evidence or admission by any of the parties with respect to any of the issues involved in the litigation.

A good coverage of the government's suit to sever connections between American Telephone & Telegraph Co., and Western Electric Co. Over 150 pages are devoted to the "Oil Pipe Line" consent decree.

U.S. Congress. House. Antitrust Subcommittee (Subcommittee No. 5) of the Committee on the Judiciary. CORPORATE AND BANK MERGERS. Interim report of above subcommittee pursuant to H. Res. 22 (84th Cong., 1st Sess.) Washington, D.C.: Government Printing Office, 1955. 188 p.
    Discusses wave of mergers in industry and banking particularly during period 1948-1955. Draws heavily on statistics from the Federal Trade Commission's Report on Corporate Mergers and Acquisitions.

U.S. Congress. House. Antitrust Subcommittee (Subcommittee No. 5) of the Committee on the Judiciary. INTERLOCKS IN CORPORATE MANAGEMENT. A staff report to the above subcommittee (89th Cong., 1st Sess.) Committee Print. March 12, 1965. Washington, D.C.: Government Printing Office, 1965. 270 p.
    Objectives of this study are: (1) to assemble, analyze, and to examine operating experience under the Clayton Act and ancillary legislation as it affects corporate management interlocks; (2) to collect and analyze the information, conclusions, and recommendations of studies of interlocks made since the passage of the Clayton Act, some of which are relatively recent; and (3) to delineate the steps that need to be taken to reach an informed judgment on the desirability or necessity for amendments to existing legislation and, if so, the legislative policy and approach to such amendments. Report covers the legislative history and analyzes Sections 8 and 10 of the Clayton Act, which apply to interlocking corporate managements. Ancillary legislation and implementing regulations of agencies other than the Federal Trade Commission are also set forth. Chapter III entitled "Experience" discusses important cases involving interlocking directorates. A survey of the current status of corporate management interlocks is covered by Chapter IV which analyzes interlocks in such companies as General Motors Corp., General Electric Co., United States Steel Corp., E.I. duPont de Nemours & Co., and many others. Part B of this chapter surveys the banking industry, and Part C surveys the insurance industry.

U.S. Congress. House. Antitrust Subcommittee (Subcommittee No. 5) of the Committee on the Judiciary. JUDICIAL DOCTRINE OF PRIMARY JURISDICTION AS APPLIED IN ANTITRUST SUITS. A staff report of the above subcommittee. (84th Cong., 2nd Sess.) Committee Print. October 15, 1956. Washington, Government Printing Office, 1957. 31 p.
    Examines the origin, scope, and nature of the "primary jurisdiction" doctrine and its effect on the administration of the antitrust laws in regulated industries.

U.S. Congress. House. Antitrust Subcommittee (Subcommittee No. 5) of the Committee on the Judiciary. THE MERGER MOVEMENT IN THE TEXTILE INDUSTRY. A staff report of the above subcommittee (84th Cong., 1st Sess.) Committee Print. Washington, D.C.: Government Printing Office, 1955. 43 p.

> This report attempts to outline the background out of which the textile merger movement has grown. Deals with the scope of the movement, together with the effect of the merger move- ment, on the pattern of concentration in industry. Describes certain specific mergers, primarily those involving Textron Ameri- can and Burlington Industries.

U.S. Congress. House. Antitrust Subcommittee (Subcommittee No. 5) of the Committee on the Judiciary. PROPOSED MERGER OF EASTERN AIRLINES AND AMERICAN AIRLINES. A staff report to the above subcommittee. (87th Cong., 2nd Sess.) Committee Print. March 23, 1962. Washington, D.C.: Government Printing Office, 1962. 35 p.

> Report on the economic, political, and legal consequences of the union of the second and fourth largest domestic airlines in the Nation.

U.S. Congress. House. Antitrust Subcommittee (Subcommittee No. 5) of the Committee on the Judiciary. WOC'S AND GOVERNMENT ADVISORY GROUPS. Interim report of above subcommittee pursuant to H. Res. 22 (84th Cong., 2nd Sess.) April 24, 1956. Washington, D.C.: Government Printing Office, 1956. 166 p.

> The utilization by the Government of representatives from business and industry for temporary periods without compensation, provides the Government, during an emergency, with special business and industrial knowledge and technology not otherwise available. However, such representatives continue to be paid regular salaries by their private employers during their time with the Government. The problem of this dual allegiance is the subject of the report.

U.S. Congress. House. Subcommittee on Study of Monopoly Power of the Committee on the Judiciary. NEWSPRINT. Report of above subcommittee pursuant to H. Res. 95 (82nd Cong., 1st Sess.) Report No. 505, Part 1. May 28, 1951. Washington, D.C.: Government Printing Office, 1951. 132 p.

> The report is divided into four parts as follows: I. The shortage of newsprint; II. The newsprint industry (covers technology and resources, history, structure, and financial characteristics of the industry); III. Monopoly problems (contracts, pricing); and IV. Conclusions and recommendations.

U.S. Congress. Senate. Subcommittee on Patents, Trademarks, and Copy- rights of the Committee on the Judiciary. COMPULSORY PATENT LICENS- ING UNDER ANTITRUST JUDGMENTS. Staff report of above subcommittee pursuant to S. Res. 240 (86th Cong., 2nd Sess.) Committee Print. Washing- ton, D.C.: Government Printing Office, 1960. 78 p.

> Considers how much use has been made of the compulsory patent licensing provision in antitrust decrees, entered during the years 1941–57. Represents the first publication of the efforts of the

patents Subcommittee and the Antitrust Division to determine the practical effects of these antitrust decrees. Lists in the appendix all of the decrees which were the subject of the study, together with the kind of patent provisions contained in each. Contains an account of all the judicial proceedings which have been brought to determine royalty rates.

U.S. Congress, Senate. Subcommittee on Patents, Trademarks, and Copyrights of the Committee on the Judiciary. THE RESEARCH AND DEVELOPMENT FACTOR IN MERGERS AND ACQUISITIONS. Study of above subcommittee pursuant to S. Res. 236 (85th Cong., 2nd Sess.) Study No. 16. Committee Print. Washington, D.C.: Government Printing Office, 1958. 35 p.

This study was prepared by Murray N. Friedman of the Department of Economics, Queens College, New York City. A reason frequently given for intercorporate acquisitions and mergers is that such transactions can make possible more extensive, effective, and diversified research and development. Out of a large number of mergers and acquisitions examined by him, Professor Friedman has selected for discussion sixteen in which advantages in terms of future research were envisioned in various degrees.

U.S. Congress. Senate. Select Committee on Small Business. DISCOUNT-HOUSE OPERATIONS. Report of the above committee. (85th Cong., 2nd Sess.) Report No. 2504. November 28, 1958. Washington, D.C.: Government Printing Office, 1958. 24 p.

Examination of the growth of discount houses and their effect on the independent businessman.

U.S. Congress. Senate. Select Committee on Small Business. FAIR TRADE. Report of above committee on a study on fair trade, based on a survey of manufacturers and retailers. (84th Cong., 2nd Sess.) Report No. 2819. Washington, D.C.: Government Printing Office, 1956. 27 p.

Describes what fair traders thought of fair trade in mid-1956.

U.S. Congress. Senate. Select Committee on Small Business. THE IMPACT OF SUBURBAN SHOPPING CENTERS ON INDEPENDENT RETAILERS. Report of above committee on alleged discriminatory practices against small-business concerns in suburban shopping centers. (86th Cong., 1st Sess.) Report No. 1016. January 5, 1960. Washington, D.C.: Government Printing Office, 1960, 41 p.

Deals with problem of independent retailers who cannot rent space in new suburban shopping centers because of the policy of major financial institutions, before granting a long-term loan on a new building in a choice location, to require the owner or developer to have fixed-minimum and guaranteed rentals from AAA tenants (those having a net worth of at least $1,000,000) to cover taxes, insurance, and amortization of loan.

Also considers complaint of independents that they are often charged higher rents than department stores and chain stores who meet the AAA requirement, since the latter, knowing the developer must have AAA tenants, are in a strong bargaining position when negotiating the lease.

U.S. Congress. Senate. Select Committee on Small Business. MATERIALS RELATIVE TO COMPETITION IN THE REGULATED CIVIL AVIATION INDUS-TRY, 1956, transmitted by the Civil Aeronautics Board to the above committee. (84th Cong., 2nd Sess.) Committee Print. April 18, 1956. Washington, D.C.: Government Printing Office, 1956. 228 p.

> Includes a list of 34 questions transmitted to the Civil Aeronautics Board and the replies of the board to the questionnaire.

U.S. Congress. Senate. Select Committee on Small Business. MONOPOLY AND TECHNICAL PROBLEMS IN THE SCRAP STEEL INDUSTRY. Report of above committee. (86th Cong., 1st Sess.) Report No. 1013, October 16, 1959. Washington, D.C.: Government Printing Office, 1959. 34 p.

> The two problems oppressing the scrap steel industry were (a) the changing technology in the manufacture of steel, and (b) the increasing concentration and control of the scrap industry by Luria Bros. & Co., Inc. Report deals with these problems.

U.S. Congress. Senate. Select Committee on Small Business. RECENT DEVELOPMENTS IN THE STRUCTURE OF BANKING. (A supplement to "Concentration of Banking in the United States.") Special staff report of the Board of Governors of the Federal Reserve System submitted to the above committee. (87th Cong., 2nd Sess.) Committee Print. January 5, 1962. Washington, D.C.: Government Printing Office, 1962. 30 p.

> Supplements Committee Print No. 7 of September 10, 1952. (See p. 111) Report for most part covers period since 1951 through June 30, 1961. Statistics, table numbers, format, text generally follow previous report.

U.S. Congress. Senate. Select Committee on Small Business. THE RIGHT TO BUY--AND ITS DENIAL TO SMALL BUSINESS. Report prepared by Dr. Vernon A. Mund for the above committee. (85th Cong., 1st Sess.) Document No. 32. March, 1957. Washington, D.C.: Government Printing Office, 1957. 118 p.

> The study holds that new legislation is required to provide effective, general relief for the discriminatory practice of refusal to sell, if small business is to enjoy the right to buy, analogous to that found in open markets.

U.S. Congress. Senate. Select Committee on Small Business. THE RIGHT TO BUY--1959. Staff report prepared for the above committee. (86th Cong., 1st Sess.) Committee Print. July 9, 1959. Washington, D.C.: Government Printing Office, 1959. 47 p.

> (Updates through February 1959 "The Right to Buy--and Its Denial to Small Business.") Presents, in a series of tables, the names of products which have been denied to buyers in recent years, as reported in complaints filed (a) with the Federal Trade Commission, and (b) with the Antitrust Division, Department of Justice. The captions indicate the business status of the alleged violator and of the firm making the complaint.

U.S. Congress. Senate. Select Committee on Small Business. THE ROLE OF PRIVATE ANTITRUST ENFORCEMENT IN PROTECTING SMALL BUSINESS--1958. Report of the above committee (85th Cong., 2nd Sess.) Report No.

No. 1855. July 19, 1958. Washington, D.C.: Government Printing Office, 1958. 13 p.

> Deals with problem of businessman who, though permitted under the Sherman Act and the Clayton Act to bring suit against anti-trust violators, does not do so, because in most cases he will come out the loser (even though he wins the suit) due to a long drawn out legal contest, which will bring him to the verge of bankruptcy or end in it.

U.S. Congress. Senate. Select Committee on Small Business. SMALL BUSI-NESS LEASE GUARANTEES. Report of above committee re feasibility of a program of federal guarantees for small business leases. (87th Cong., 2nd Sess.) Report No. 1532. May 24, 1962. Washington, D.C.: Government Printing Office, 1962. 42 p.

> Cites difficulties confronting small businessman when he seeks to obtain a lease on first-class commercial space. Favors a program of participating, and if necessary direct federal guarantees of small business leases.

U.S. Congress. Senate. Select Committee on Small Business. STUDIES OF DUAL DISTRIBUTION: THE FLAT GLASS INDUSTRY. Report of the above committee on dual distribution methods of flat-glass producers and competitive problems of independent flat-glass dealers and distributors. (86th Cong., 1st Sess.) Report No. 1015. December 31, 1959. Washington, D.C.: Govern-ment Printing Office, 1960. 104 p.

> "Dual distribution," a term of increasing currency in several in-dustries, including the flat-glass industry, describes a marketing situation in which the manufacturer competes directly with his customers at either the wholesale or retail level or both. The term is also applied to competition by wholesalers with their re-tailer customers at the latter's resale level.

U.S. Congress. Senate. Subcommittee on Monopoly of the Select Committee on Small Business. CONCENTRATION OF BANKING IN THE UNITED STATES. Staff report of the Board of Governors of the Federal Reserve System submitted to the above subcommittee. (82nd Cong., 2nd Sess.) Committee Print No. 7. September 10, 1952. Washington, D.C.: Government Printing Office, 1952. 50 p.

> Covers measurement of concentration changes in banking structure (number of banking offices, mergers and consolidations, groups and chains) and banking as a small business. Appendix sets forth the Clayton Act proceeding against Transamerica Corp.

U.S. Congress. Senate. Subcommittee on Monopoly of the Select Committee on Small Business. FOREIGN LEGISLATION CONCERNING MONOPOLY AND CARTEL PRACTICES. Report of the Department of State to the above subcommittee. (82nd Cong., 2nd Sess.) Subcommittee Print No. 5. July 9, 1952. Washington, D.C.: Government Printing Office, 1952. 253 p.

> A study of the development of legislation in the general area of monopoly power and restrictive business practices in a selected group of foreign countries. Factual information concerning the administration of these laws is presented, and brief notes con-cerning the attitudes of leading groups in these countries have

been appended where sufficient information is available to make this useful.

U.S. Congress. Senate. Subcommittee on Monopoly of the Select Committee on Small Business. THE INTERNATIONAL PETROLEUM CARTEL. Staff report to the Federal Trade Commission submitted to the above subcommittee. (82nd Cong., 2nd Sess.) Committee Print No. 6. August 22, 1952. Washington, D.C.: Government Printing Office, 1952. 310 p.

> Deals with the following questions: (1) whether or not five major integrated American oil companies joined two foreign companies in a series of international monopoly agreements; (2) whether or not the structure of international oil prices imposed an excessive burden on the economies of friendly nations, and thus on the American public which was extending economic and military assistance to these nations; and, perhaps most important of all, (3) whether or not the dumping of foreign oil in the United States, at a net cost far below the price charged in Europe and the Middle East caused injury to independent American oil producers.

U.S. Congress. Senate. Subcommittee on Monopoly of the Select Committee on Small Business. MONOPOLISTIC PRACTICES AND SMALL BUSINESS. Staff report to the Federal Trade Commission for the above subcommittee. March 31, 1952. Washington, D.C.: Government Printing Office, 1952. 88 p.

> Divided into five chapters, as follows: I. Changes in economic concentration, 1935–47; II. Denial of supplies; III. The price squeeze; IV. Price and other discriminations; V. Coercive and predatory practices.

U.S. Congress. Senate. Subcommittee on Monopoly of the Committee on Small Business. THE PUBLIC UTILITY HOLDING COMPANY ACT OF 1935. Report of the Securities and Exchange Commission to the above subcommittee. (82nd Cong., 2nd Sess.) Subcommittee Print No. 4. June 3, 1952. Washington, D.C.: Government Printing Office, 1952. 25 p.

> Contains a description of the statute, the problems presented by the reorganization of the holding companies, and the accomplishments of the Securities and Exchange Commission in enforcing the Act.

U.S. Congress. Senate. Subcommittee on Monopoly of the Select Committee on Small Business. A STUDY OF THE DEVELOPMENT OF THE ANTITRUST LAWS AND CURRENT PROBLEMS OF ANTITRUST ENFORCEMENT. (82nd Cong., 2nd Sess.) Subcommittee Print No. 3, May 23, 1952. Washington, D.C.: Government Printing Office, 1952. 58 p.

> Covers the history of antitrust enforcement and activities in antitrust enforcement. Appendix includes statistical evidence of concentration of power, sources of monopoly power, and examples of concentration. Standard Oil Co. and United States Steel Corp. are given as examples of integration. A chart sets forth the principal affiliates and main areas of operation of Standard Oil Co.

U.S. Congress. Senate. Special Committee to Study Problems of American Small Business. ANTI-TRUST CASES IN THE CONSTRUCTION INDUSTRY.

Report of above committee pursuant to S. Res. 28 (79th Cong., 2nd Sess.) September 12, 1946. Washington, D.C.: Government Printing Office, 1946. 54 p.

A list of cases in the construction field which have required the attention of the Antitrust Division, and which illustrate various forms of restrictive practices.

U.S. Congress. Senate. Special Committee to Study Problems of American Small Business. FUTURE OF INDEPENDENT BUSINESS. Progress report of the chairman of the above committee. (79th Cong., 2nd Sess.) Committee Print No. 16. January 2, 1947. Washington, D.C.: Government Printing Office, 1947. 379 p.

The student seeking a birds-eye view of the history of the antitrust laws and developments up to 1946 will find this report most useful. Includes lists of small business committee publications during 77th, 78th, and 79th Congresses.

U.S. Congress. House. Select Committee on Small Business. ANTITRUST COMPLAINTS. Staff report to the above committee on the volume of Federal Trade Commission antitrust complaints, pursuant to H. Res. 114 (84th Cong., 1st Sess.) Washington, D.C.: Government Printing Office, 1956. 8 p.

Examines record of Federal Trade Commission's antitrust complaints for a period of five and one-half years.

U.S. Congress. House. Select Committee on Small Business. ANTITRUST LAW ENFORCEMENT BY THE FEDERAL TRADE COMMISSION AND THE ANTITRUST DIVISION, DEPARTMENT OF JUSTICE. A preliminary report by the above committee pursuant to H. Res. 22 (81st Cong., 2nd Sess.) Washington, D.C.: Government Printing Office, 1951. 95 p.

Divided into two main parts. Part I is confined exclusively to the Federal Trade Commission. Part II is devoted to the Antitrust Division, with a brief report on relations between the two agencies and the problem of developing a unified antitrust policy. Parts III and IV include exhibits containing statistical and other data on key issues.

U.S. Congress. House. Select Committee on Small Business. BANKING CONCENTRATION AND SMALL BUSINESS. A staff report to the above committee pursuant to H. Res. 51 (86th Cong., 2nd Sess.) Committee Print. December 23, 1960. Washington, D.C.: Government Printing Office, 1960. 97 p.

Holds that multiunit chain banking possesses two-thirds of all of the commercial bank resources of the nation and about three-fourths of all the loans; and that in many states, the total resources of the independent unit banks represent less than 10 percent of the total for the State. Tabulations and tables are listed showing the concentration existing in each of the larger cities, in each of the states and in the United States as a whole.

U.S. Congress. House. Select Committee on Small Business. CHAIN BANKING, STOCKHOLDER AND LOAN LINKS OF 200 LARGEST MEMBER BANKS. Report by Honorable Wright Patman to the above committee. (87th Cong., 2nd Sess.) Committee Print. Washington, D.C.: Government Printing Office, 1963. 541 p.

Holds that the picture of a trend toward greater banking concentration is incomplete because chain banking has been omitted. Chain banking is defined as a "situation where the same individual or group of individuals controls two or more banks. In a broader sense, however, chain banking could be construed as any community of interest or links among banks arising directly, or indirectly, from stock ownership."

U.S. Congress. House. Select Committee on Small Business. CONGRESS AND THE MONOPOLY PROBLEM—FIFTY-SIX YEARS OF ANTITRUST DEVELOPMENT, 1900-1956. History of Congressional Action in the Antitrust Field since 1900. Report of above committee pursuant to H. Res. 114 (84th Cong., 2nd Sess.) Washington, D.C.: Government Printing Office, 1957. 662 p.

This documental survey includes major pertinent legislative data on the antitrust laws from 1900 through 1956. The study was planned for the purpose of enabling the House Small Business Committee and those having responsibility in the area of small business and antimonopoly problems, (1) to evaluate properly what further legislation is needed in the general field of antitrust to protect small business, and (2) to judge properly the effectiveness of the administration of present antitrust laws by the executive agencies and departments.

Part I consists of an analytical summary of all antitrust laws now in force. Part II contains a detailed statement relating to the executive department or agency having jurisdiction. Part III is a complete list of statutory exemptions from the antitrust laws. Part IV contains a listing of all legislative proposals in the antitrust field which were reported by a House or Senate committee from 1900 to 1950. From 1950 through 1956, similar treatment has been given to all pertinent legislative proposals, whether or not they were reported by a committee. Part V is a compilation of important supplementary recommendations. Part VI sets out the texts of the statutes covered in this document. Part VII includes a list of reference to pertinent hearings and reports. Part VIII contains a subject grouping of all bills treated in Part IV. Part IX consists of statistics on federal antitrust activities which were prepared and compiled by the Staff of the House Small Business Committee. The statistics include a record of the antimonopoly charges filed by the Antitrust Division of the Department of Justice and the Federal Trade Commission during each year of their operations, and a showing of how the proceedings were terminated.

U.S. Congress. House. Select Committee on Small Business. FAIR TRADE: THE PROBLEM AND THE ISSUES. Report of above committee pursuant to H. Res. 33 (82nd Cong., 2nd Sess.) Washington, D.C.: Government Printing Office, 1952. 70 p.

Part I reviews the nature of the "fair trade problem," gives a brief account of its historical development and states the present issue. Part II analyzes the legal basis of fair trade including the status of resale price maintenance under the antitrust laws as amended and state fair trade laws. Part III presents the arguments pro and con on the basic issues of fair trade.

U.S. Congress. House. Select Committe on Small Business. FTC ADVISORY OPINION ON JOINT ADS. A report of the above committee pursuant to H. Res. 13 (88th Cong., 1st Sess.) Report No. 699. August 22, 1963. Washington, D.C.: Government Printing Office, 1963. 32 p.
>   Deals with Federal Trade Commission ruling holding that it is illegal for small business retailers to engage in cooperative advertising if prices for merchandise are quoted. Also discusses the Antitrust Division's disagreement with this ruling.

U.S. Congress. House. Select Committee on Small Business. INTERLOCKING DIRECTORS AND OFFICIALS OF 135 LARGE FINANCIAL COMPANIES OF THE UNITED STATES. Part I of a preliminary report of the above committee pursuant to H. Res. 56 (85th Cong., 1st Sess.) Report No. 1278. November 30, 1957. Washington, D.C.: Government Printing Office, 1957. 176 p.
>   Major portion of report consists of a table entitled "Interlocks Between 135 Top Financial Institutions and other Large Companies by Industry Group." Does not attempt to evaluate or pass judgment on any particular interlock.

U.S. Congress. House. Select Committee on Small Business. LIST OF PUBLICATIONS ISSUED BY SELECT COMMITTEE ON SMALL BUSINESS. HEARINGS, REPORTS, STAFF STUDIES, AND DOCUMENTS. 77th-88th CONGRESSES (1941-63) (88th Cong., 1st Sess.) Committee Print. November 1963. Washington, D.C.: Government Printing Office, 1963. 23 p.
>   Indexed alphabetically and also by Congresses for ready reference. Includes 65 hearings and 97 reports of this committee.

U.S. Congress. House. Select Committee on Small Business. MERGERS AND SUPERCONCENTRATION. ACQUISITIONS OF 500 LARGEST INDUSTRIAL AND 50 LARGEST MERCHANDISING FIRMS. Staff report of the above committee. (87th Cong., 2nd Sess.) Committee Print. November 8, 1962. Washington, D.C.: Government Printing Office, 1962. 272 p.
>   Presents voluminous data on merger actions of large firms during the 11-year period since the passage of the Celler-Kefauver Act.

U.S. Congress. House. Select Committee on Small Business. OPERATION AND EFFECT OF CONSENT DECREE IN WEST COAST OIL CASE. Report of the above committee pursuant to H. Res. 46 (87th Cong., 2nd Sess.) Report No. 2522. October 3, 1962. Washington, D.C.: Government Printing Office, 1962. 45 p.
>   Report concludes that, although this judgment had been productive of results which had been beneficial to both the service station operators and the petroleum suppliers, it appeared that some petroleum suppliers had failed to fully comply with one or more provisions of the judgment--thereby causing certain coercive and unfair practices to continue.

U.S. Congress. House. Select Committee on Small Business. PRICE DISCRIMINATION, THE ROBINSON-PATMAN ACT, AND THE ATTORNEY GENERAL'S NATIONAL COMMITTEE TO STUDY THE ANTITRUST LAWS.

Report of the above committee pursuant to H. Res 114 (84th Cong., 2nd Sess.) Report No. 2966. December 19, 1956. Washington, D.C.: Government Printing Office, 1956. 304 p.

> A critical appraisal of the report of the Attorney General's National Committee To Study the Antitrust Laws. Analyzes the Attorney General's Committee's attack on the Robinson-Patman Act. Appendix B lists the members of the Attorney General's Committee and the law firms, institutions and agencies with which they were affiliated. It also lists antitrust cases in which the members of the Committee or their law firms had participated. Appendix D is entitled "Tabular showing of how the Robinson-Patman Act has been interpreted away (with particular reference to interpretations of subsection 2 (b)."

U.S. Congress. House. Select Committee on Small Business. STATISTICS ON FEDERAL ANTITRUST ACTIVITIES. Staff report to the above committee pursuant to H. Res. 114 (84th Cong., 1st Sess.) Committee Print. Washington, D.C.: Government Printing Office, 1956. 6 p.

> Divided into three parts as follows: I. Appropriations and expenditures for antimonopoly law enforcement by the Antitrust Division of the Department of Justice and the Federal Trade Commission for the entire period of time for which statistics are available. II. A record of the total number of charges of antimonopoly law violations filed and disposed of by the Antitrust Division of the Department of Justice and the Federal Trade Commission since those agencies were established. III. The record of the total number of antitrust cases filed in Federal courts for each year during the 5-year period ending June 30, 1955, by the Government and by private parties.

U.S. Congress. House. Special Subcommittee of the Select Committee on Small Business. PRICE DISCRIMINATION IN THE DISTRIBUTION OF DAIRY PRODUCTS. Report of the above subcommittee pursuant to H. Res. 56 (85th Cong., 2nd Sess.) Report No. 2713. January 3, 1959. Washington, D.C.: Government Printing Office, 1959. 49 p.

> Report on investigation of complaints alleging that large, powerful processors and distributors of dairy products were discriminating in prices, and in that connection were making sales in some areas at unreasonably low prices and at levels below cost, with the result of destroying competition.

U.S. Congress. House. Special Subcommittee of the Select Committee on Small Business. SMALL BUSINESS PROBLEMS IN THE DAIRY INDUSTRY. Report of the above subcommittee pursuant to H. Res. 51 (86th Cong., 2nd Sess.) Report No. 2231. December 22, 1960. Washington, D.C.: Government Printing Office, 1960. 128 p.

> Deals with findings and conclusions of subcommittee which investigated complaints that large concerns engaged in the processing and distribution of dairy products were using unfair pricing practices to eliminate small, competing processors and distributors.

U.S. Congress. House. Subcommittee No. 1 of the Select Committee on Small Business. LAW-ENFORCEMENT ACTIVITIES AFFECTING SMALL BUSINESS. Report of Subcommittee No. 1 on Law Enforcement and Subsidies Affecting Small Business to the above committee pursuant to H. Res. 56 (85th Cong., 2nd Sess.) Report No. 2714. January 3, 1959. Washington, D.C.: Government Printing Office, 1959. 69 p.

> Report on investigation of complaints about the alleged failure of law enforcement agencies to act timely and effectively under our antimonopoly laws to protect small-business firms from predatory and other unfair trade practices.

U.S. Congress. House. Subcommittee No. 1 of the Select Committee on Small Business. THE ORGANIZATION AND PROCEDURES OF THE FEDERAL REGULATORY COMMISSIONS AND AGENCIES AND THEIR EFFECT ON SMALL BUSINESS. Report of Subcommittee No. 1 on Regulatory Agencies and Commissions to the above committee, pursuant to H. Res. 114 (84th Cong., 2nd Sess.) Report No. 2967. December 24, 1956. Washington, D.C.: Government Printing Office, 1956. 91 p.

> This report proposes no action against any person. It is directed toward effort for improvement in a system. The improvement would insure that regulation over commerce by the Federal Trade Commission, Federal Power Commission, Federal Communications Commission, Civil Aeronautics Board, Securities and Exchange Commission, and other federal regulatory commissions and agencies would be made more independent of the executive branch and more responsive to Congress. Investigates Hoover Commission plan to make chairman of each regulatory commission and agency responsible to the President, to serve at the pleasure of the President.

U.S. Congress. House. Subcommittee No. 3 of the Select Committee on Small Business. SMALL BUSINESS AND THE ALUMINUM INDUSTRY. Report of Subcommittee No. 3 on Minerals and Raw Materials to the above committee pursuant to H. Res. 114 (84th Cong., 2nd Sess.) Report No. 2954. July 27, 1956. Washington, D.C.: Government Printing Office, 1956. 150 p.

> Report on investigation of complaints of small-businessmen that they could not obtain enough primary aluminum needed for fabrication from the three integrated aluminum producers who were their only domestic sources of supply.

U.S. Congress. House. Subcommittee No. 3 of the Select Committee on Small Business. SMALL-BUSINESS PROBLEMS IN THE ALUMINUM INDUSTRY. Report of Subcommittee No. 3 on Minerals and Raw Materials to the above committee, pursuant to H. Res. 56 (85th Cong., 2nd Sess.) Report No. 2716. January 3, 1959. Washington, D.C.: Government Printing Office, 1959. 19 p.

> Explores, among others, the problem of the overabundance of aluminum which causes integrated producers to tender aluminum to the government under expansion contracts which were made at a time when there was a critical shortage of the metal.

U.S. Congress. House. Subcommittee No. 4 of the Select Committee on Small Business. THE IMPACT UPON SMALL BUSINESS OF DUAL DISTRIBU-

TION AND RELATED VERTICAL INTEGRATION. Report of Subcommittee No. 4 on Distribution Problems to the above committee, pursuant to H. Res. 13 (88th Cong., 2nd Sess.) Report No. 1943, December 30, 1964. Washington, D.C.: Government Printing Office, 1964. 124 p.

Dual distribution exists when a vertically integrated firm operates in two successive stages of production and/or distribution of a good, but also sells some of its output from the first stage to independent firms, who then sell in competition with the supplying firm's second stage operations. Thus the independent is in competition with his supplier. Dual distribution also exists when the manufacturer of a branded good sells that brand through two or more competing distribution channels, or when a manufacturer sells two brands of basically the same product through two competing kinds of distribution networks. This report considers the extent and effect of dual distribution and related practices arising from vertical integration on small business.

U.S. Congress. House. Subcommittee No. 5 of the Select Committee on Small Business. DISTRIBUTION PRACTICES IN THE PETROLEUM INDUSTRY. Interim report of Subcommittee No. 5 on Distribution Problems the above committee, pursuant to H. Res. 56 (85th Cong., 1st Sess.) Report No. 1157. August 14, 1957. Washington, D.C.: Government Printing Office, 1957. 40 p.

Report on investigation of complaints which included, among others, alleged oppressive leases, lack of financing from private sources, competitive allowances, large retail dealer turnover, price manipulations, coercive sales of tires, batteries and accessories to dealers and lessees by some major oil companies.

U.S. Congress. House. Subcommittee No. 5 of the Select Committee on Small Business. SMALL BUSINESS PROBLEMS IN FOOD DISTRIBUTION. Report of the Subcommittee No. 5 on Distribution Problems Affecting Small Business to the above committee, pursuant to H. Res. 51 (86th Cong., 2nd Sess.) Report No. 2234. December 27, 1960. Washington, D.C.: Government Printing Office, 1960. 225 p.

A study of alleged unfair competitive trade practices in food distribution. Covers pricing practices, trade practices, financing of small business, and the economic significance of the concentration of economic power in food distribution.

U.S. Congress. House. Subcommittee No. 5 of the Select Committee on Small Business. SMALL BUSINESS PROBLEMS IN THE PETROLEUM INDUSTRY (TIRES, BATTERIES, AND ACCESSORIES). Report of Subcommittee No. 5 on Distribution Problems Affecting Small Business to the above committee, pursuant to H. Res. 51 (86th Cong., 2nd Sess.) Report No. 2233. December 22, 1960. Washington, D.C.: Government Printing Office, 1960. 66 p.

In general the report covers: (a) the economic position of major petroleum corporations; (b) meagerness of profits of service station operators; (c) service station leases; (d) effect of petroleum companies' sponsorship of specified brands of tires, batteries, and accessories upon lessee-dealers.

U.S. Congress. House. Subcommittee No. 6 of the Select Committee on
Small Business. PROBLEMS IN THE POULTRY INDUSTRY. Report of Sub-
committee No. 6 on Food Industries to the above committee, pursuant to H.
Res. 56 (85th Cong., 2nd Sess.) Report No. 2717. January 3, 1959.
Washington, D.C.: Government Printing Office, 1959. 11 p.
> Report on investigation of complaints that overproduction and
> declining prices in the poultry industry were due to unfair tac-
> tics and practices which had the effect of driving the indepen-
> dents out of the industry.

Reports and Studies of Government Departments and Agencies

U.S. Advisory Committee on Cost Justification. REPORT TO THE FEDERAL
TRADE COMMISSION. February, 1958. 26 p.
> Committee was formed for the purpose of ascertaining whether
> it was "feasible for the Federal Trade Commission to develop
> standards of proof and procedures for costing" which would serve
> as guides to business enterprises.

U.S. Attorney General. IDENTICAL BIDDING IN PUBLIC PROCUREMENT.
Report of the Attorney General under Executive Order 10936. Washington,
D.C.: Government Printing Office, July, 1962. 434 p.
> Explains origin of the executive order and its implementation,
> as well as the nature of identical bidding. Includes tabulations
> of identical bidders and details of identical bids. Covers period
> from July 15, 1961 to February 9, 1962.

U.S. Attorney General. IDENTICAL BIDDING IN PUBLIC PROCUREMENT.
Second report of the Attorney General under Executive Order 10936. Washington, D.C.: Government Printing Office, July, 1964. 401 p.
> Reveals the pertinent details of each of the publishable identical
> bids affecting procurements consummated in calendar year 1962.
> The general format of presentation of these details is similar to
> that utilized in the first report.

U.S. Attorney General. IDENTICAL BIDDING IN PUBLIC PROCUREMENT.
Report of the Attorney General under Executive Order 10936. Washington,
D.C.: Government Printing Office, February, 1965. 347 p.
> Includes 1675 reports filed by federal, state, and local govern-
> ments; reveals the details of the identical bidding affecting
> 2504 line items of procurement; and identifies 2503 firms which
> submitted identical bids to public agencies in calendar year
> 1963. General format is similar to first and second reports.

U.S. Department of Agriculture. Agricultural Marketing Service, Marketing
Research Division. OWNERSHIP CHANGES BY PURCHASE AND MERGER
IN SELECTED FOOD INDUSTRIES. (Marketing Research Report No. 369)
Washington, D.C.: Government Printing Office, 1959. 24 p.
> Results of a survey of eight food industries representing all levels
> of food marketing. Of the companies covered, 26 percent re-
> ported making acquisitions, disposals, or both, during 1952-58.
> Survey found that the methods of acquisition and disposition

most frequently adopted were through purchase, and that the vast majority of acquisitons were of companies within the same industry and at the same market level.

U.S. Department of Commerce. SELF-REGULATION IN ADVERTISING. A report on the operations of private enterprise in an important area of public responsibility. Washington, D.C.: Government Printing Office, 1964. 105 p.

Includes a chapter entitled "Self-Regulation and Government Regulation."

BIBLIOGRAPHIES

American Marketing Association. A SPECIAL INTEREST BIBLIOGRAPHY ON DISCOUNT SELLING, RETAIL PRICE-CUTTING AND RESALE PRICE CONTROLS, compiled by Stanley C. Hollander. (AMA Bibliog. Series, No. 3). Chicago: 1956. 52 p.

Does not cite literature on the chain store question. Was originally intended as a bibliography on discount selling, but was broadened to include such retail selling techniques as differential pricing, diversion of trade from conventional channels and noncompliance with manufacturer-set minimum prices. Standard college texts in marketing, retailing and government regulation of business are omitted. Recent materials are emphasized. Compiler is a Visiting Associate Professor of Marketing at the University of Pennsylvania.

The Association of the Bar of the City of New York. THE RECORD. The Library. "Recent Literature on Antitrust Law, 1953-1957." May, 1957. pp. 303-309.

Federal Trade Commission. SELECTED REFERENCES RELATING TO CLAYTON ACT, SECTION 7 AND THE CURRENT MERGER PROBLEM. Special Reference List No. 3. Prepared under the direction of Amy Jennings, Librarian. Washington, D.C.: Library, Federal Trade Commission, revised March, 1958. 52 p.

This list of material was originally prepared in response to numerous requests from members of the Commission Staff for books and articles on the merger problems. Revised and brought up-to-date. Includes largely material published subsequent to the Clayton Act Amendment of 1950.

Federal Trade Commission. TWENTY YEARS OF ROBINSON-PATMAN ACT LITERATURE, 1936-56. Special Reference List No. 4. Compiled by Amy R. Jennings, Librarian. Washington, D.C.: Library, Federal Trade Commission, revised October, 1957. 71 p.

Includes books and miscellaneous publications, articles from legal and non-legal periodicals and magazines, and a list of bibliographies. A good coverage of government publications on the subject.

The Library of Congress. General Reference and Bibliography Division. CAR-
TELS, COMBINES AND TRUSTS. A Selected List of References compiled by
Frances Cheney. Washington, D.C. September 28, 1944.
> Bibliography is divided into following parts: Part I, Bibliographies;
> Part II, The Cartel Movement Prior to World War II; Part III,
> Impact of the Cartel Movement on World War II; Part IV, The
> Cartel Movement in the Postwar Period; Part V, Index.

National Industrial Conference Board. SELECTED BIBLIOGRAPHY. ECONOM-
IC EVIDENCE IN ANTITRUST CASES. New York: September, 1962. 7 p.
> Divided into four parts as follows: Part I. General Considerations;
> Part II. Evidentiary Problems; Part III. Basic Evidentiary Data;
> and Part IV. A Handful of Cases (and books and articles by
> economists serving on cases).

Packer, Herbert L. THE STATE OF RESEARCH IN ANTITRUST LAW. New
Haven: Walter E. Meyer Research Institute of Law, 1963. 185 p.
> Includes chapters on the following: Pre-1945 Antitrust Law and
> Research; Economics, Economists and Antitrust; Work Patterns in
> Antitrust, The Literature and the Issues. Appendix I lists anti-
> trust casebooks, and Appendix II is "A Compilation of Outstand-
> ing Work in the Antitrust Field: 1945-60."

PERIODICALS AND SERVICES

American Bar Association, Section of Antitrust Law. BULLETIN. Chicago:
Semi-annual.
> Two volumes are published each year, covering the proceedings
> and symposiums held at the spring and annual meetings. Pro-
> grams include papers by government officials, leading lawyers,
> and eminent law professors who are considered outstanding in
> the field of antitrust and trade regulation. A cumulative index
> covers volumes 1 through 15 (1952-1959).

ANTITRUST AND TRADE REGULATION NEWSLETTER. Boston: Management
Reports, Inc., 1962-   . Monthly.
> A four page letter, summarizing outstanding court and commission
> cases in the antitrust field and reporting developments both in
> this country and abroad.

ANTITRUST BULLETIN. New York: Federal Legal Publications. Bimonthly.
> Devoted exclusively to articles on antitrust matters. A section
> entitled "Bibliographia" lists new antitrust books and articles
> from legal and nonlegal periodicals. Includes book reviews.

BNA'S ANTITRUST & TRADE REGULATION REPORT. Washington, D.C.:
Bureau of National Affairs. Weekly.
> A report letter which meets the need for prompt and comprehen-
> sive antitrust and trade regulation coverage. Important court
> and Federal Trade Commission decisions, pending court and
> agency proceedings, Congressional activity, statements and ad-
> dresses by Justice Department officials, Congressmen and others
> are reported. Includes frequent bibliographies.

New York State Bar Association. ANTITRUST LAW SECTION. Chicago:
Commerce Clearing House, Inc. 1946-
>The above section holds antitrust symposiums annually. The re-
>port of their meetings consisting mainly of contributions from
>many outstanding authorities adds up to monographs each year
>on a particular aspect of antitrust law.

Potter's Supreme Court News Service. ANTITRUST NEWS SERVICE. Chevy
Chase, Maryland. Frequent mailings while the United States Supreme Court
is in session.
>Coverage is limited to antitrust and related cases in the United
>States Supreme Court. Mimiographed copies of briefs filed in
>the above cases in the Supreme Court are supplied to subscribers.
>Service also includes lists of pending cases and their status to
>date, as well as tentative lists of cases expected to be reached
>for argument during a stated period. Reproductions of selected
>Department of Justice press releases are another feature of the
>service.

Reed, Stanley Foster, ed. MERGERS & ACQUISITIONS. THE JOURNAL OF
CORPORATE VENTURE. Washington, D.C.: Stanley Foster Reed. Quarterly.
>A "how-to" journal written, edited, and published by business-
>men, professional writers, and experts in the special fields sur-
>rounding corporate venture here and abroad.

TRADE REGULATION REPORTER. Chicago: Commerce Clearing House, Inc.
>A looseleaf service kept current by insertion of pages issued
>weekly. Includes the antitrust laws in full text with annotations.
>The reporter, supplemented by a transfer binder and "Blue Books,"
>digests all federal antitrust complaints and indictments filed since
>1898. A report letter accompanying the weekly insertion sheets
>highlights important developments in the antitrust and trade regu-
>lation field. Federal Trade Commission complaints are listed by
>docket number and a respondent section lists firms or individuals
>alphabetically by name. A section covering the state fair trade
>laws is also included in the service. At the end of each year,
>bound volumes entitled Trade Cases have been published since
>1932. These contain texts of decisions rendered by federal and
>state courts, consent decrees, and state attorney general opin-
>ions which were reported in the service during the year.

Section 4

FEDERAL COMMUNICATIONS COMMISSION

Section 4

FEDERAL COMMUNICATIONS COMMISSION

The Federal Communications Commission came into existence in 1934 with the passage of the Federal Communications Act of 1934.

Its powers include the authority and duty to regulate interstate telephone and telegraph rates on a reasonable basis. It also regulates radio and television frequencies and licenses such station operations.

In addition, the commission has jurisdiction over service connections, and can and has set up accounting systems and prescribed depreciation methods. It passes on applications for mergers between Bell and independent companies, deciding whether public interest is protected or assisted by the proposed sale or merger of telephone properties or operations in interstate commerce.

The Federal Communications Act of 1934 reserved all jurisdiction over local telephone exchange service to the state commissions, which take care of such local exchange regulations. Only the interstate long-distance phase of the telephone operations comes under the service and rate control of the Federal Communications Commission.

The operations of Western Union are entirely within the regulatory control of the Federal Communications Commission.

TEXTS

Clemens, Eli W. ECONOMICS AND PUBLIC UTILITIES. New York: Appleton-Century-Crofts, 1950. 765 p.
> The author, a professor of economics at the University of Maryland, has based this book on his teaching program designed to train economists, accountants, and technicians for public service. His underlying philosophy is a belief in continuous disciplined competition between public and private ownership. Among the topics treated are: the nature of commission regulation; public utility finance; valuation; rate of return; the state commissions; federal regulation; regulation of accounting, securities, and finance; problems of the holding company; regional public power; the Tennessee

Valley Authority; the Columbia River project; and other regional
power projects.

Edelman, Murray. THE LICENSING OF RADIO SERVICES IN THE UNITED
STATES, 1927 to 1947. A STUDY IN ADMINISTRATIVE FORMULATION OF
POLICY. Urbana: University of Illinois Press, 1950. 229 p.
Deals with the manner of development of the body of rules and
decisions which govern the licensing of broadcasting and the lesser
known radio services in the United States. Offers a basis for determining to what degree the licensing authority in this field has
found it possible to reduce its discretion to rule.

Emery, Walter B. BROADCASTING AND GOVERNMENT. Lansing: Michigan
State University Press, 1961. 482 p.
Author was a member of the legal staff of the Federal Communications Commission. Concerned with what has been, and what should
be function of government in regulation of broadcasting. Designed
to bring together, in one handy volume, basic information essential
to an understanding of how our regulatory system developed and
how it operates. Generally deals with what qualification tests
and rules of conduct must be complied with by those who operate
these communications media.

Emery, Edwin and others. INTRODUCTION TO MASS COMMUNICATIONS.
New York: Dodd, Mead, 1960. 435 p.
Part One deals with communications and society; Part Two, with
the historical perspective; Part Three, with the mass communications industries and professions; and Part Four, with education for
mass communications.

Garfield, Paul J. and Lovejoy, Wallace F. PUBLIC UTILITY ECONOMICS.
Englewood Cliffs, New Jersey: Prentice-Hall, 1964. 505 p.
A textbook intended for use by students in universities, and in the
training programs of commissions and utilities. Pricing is given a
prominent place and expanded treatment, as a central problem in
economics. Developing problems, in the areas where utility regulatory policies and antitrust policies overlap, are surveyed. The
problems in the dual regulation of telephone rates are discussed.

Head, Sydney W. BROADCASTING IN AMERICA. A SURVEY OF TELEVI-
SION AND RADIO. Boston: Houghton Mifflin, 1956. 502 p.
Chapter 8 of this volume deals with the origin of government regulation of broadcasting, chapter 21 with the law of broadcasting,
and chapter 22 with the administration of the law. Other chapters
are grouped under the five major categories: physical bases of
braodcasting; origin and growth of broadcasting; the economy of
the broadcasting industry; social control of broadcasting; evaluating
the broadcasting service.

Levin, Harvey J. BROADCAST REGULATION AND JOINT OWNERSHIP OF
MEDIA. New York: New York University Press, 1960. 219 p.
A case study in the economics of public regulation, of interest to
those who wish to study the role and limitations of economic analysis in the formulation of policy in a regulated industry. It is

also intended for students of mass communications. Chapter 7 deals with broadcast regulatory policy.

Minow, Newton N. EQUAL TIME: THE PRIVATE BROADCASTER AND THE PUBLIC INTEREST. Edited by Lawrence Laurent. New York: Atheneum, 1964. 316 p.

A collection of the speeches and writings of the former Chairman of the Federal Communications Commission, beginning with the famous "Vast Wasteland" address of 1961.

Phillips, C.F. THE ECONOMICS OF REGULATION: THEORY AND PRACTICE IN THE TRANSPORTATION AND PUBLIC UTILITY INDUSTRIES. Homewood, Illinois: Irwin, 1965. 783 p.

This book resulted from a one-semester course given by the author at Washington and Lee University. It concentrates on the theory and practice of regulation, and on current regulatory problems.

Topics discussed are: the economic and legal concepts of public regulation; the independent regulatory commissions; accounting and financial control; operating costs; rate base; rate of return; rate structure; service and safety regulation; regulation of transportation industries; public policy and transportation. Separate chapters are devoted to the electric power industry, the natural gas industry, and communications.

University of Michigan Law School. Summer Institute on International and Comparative Law. COMMUNICATIONS MEDIA, LEGAL AND POLICY PROBLEMS. Ann Arbor: University of Michigan Law School, 1954. Lectures delivered June 16-18, 1954. 234 p.

Lectures in the field of official controls versus self-regulation of communications media comprise one part of this book.

Warner, Harry P. RADIO AND TELEVISION LAW. A Standard Reference Book on the Legal and Regulatory Structure of the Radio Industry. New York: Matthew Bender, 1948 with 1949 supplement. 1216 p. plus 127 p. supplement.

Covers administrative practice and procedure of the Commission, the administrative process, administrative control of program standards; network regulations; transfer and assignment of broadcasting licenses; frequency modulation; television; judicial review of the Federal Communications Commission; the legislative basis of broadcast regulation; and proposals to amend the Communications Act of 1934.

Wilcox, Clair. PUBLIC POLICIES TOWARD BUSINESS. Rev. ed. Homewood, Illinois: Irwin, 1960. 907 p.

Chapter 25 of this general textbook deals with the regulation of radio and television.

Wilson, G. Lloyd. TRANSPORTATION AND COMMUNICATIONS. New York: Appleton-Century-Crofts, 1954. 757 p.

Designed for students who have not had a course in transportation and communications. Gives a comprehensive and factual presentation of the structure and services of these utilities, discussing the principles of economic theory characteristic of these industries, sketching the development of each form of transportation and communication, and discussing the services rendered by each. Also describes the bases upon which their rates are made, and outlines the organization and management patterns. The relations of the utilities with each other and the public they serve are taken up. Finally, the regulation of the various instrumentalities of transportation and communications, and the administrative control, by regulatory commissions and the courts, are discussed through the media of statutory law, and commission and court decisions. References are given for further study at the conclusion of each part.

GOVERNMENT PUBLICATIONS

A list of the publications of the Federal Communications Commission, available from the Government Printing Office, may be obtained from the Federal Communications Commission in Washington, D.C.

Administrative Conference of the United States. Committee on Licenses and Authorizations. LICENSING OF MAJOR BROADCAST FACILITIES BY THE FEDERAL COMMUNICATIONS COMMISSION, by William K. Jones. Washington, D.C.: September 1962. 233 p. Mimeo.
> Covers only primary broadcast facilities--standard AM broadcasting, FM broadcasting, and television. Begins with the background of broadcast regulation and the statutory framework within which it functions. Reviews the substantive policies used in granting broadcast licenses, and the procedures employed in implementing these policies. Prospects for improvement and recommendations conclude the report.

Federal Communications Commission. ANNUAL REPORTS. Washington, D.C.: Government Printing Office. 1934-
> Summarize developments in the field of communications for the prior year. Outline legislation, enacted and pending, and litigation to which the Commission was a party. Also describe developments in national defense, space communication, broadcast services, safety and special radio services, common carrier services, field engineering, research and laboratory; and frequency allocation and use.

Federal Communications Commission. REPORTS. Washington, D.C.: Government Printing Office. Vol. 1- , 1935-
> Compilations of Federal Communications Commission docket case decisions. Weekly advance parts, with the same pagination as the bound volumes, are also available on a subscription basis.

Federal Communications Commission. RULES AND REGULATIONS. Washington, D.C.: Government Printing Office. 10 vols. Current.
> Issued in categories. Volume I contains the statement of organization and rules of practice and procedure. Volume VIII contains the uniform system of accounts for classes A and B, and for Class C telephone companies. Volume IX contains the uniform system of accounts for radiotelegraph carriers and for wire-telegraph and ocean cable carriers.

FEDERAL COMMUNICATIONS COMMISSION

Federal Communications Commission. STATISTICS OF COMMUNICATIONS COMMON CARRIERS. Washington, D.C.: Government Printing Office. Annual.
>Summary data and data for individual common carriers.

>Formerly "Statistics of Communications Industry in the United States."

Federal Communications Commission. OPERATING DATA FROM MONTHLY REPORTS OF 47 TELEPHONE CARRIERS FILING ANNUAL AND MONTHLY REPORTS. Washington, D.C. Revisions issued.
>Based on data taken from FCC Forms 81-1 and 81-2.

Federal Communications Commission. OPERATING DATA FROM MONTHLY REPORTS OF LARGE TELEGRAPH CARRIERS. Washington, D.C. Revisions issued.
>Cover those telegraph carriers having annual operating revenues in excess of $250,000.

>Based on FCC Form 82.

Federal Communications Commission. RELEASES. Washington, D.C. Daily.
>Consists chiefly of required public notices of commission actions, receipt of certain applications and petitions, etc. No mailing list is maintained, but arrangements may be made to have them picked up as issued.

President's Communications Policy Board. TELECOMMUNICATIONS, A PROGRAM FOR PROGRESS. Washington, D.C.: Government Printing Office, March 1951. 238 p.
>A report on policies and practices recommended to be followed by the federal government in the communications field. Telephone, telegraph, radio, and television are studied. Chapter III examines the telephone and telegraph systems as well as the domestic telecommunication systems of the federal government. Chapter IV discusses United States telecommunication abroad, both commercial and government. Chapter V takes up the nature and functions of the various existing government agencies concerned with telecommunications.

U.S. Congress. House. Committee on Interstate and Foreign Commerce. NETWORK BROADCASTING. (85th Cong., 2nd Sess.) Report No. 1297. Washington, D.C.: Government Printing Office, 1958. 737 p.
>A report by the network study staff to the network study committee. Covers the structure, operations, and practices of the networks in their relationships with other components of the industry. Emphasis is given to the opportunities for effective competition in the broadcasting industry. The basic problem taken up is whether, under the existing structure and practices of the industry, there is effective competition; and if not, whether the public interest would be served by legislation or rules issued by the Federal Communications Commission, designed to insure the degree of competition necessary to effectuate the commission's policy.

U.S. Congress. House. Committee on Interstate and Foreign Commerce. REGULATION OF BROADCASTING. HALF A CENTURY OF GOVERNMENT

FEDERAL COMMUNICATIONS COMMISSION

REGULATION OF BROADCASTING AND THE NEED FOR FURTHER LEGISLA-
TIVE ACTION, prepared by Robert S. McMahon, Research Assistant, Special
Subcommittee on Legislative Oversight. (85th Cong., 2nd Sess.) Subcommittee
print. Washington, D.C.: Government Printing Office, 1958. 171 p.
> This study was done in response to the committee's direction to its
> staff to prepare a full analysis of the trends and developments of
> 50 years of broadcast regulation. It contains a legislative history
> of broadcasting, and makes recommendations for future enactment
> by Congress.

U.S. Congress. Senate. Committee on Interstate and Foreign Commerce.
THE NETWORK MONOPOLY. (84th Cong., 2nd Sess.) Committee print.
Washington, D.C.: 1956. 27 p.
> A report prepared for the use of the committee by Senator John W.
> Bricker. Based on 1954 figures, it outlines the economic grip on
> the television industry held by two major networks and a selected
> group of large affiliated television stations. The information set
> out was intended to be of assistance to the committee in examin-
> ing the responsible officials of the two major networks who were
> to testify before it in connection with an overall study of the
> television industry. The appendix contains a chart showing broad-
> cast revenues, expenses, and income of the entire television net-
> work industry (1953-1954). A map of the top 100 television mar-
> ket areas is also included.

U.S. Congress. Senate. Committee on Interstate and Foreign Commerce.
THE TELEVISION INQUIRY. ALLOCATIONS PHASE. (84th Cong., 2nd
Sess.) Report No. 2769. Washington, D.C.: Government Printing Office,
1956. 67 p.
> An interim report submitted to the Federal Communications Com-
> mission, commending the commission for the constructive steps it
> had taken, urging it to push its program, and indicating the intent
> of the committee to follow the course of the commission's work
> very closely. Based on the committee's inquiry into television
> during the preceding six months.

MISCELLANEOUS

American Bar Association, Section of Public Utility Law. ANNUAL
REPORT. Chicago.
> Contains articles and reviews of the year's developments in the
> field of public utilities, including telecommunications.

Blum, Eleanor. REFERENCE BOOKS IN THE MASS MEDIA. Urbana: University of Illinois Press, 1962. 103 p.
> An annotated, selected booklist covering book publishing, broad-
> casting, films, newspapers, magazines, and advertising. General
> and background books are listed first, followed by materials listed
> by media.
>
> Intended to provide sources for facts and figures, names and ad-
> dresses, and other biographical information; and to suggest starting
> points for research.

An alphabetical index at the end refers to the number of each item. Addresses of publishers are also given.

National Association of Railroad and Utilities Commissioners. PROCEEDINGS. Washington, D.C. Annual.

Papers presented at the annual meetings of the association, which consists of commissioners on both the federal and state level who head commissions regulating public utilities. On the federal level, the Interstate Commerce Commission, the Federal Communications Commission, the Federal Power Commission, the Securities and Exchange Commission, and the Civil Aeronautics Board are represented.

RADIO REGULATION. Second Series. Washington, D.C.: Pike & Fischer. Current.

A comprehensive reference work covering every aspect of radio and television regulation. Contains the laws concerning radio and television, amended to date and annotated with legislative history; the regulations of the Federal Communications Commission concerning radio and television, amended to date; proposed rules of the commission not yet adopted but the subject of rule-making proceedings before the agency; the reports, decisions, opinions, and other forms of rulings of the Commission, its review board and its examiners, handed down since July 1963, reported in full text or relevant part; the decisions of courts, federal and state, and of federal government agencies, handed down since July 1963, and directly concerning radio and television, reported in full text or relevant part. A digest and finding aids give access to the material in the service. A consolidated digest gives access to reports, opinions, rulings, and decisions handed down prior to the Second Series.

PERIODICALS

ACA NEWS. New York: American Communications Association. Monthly, except August.

Published in a newspaper format, usually of eight pages, by the association of employees of the telegraph industry. In addition to labor news, it contains excellent coverage of congressional activities in the communications field.

FEDERAL COMMUNICATIONS BAR JOURNAL. Washington, D.C.: Federal Communications Bar Association. Quarterly.

Contains articles, reviews, news items, and digests of recent decisions.

JOURNAL OF BROADCASTING. Washington, D.C.: Association for Professional Broadcasting Education. Quarterly.

Contains scholarly articles and book reviews.

PUBLIC UTILITY FORTNIGHTLY. Washington, D.C.: Public Utilities Reports. Biweekly.

A magazine published every other Thursday. Contains articles, news items, and comments on recent cases and rulings.

RADIO TELEVISION DAILY. New York: Radio Daily Corporation. Daily except Saturday, Sunday, and holidays.
Printed in a newspaper format. Contains news items of current happenings in the industry.

RADIO & TELEVISION WEEKLY. Jersey City, New Jersey: Radio & Television Weekly. Weekly.
A newspaper type of format. Contains some very short articles, and news items.

TELECOMMUNICATIONS REPORTS. Washington, D.C.: Telecommunications Publishing Co. Weekly. Vol. 1-   , 1934-   .
A news service covering the telephone, telegraph and radio communications fields and providing prompt and comprehensive coverage of all developments affecting them. Each issue contains between 30 and 50 pages, with an index on the first page.

TELEPHONE ENGINEER & MANAGEMENT. Wheaton, Illinois: Brookhill Publishing Company, Semimonthly.
Edited for the administrative executives in every department of the operating telephone industry--management, engineering, plant. Contains short articles and special features. The "Washington Report" summarizes the work currently before the Federal Communications Commission. Another feature entitled "Regulatory News Front" summarizes the work of the state regulatory commissions.

TELEPHONY. THE JOURNAL OF THE TELEPHONE INDUSTRY. Chicago: Telephony Publishing Corp. Weekly.
This journal contains short articles on all phases of the telephone industry. A feature entitled "Courts and Commissions" summarizes proceedings before both bodies. Another feature entitled "In the Nation's Capital" summarizes events in Washington which affect the telephone industry.

TELEVISION AGE. Baltimore: Television Editorial Corp. Biweekly.
Contains articles and news items. A feature entitled "Television Age Spot Report" reviews current activity in national spot television. Ratings of various programs are discussed.

TELEVISION QUARTERLY. Syracuse: National Academy of Television Arts and Sciences in cooperation with the Television and Radio Department, Newhouse Communications Center. Quarterly.
Contains articles on matters relating to television; e.g. current programs, self-regulation in advertising, foreign markets. Also has regular departments of comments and book reviews.

TRADE ASSOCIATIONS

The trade association in the radio and television field is the National Association of Broadcasters, 1771 N Street, N.W., Washington, D.C. 20036; formerly known as the National Association of Radio and Television Broadcasters. It was founded in 1922, has 3239 members, and a staff of 85.

Radio and television stations, and all seven national radio and television networks, are members, to the total of 1986. Frequency modulation radio members total 687. Members subscribing to the association's Television Code number 428.

The association institutes voluntary codes for radio and television which provide broadcasters with guideposts in determining acceptable programming and advertising practices.

Its purpose is to uphold the American system of broadcasting, free from government censorship; and to combat discriminatory legislative proposals against advertising.

The trade association for the independent telephone systems is the United States Independent Telephone Association, 438 Pennsylvania Building, Washington 4, D.C. It was founded in 1897, has 1207 members, and a staff of 17.

Members are independent (non-Bell) operating telephone companies, and their manufacturers and suppliers. Members represent a total of 13,000,000 independent telephones, with a total of 10,000,000 individual subscribers. Membership is concentrated in the smaller communities and rural areas.

This association maintains agreements with the Bell System toll network on routings and divisions of revenue on interchanged business. It also publishes news bulletins, booklets, brochures, and an annual statistical volume.

Section 5

FEDERAL POWER COMMISSION

Section 5

FEDERAL POWER COMMISSION

The Federal Power Commission regulates the rates, services and accounting practices of the water, gas and electric utilities; and the securities issues of certain electric utilities.

ELECTRIC AND GAS UTILITIES

Texts

Bary, Constantine W. OPERATIONAL ECONOMICS OF ELECTRIC UTILITIES. New York: Columbia University Press, 1963. 221 p.
    Describes and illustrates conceptual models, methods, principles and procedures developed by the author in years of study of the most probable incidence of costs for electric utility services, and in designing equitable and compensatory rates therefor. It appraises the probable economic impact of foreseeable developments in the fields of production, transmission and distribution of electric services by utilities.

Bauer, John. PUBLIC ORGANIZATION OF ELECTRIC POWER. New York: Harper, 1949. 263 p.
    The author presents his views of the advantages of properly established public organization of the utility industry. His proposal would avoid central authoritarian control, separating the federal, state and local systems, while providing for comprehensive coordination. Written for the practical purpose of influencing public policy in the utility industry.

Bauer, John. TRANSFORMING PUBLIC UTILITY REGULATION. New York: Harper, 1950. 367 p.
    Attempts to present the needed pattern of regulation and public utility organization if the system of private ownership and operation is to be maintained against the inherent advantages of outright public ownership and operation. Proposals are presented, not in opposition to public ownership and operation, but as alternative means through which the same public objectives can be attained under readjusted private organization and management.

Bonbright, James C. PRINCIPLES OF PUBLIC UTILITY RATES. New York: Columbia University Press, 1961. 433 p.

> A survey which centers attention on the basic criteria of reasonable rates rather than on the many problems of application and administration. Concerned especially with the electric utilities.

Caywood, Russell E. ELECTRIC UTILITY RATE ECONOMICS. New York: McGraw-Hill, 1956. 236 p.

> The object of this volume is to make available a concise, practical, up-to-date guide to electric rate-making; and to present the economics of the electric utility business, including regulatory aspects, as a framework on which rates are built and as a summary of the fundamentals of the business. The fundamentals of the electric utility business are first outlined, and then rate principles and problems are discussed.

Clemens, Eli W. ECONOMICS AND PUBLIC UTILITIES. New York: Appleton-Century-Crofts, 1950. 765 p.

> The author, a professor of economics at the University of Maryland, has based this book on his teaching program designed to train economists, accountants and technicians for public service. His underlying philosophy is a belief in continuous disciplined competition between public and private ownership.
>
> Among the topics treated are: the nature of commission regulation; public utility finance; valuation; rate of return; the state commissions; federal regulation; regulation of accounting, securities and finance; problems of the holding company; regional public power; the Tennessee Valley Authority; the Columbia River project; and other regional power projects.

Cook, Franklin H. THE ELECTRIC POWER INDUSTRY IN THE UNITED STATES. University Park: Bureau of Business Research, Pennsylvania State University, 1964. 83 p.

> The author, an economist, gives the economic dimensions of the electric utility business, by text and statistics, emphasizing expense analysis, plant investment and utilization, and revenue and consumption characteristics.

Davidson, Ralph K. PRICE DISCRIMINATION IN SELLING GAS AND ELECTRICITY. Baltimore: Johns Hopkins Press, 1955. 254 p.

> Utilities charge their customers different rates for their services, depending on the use for which purchased, or the quantity used. This book discusses the case for and against this price discrimination in the setting of gas and electric rates.

Davidson, Sidney. THE PLANT ACCOUNTING REGULATIONS OF THE FEDERAL POWER COMMISSION. Ann Arbor: University of Michigan School of Business Administration, 1952. 163 p.

> The purpose of this study is to describe and analyze the Uniform System of Accounts adopted by the Federal Power Commission in order to obtain adequate and accurate financial information about the regulated firms. Major attention in the Uniform System centers on accounting for plant assets, since utilities require unusually

large amounts of plant investment. Therefore, this study is confined to property account problems.

ELECTRIC POWER AND GOVERNMENT POLICY. A SURVEY OF THE RELA-
TIONS BETWEEN THE GOVERNMENT AND THE ELECTRIC POWER INDUSTRY.
New York: Twentieth Century Fund, 1948. 860 p.
Based on the findings of a comprehensive survey of the relations
between government--national, state and local--and the electric
power industry. The project was designed to give the public an
unbiased picture of how these relations have worked out--rate
regulation, control of security issues, and direct government ownership and operation--and to construct some planks for a national
power policy platform in the interest of the public as a whole.

Foster, J. Rhoads and Rodey, Bernard S. PUBLIC UTILITY ACCOUNTING.
New York: Prentice-Hall, 1951. 690 p.
Combines procedural explanation with attention to alternative
accounting policies and the significance of accounting results.
Intended for public utility accountants in and outside the industries, accountants employed by regulatory agencies, lawyers,
engineers, and others interested in the management and regulation of public utility industries.

Garfield, Paul J. and Lovejoy, Wallace F. PUBLIC UTILITY ECONOMICS.
Englewood Cliffs, New Jersey: Prentice-Hall, 1964. 505 p.
A textbook intended for use by students in universities, and in
the training programs of commissions and utilities. Pricing is
given a prominent place and expanded treatment as a central
problem in economics. Developing problems in the areas where
utility regulatory policies and antitrust policies overlap, are surveyed. The problems in the dual regulation of telephone rates
are discussed, and the regulatory policies of the Atomic Energy
Commission are taken up. It also covers the development and
regulation of the natural gas pipeline industry and the regulation
of independent producers of natural gas.

Garwood, John D. and Tuthill, W. C. THE RURAL ELECTRIFICATION AD-
MINISTRATION, AN EVALUATION. Washington, D.C.: American Enterprise
Institute, 1963. 75 p.
The authors consider the evolution of REA, the change in orientation from farm to non-farm customers, the agency's promotional
activities, its achievements and costs. They conclude that it has
fulfilled its original purpose, and is now spreading out in directions
only remotely related to its original statutory authorization.

Glaeser, Martin G. PUBLIC UTILITIES IN AMERICAN CAPITALISM. New
York: Macmillan, 1957. 624 p.
An introduction to the problems associated with public utilities,
including various branches of the transport industries. Sets forth
the economic and legal principles underlying public utilities, and
traces essentials in development of technology on which these industries are based. Designed primarily to orient college students
beginning to study utilities.

Kolb, Burton A. and Lipstreu, Otis, editors. NEW CONCEPTS AND CUR-
RENT ISSUES IN PUBLIC UTILITY REGULATION. Denver: Peerless, 1963.
256 p.
> Contains the papers presented at a conference held in November
> 1962, designed to stimulate creative thinking and to give a free
> and open airing to all points of view regarding the regulation of
> public utility enterprises. The edited discussions held after the
> presentation of the papers, are also included. Deans and profes-
> sors of Economics and Business Administration were the participants.

Murphy, Blakely M., ed. CONSERVATION OF OIL & GAS. A LEGAL
HISTORY, 1948. Chicago: American Bar Association, Section of Mineral
Law, 1949. 754 p.
> Presents the conservation records of the producing states, covering
> the legislation, rules and regulations and judicial interpretations
> of each. A section is included which describes federal conserva-
> tion activities. Another is devoted to the history, findings, and
> recommendations of the Interstate Oil Compact Commission.

McKeage, Everett C. PUBLIC UTILITY REGULATORY LAW, REGULATORY
PROCEDURE AND JUDICIAL REVIEW. New York: Vantage, 1956. 107 p.
> A consolidation of articles written and addresses given by the
> author who, among other things, was chief counsel of the Cali-
> fornia Public Utilities Commission. Intended primarily for the
> practitioner of public utility and administrative law. The authori-
> ties cited will be of great assistance in preparing for a regulatory
> proceeding, formulating oral argument and writing briefs both
> before the regulatory body in the trial of the proceeding, and
> before the courts on judicial review.

Nichols, Ellsworth. PUBLIC UTILITY SERVICE AND DISCRIMINATION.
Washington, D.C.: Public Utilities Reports, 1928. 1087 p.
> Examines rulings of the public service commissions and the deci-
> sions of the courts as to the principles that utilities must serve
> without discrimination and each customer must recognize the rights
> of the utility and the rights of other customers.

Nichols, Ellsworth. RULING PRINCIPLES OF UTILITY REGULATION--RATE
OF RETURN. Washington, D.C.: Public Utilities Reports, 1955. 502 p.
1964 supplement - 373 p.
> Emphasis is placed on the views of courts and commissions regard-
> ing various factors to be considered, the weight to be accorded
> such factors, and illustrations of the application of the principles
> discussed. The text includes quotations from court and commission
> decisions.

Pegrum, Dudley F. PUBLIC REGULATION OF BUSINESS. Rev. ed. Homewood, Illinois: Irwin, 1965. 766 p.
> Part V, entitled "The Regulation of Transportation and Public
> Utilities," covers: (a) The Transport System; (b) The Pricing
> of Transport Services; (c) The Regulation of Transport; (d) The
> National Transport Problem; (e) The Regulation of Public Utilities;
> (f) Public Utility Rate Making; and (g) Public Ownership of Utili-
> ties.

Phillips, C.F. THE ECONOMICS OF REGULATION: THEORY AND PRAC-
TICE IN THE TRANSPORTATION AND PUBLIC UTILITY INDUSTRIES. Homewood, Illinois: Irwin, 1965. 783 p.
> This book resulted from a one semester course given by the author
> at Washington and Lee University. It concentrates on the theory
> and practice of regulation, and on current regulatory problems.
>
> Topics discussed are: the economic and legal concepts of public
> regulation; the independent regulatory commissions; accounting and
> financial control; operating costs; rate base; rate of return; rate
> structure; service and safety regulation; regulation of transporta-
> tion industries; public policy; and transportation. Separate chap-
> ters are devoted to the electric power industry, the natural gas
> industry, and communications.

Shipman, William D. AN INQUIRY INTO THE HIGH COST OF ELECTRICITY
IN NEW ENGLAND. Middletown, Connecticut: Wesleyan University Press,
1962. 219 p.
> An economic study undertaken to measure the extent to which
> electric rates in New England exceed those elsewhere in the coun-
> try; to analyze the reasons for the difference; and to suggest a
> regional power policy. The author bases his work on data pub-
> lished by the Federal Power Commission, area studies by state and
> quasi-public agencies, and private sources in the power industry.
> A regional policy is suggested.

Vennard, Edwin. THE ELECTRIC POWER BUSINESS. New York: McGraw-
Hill, 1962. 280 p.
> The aim of this book is to present basic facts about the power
> business and the economic principles that govern it. The eco-
> nomics of the electric utility business are set against an opera-
> tional background. Considers engineering, accounting, financing,
> sales and legal phases of the business.

Welch, Francis X. CASES AND TEXT ON PUBLIC UTILITY REGULATION.
Washington, D.C.: Public Utilities Reports, 1961. 704 p.
> This book is one of the best sources of general information about
> the regulation of utilities. Emphasis is placed on the text with
> cases used as examples. Its major headings are: utility status
> and service; determination of reasonable rates; the rate-fixing
> process; the utility rate structure; regulation by commissions; and
> federal-utility relations.

Welch, Francis X., ed. CONDUCT OF THE UTILITY RATE CASE. Washington, D.C.: Public Utilities Reports, 1955. 383 p.
> A companion work to "Preparing for the Utility Rate Case," with
> inevitable overlapping. Concerned with the presentation and
> completion of the public utility rate case before the regulatory
> tribunal, and supplemental matters after conclusion and decision,
> especially with respect to appellate relief. Based on paraphrased
> excerpts from, and references to, actual rate case material selected
> by the editor. It stresses tactics which may be used.

Welch, Francis X., ed. PREPARING FOR THE UTILITY RATE CASE. Washington, D.C.: Public Utilities Reports, 1954. 323 p.
> Deals entirely with the preparation of the rate case, from the time it is found necessary, to the time of filing documentary pleadings. Based on the records of a hand-picked selection of representative rate cases. Stresses strategy and planning.

Government Publications

The Federal Power Commission issues a monthly Publications List, which may be obtained from the Office of Public Information, Federal Power Commission, Washington, D.C. 20426. This lists all publications of the commission which are distributed by the Government Printing Office, indicating the price. It also includes publications sent out by the commission, such as press releases and formal documents.

Federal Power Commission. ACCOUNTING RELEASES. Washington, D.C.: irregular.
> Informal interpretations by the chief accountant of the Federal Power Commission, of the uniform systems of accounts to be followed in the absence of specific references in the prescribed accounting regulations, and other authoritative decisions of the commission.

Federal Power Commission. ALL ELECTRIC HOMES, ANNUAL BILLS. Washington, D.C.: Government Printing Office, 1964. 26 p.
> Includes compilation of annual bills for electric power consumption in all-electric homes; data for individual utilities on the number of homes served, with estimates of the average annual kw-h consumption; and amounts used, with estimated normal figures, for heating and cooling.

Federal Power Commission. ANNUAL REPORTS. Washington, D.C.: Government Printing Office. 1921-
> These reports outline the establishment and working of the commission, summarize legislation in the field in the preceding year, set out legislative recommendations to be made to the next Congress, and summarize the work of the Commission during the preceding year. They also contain an appendix which summarizes litigation and rule making.

Federal Power Commission. DEPRECIATION PRACTICES OF ELECTRIC UTILITIES. Washington, D.C.: Government Printing Office, 1961. 10 p.
> A report on the depreciation practices of electric utilities under Federal Power Commission jurisdiction having annual operating revenues of one million dollars. Covers Classes A and B privately owned companies.

Federal Power Commission. ELECTRIC POWER STATISTICS. Washington, D.C.: Government Printing Office. Monthly.
> Pamphlets which summarize the production and sale of electric

energy, capacity of generating plants, consumption of fuel for production of energy, and electric utility system loads for all utilities of all types of ownership; also sales, revenues, and income of privately owned electric utilities, by states and geographic divisions.

Federal Power Commission. FEDERAL POWER ACT. Washington, D.C.: Government Printing Office, 1963. 150 p.
A pamphlet with index.

Federal Power Commission. FORMAL DOCUMENTS ISSUED. Washington, D.C. Daily.
A daily listing of formal documents issued, such as orders, notices, decisions, and opinions, mailed out weekly. Documents desired are encircled, and the lists returned to the Commission, which then sends out the items encircled.

Federal Power Commission. HYDROELECTRIC PLANT CONSTRUCTION COST AND ANNUAL PRODUCTION EXPENSES, 1953-56. Washington, D.C.: Government Printing Office, 1958. 257 p. Annual supplements through 1961. A combined 6th and 7th annual supplement covers 1962 and 1963.
Gives cost of plant and production expenses, statistics on plant capacity, plant output, and characteristics for 310 plants in the United States and Puerto Rico. Plant data are based on annual reports and statements filed with the Federal Power Commission.

Federal Power Commission. NATIONAL ELECTRIC RATE BOOK. Washington, D.C.: Government Printing Office. Current.
Gives rates charged in each state by publicly and privately owned electric utilities, in communities of 2500 or more.

LIST OF ELECTRIC POWER SUPPLIERS WITH ANNUAL OPERATING REVENUES OF $2,500,000 OR MORE CLASSIFIED AS PUBLIC UTILITIES UNDER THE FEDERAL POWER ACT. Washington, D.C.: Federal Power Commission, January 1963. 9 p.
Lists the electric utility systems that are classified as "public utilities" for purposes of the Federal Power Act.

Federal Power Commission. NATIONAL POWER SURVEY. Washington, D.C.: Government Printing Office, 1964. In two parts.
A study designed to illustrate a possible pattern of efficient development, and to promote interest in the opportunities for savings. It outlines a plan for the coordinated growth of the electric power industry.

Part II contains the 24 advisory reports. In addition, an interim report on defense implications of the national power survey was prepared for the Federal Power Commission, in September 1963, by F. J. Lewis and K. E. Willis, of the Research Triangle Institute, Operations Research Division, Durham, North Carolina. Its purpose was to determine the vulnerability of the power industry to thermonuclear attack.

Federal Power Commission. NEWS DIGEST. Washington, D.C.: Weekly.
The only publication issued directly by the Commission for which

there is a charge. A weekly mailing of a day-by-day summary
of electric power and natural gas news, taken from various press
and periodical sources; e.g. Wall Street Journal, Tulsa World,
Houston Post, etc.

Federal Power Commission. PRESS RELEASES. Washington, D.C.
These releases, which are distributed by the Commission. summarize
the action of the Commission on various applications; give statistics
about consumption of electricity; set out new rules, both proposed
and final; give information about personnel, etc.

Federal Power Commission. REGULATIONS UNDER THE FEDERAL POWER
ACT. Washington, D.C.: Government Printing Office, March 31, 1964.
107 p.
A convenient pamphlet edition of the regulations, designed to be
kept up to date by looseleaf supplements.

Federal Power Commission. REGULATIONS TO GOVERN THE PRESERVATION
OF RECORDS OF PUBLIC UTILITIES AND LICENSEES. Washington, D.C.:
Government Printing Office, December 12, 1962. 18 p.

Federal Power Commission. REGULATIONS TO GOVERN THE PRESERVATION
OF RECORDS OF NATURAL GAS COMPANIES. Washington, D.C.: Government Printing Office, December 12, 1962.

Federal Power Commission. REPORTS. Washington, D.C.: Government Printing Office. Vol. 1- , 1940-
Bound volumes containing all the formal opinions, and accompany-
ing orders, of the Federal Power Commission. Also include inter-
mediate decisions which have become final, and selected orders
of the Commission. A table of cases and index-digest, as well
as a subject index, are included in each volume. Advance sheets
are issued monthly with the same pagination as the bound volumes.

Federal Power Commission. RULES OF PRACTICE AND PROCEDURE. Washington, D.C.: Government Printing Office, January 1, 1966. Current.
This pamphlet represents a new venture into looseleaf reporting
by the commission. All additions and amendments published in
the Federal Register appear in looseleaf pages which are mailed to
subscribers.

Federal Power Commission. STATE COMMISSION JURISDICTION AND REGU-
LATION OF ELECTRIC AND GAS UTILITIES. Washington, D.C.: Government Printing Office, 1960. 39 p.
This pamphlet, which was prepared in cooperation with the National Association of Railroad and Utilities Commissioners, summarizes the powers of state commissions to regulate electric and
gas utilities in the following tabulations: regulation of rates;
regulation of service standards and extensions; accounting and
report forms; licenses and permits; financial and corporate regulation; assessment of costs of regulation; term and compensation of
state commissioners; utilities other than electric and gas regulated.
Tables in the text give information on: regulatory practices as to
competitive bidding; rate base determination; depreciation policies;
rate of return; and court review of commission decisions.

Federal Power Commission. STATISTICS OF ELECTRIC UTILITIES, PUBLICLY OWNED. Washington, D.C.: Government Printing Office. Annual.
> Contain financial and operating data for publicly owned electric utilities (municipal and federal projects) taken from annual reports filed with the Federal Power Commission.

Federal Power Commission. STEAM-ELECTRIC PLANT CONSTRUCTION COST AND ANNUAL PRODUCTION EXPENSES. Washington, D.C.: Government Printing Office, 1947. Annual supplements.
> Report operating results for steam electric plants in the U.S. and Puerto Rico. Based on data from annual reports and statements filed with the Federal Power Commission by electric utilities. Give information on capacity, demand, capability, costs, and construction.

Federal Power Commission. TABLE OF OPINIONS PUBLISHED IN THE FEDERAL POWER COMMISSION REPORTS. Washington, D.C.: June 30, 1958. 20 p.
> Indexes by name of party and by opinion number. Cites to public utilities reports and Federal Power Commission reports, with date of decision and docket number. Includes citations through volume 12 and 14 of the Federal Power Commission reports.

Federal Power Commission. TYPICAL ELECTRIC BILLS. Washington, D.C.: Annual.
> Give residential bills in cities of 2500 population and more; commercial and industrial bills in cities of 50,000 population and more.

Federal Power Commission. UNIFORM SYSTEM OF ACCOUNTS FOR CLASS A AND CLASS B PUBLIC UTILITIES AND LICENSEES. Washington, D..C: Government Printing Office, March 1, 1965. Current.
> A looseleaf pamphlet, indexed, which contains the Federal Power Commission's accounting rules and regulations in effect as of March 1, 1965. Supplemental pages will be issued if the commission amends its rules.

> Class A and Class B electric utilities are those having annual electric operating revenues of $1,000,000 or more.

Federal Power Commission. UNIFORM SYSTEM OF ACCOUNTS PRESCRIBED FOR PUBLIC UTILITIES AND LICENSEES (CLASS C) Washington, D.C.: Government Printing Office, January 1, 1961. 121 p.

Federal Power Commission. UNIFORM SYSTEM OF ACCOUNTS PRESCRIBED FOR PUBLIC UTILITIES AND LICENSEES (CLASS D). Washington, D.C.: Government Printing Office, January 1, 1961. 85 p.

FEDERAL REGULATION OF THE ELECTRIC POWER INDUSTRY UNDER PARTS II AND III OF THE FEDERAL POWER ACT. Washington, D.C.: Federal Power Commission, May 1965. 72 p.

> Outlines the commission's responsibilities under Parts II and III of the Federal Power Act, and describes the program by which the commission discharges those responsibilities. Among the topics discussed are: Congressional purpose in enacting parts II and III; public utilities subject to federal regulation; regulation of wholesale rates and the filing of rate schedules; corporate regulation and international transactions; accounting and auditing responsibilities.

U.S. Commission on Organization of the Executive Branch. Task Force on Water Resources and Power. REPORT ON WATER RESOURCES AND POWER. 1955. 3 vols.

> Volume One contains the findings, analyses and recommendations of the task force. Volume Two contains the constituent reports of the Task Groups on Power Generation and Distribution, Reclamation and Water Supply, Flood Control, and Improvements to Navigation, as well as a survey of the federal government's activities in the power field. Volume Three contains the studies on which the task force and task groups depended.

WATER RESOURCE APPRAISALS FOR HYDROELECTRIC LICENSING. PLANNING STATUS REPORTS. Washington, D.C.: Federal Power Commission, Bureau of Power. 1964-

> A series of reports for major river basins in the United States, constituting the first step in a program of water resources appraisals for hydroelectric licensing. Prepared for staff use by the Bureau of Power of Federal Power Commission, to identify those basins most in need of additional planning studies, and to provide information needed by the Commission in its hydroelectric licensing and other work. Show data on existing water resources developments and known potentials, summarize the license status of non-federal hydroelectric developments, review past and current planning studies, and identify the needs for additional planning.

Miscellaneous

American Bar Association, Section of Public Utility Law. ANNUAL REPORT. Chicago.

> Contains papers on various aspects of utility regulation, as well as reports on developments in the field during the preceding year. The fields of electric utilities and natural gas are covered, among others.

American Bar Association. Section of Public Utility Law. ABA UTILITY SECTION NEWSLETTER. Washington, D.C., irregular. [Edited by Francis X. Welch]

> Briefly discusses the highlights of current developments in the utilities field; e.g. atomic energy, communications, natural gas, railroads, telephones, REA and water. Each issue is approximately

eight pages in length.

Arthur Anderson & Co. RETURN ALLOWED IN PUBLIC UTILITY RATE CASES. 1960. New York. No pagination.

Digests rate cases by year, and then by state under each year. Covers period 1915-1959. Excludes cases involving independent natural gas producers, and cases in which the rate base is less than $1,000,000. Digests indicate the return allowed and the amount and type of rate base as designated in the order or opinion. Comments are included to clarify various factors considered by the commissions and courts in determining the rate base and allowable return. Indication is made where consideration was given to deferred income taxes in determining either the rate base or the rate of return.

Clark, Dodge & Co. AN OUTLINE OF ELECTRIC UTILITY REGULATION BY STATES. New York: 1962. 101 p.

A handy reference pamphlet for the major determinants considered by each state commission in establishing a rate base and a rate of return. Omits the five states of Iowa, Minnesota, Nebraska, South Dakota, and Texas, which have no state commission regulation; and Alaska whose recently created commission has not yet been active. Contains a glossary of terms. Arranged by states, giving the name of the appropriate commission, the names of the commissioners, how they are elected, and the political affiliation of each commissioner. The information is arranged under the following headings: rate base valuation; other items included in the rate base; other items excluded from the rate base; major factors considered in establishing the rate of return; adjustments in establishing allowable earnings; fuel adjustment clauses; recent electric utility rate cases; and principal electric utilities. Outline form is used.

Commerce Clearing House. UTILITIES SERVICE. 2 vols. Current.

One volume covers Federal and the other State material. The Federal volume contains the Federal Power Act annotated; the Natural Gas Act annotated; the Federal Power Commission regulations; the Federal Power Commission general orders; related statutes; e.g. Rural Electrification Act, Tennessee Valley Authority, etc. It also includes selected federal court decisions and selected Federal Power Commission decisions and orders. It has a table of cases and a topical index.

The State volume contains a table of cases of court and commission decisions, and of attorney general opinions which are included in the volume. The decisions are set out in comprehensive digest form except for opinions of the U.S. Supreme Court and decisions of great interest and importance, which are reported in full text. It also contains an index arranged by states, with topics under each state and reference to the paragraph at which the topic is digested. A topical index to new decisions is included.

DIRECTORY OF ELECTRIC UTILITIES. New York: McGraw-Hill, 1964.

Covers investor-owned, municipal, cooperative, and government owned utilities in the United States and Canada. Gives names and titles of officials for the key functions in all departments; addresses, telephone numbers and area codes; areas served and 1960 population, for all cities and towns of over 500 population within the system. Also includes total sales; number of residential, industrial, commercial, and rural customers; average residential rates and use; net system input; number of bulk power substations and total kw, circuit miles; peaks; capacities and fuel of each unit.

FEDERAL UTILITY REGULATION ANNOTATED (FURA). Washington, D.C.: Public Utilities Reports, 1943 to date. 2 vols.
> Volume 2 covers the Federal Power Act and the Natural Gas Act. Events leading up to the enactment of the Federal Power Act, and the Natural Gas Act are summarized. The bulk of the volume sets out the texts of both acts, with extensive annotations under each section.
>
> Supplemental volume A was issued in 1953; B, in 1958; and C, in 1964. In addition to bringing the basic volume up to date, each supplement contains the rules and regulations, and the uniform system of accounts for each act, as of the date of the volume.
>
> Semi-monthly pamphlets keep the bound volumes up to date with digests of findings and opinions of the Federal Power Commission, and of court decisions. They also contain information about new applications, supplemental proceedings, and orders.

GLOSSARY OF ELECTRIC UTILITY TERMS, FINANCIAL AND TECHNICAL. New York: Edison Electric Institute, 1961. 80 p.

HISTORICAL STATISTICS OF THE ELECTRIC UTILITY INDUSTRY. New York: Edison Electric Institute, 1962. Current.
> Gathers and reprints from the EEI Statistical Year Book all the data commonly reported there for selected years, from all the Year Books through 1960. Data for the years 1951 through the current year are reported annually in a Year Book section. The Year Book section is revised annually.

Hunt, Florine E. PUBLIC UTILITIES INFORMATION SOURCES. Detroit: Gale Research, 1965. 200 p. Management Information Guide: 7.
> An annotated guide to literature and bodies concerned with rates, economics, accounting, regulation, history, and statistics of electric, gas, telephone, and water companies. Appendices list trade associations; periodicals and periodical indexes; and government regulatory agencies.

MOODY'S PUBLIC UTILITY MANUAL. New York: Moody's Investors Service. Annual with semi-weekly supplements.
> A comprehensive source of information on public utility enterprises. Provides details of history, background, mergers and acquisitions, subsidiaries, business, construction programs, principal plants and properties. Also gives data relating to rates, franchises and con-

tracts. In addition, includes names and titles of officers and directors; as well as general counsel, auditors, date of annual meeting, latest number of stockholders and employees, and address of the corporation. Financial statements are shown for the larger electric power companies.

National Association of Railroad and Utilities Commissioners. PROCEEDINGS. Washington, D.C.: Annual.

Papers presented at the annual meetings of the association, which consists of commissioners on both the federal and state level, who head commissions regulating public utilities. On the federal level, the Interstate Commerce Commission, the Federal Communications Commission, the Federal Power Commission, the Securities and Exchange Commission, and the Civil Aeronautics Board, are represented.

PUBLIC UTILITIES REPORTS. Washington, D.C.: Public Utilities Reports.

A series of bound volumes giving the full text of selected state and federal court and commission decisions in the field of electric and gas utilities. The first series covers the period 1915–1933; the second (New Series), 1934–43; and the current (3rd Series), 1954 to date. Weekly advance sheets are issued.

PUR DIGEST, 2D SERIES, 1933–1962, with up-keep supplements. Washington, D.C.: Public Utilities Reports, Inc., 1963. Ten volumes.

Covers the 30-year interval following the appearance of the original PUR Digest, Cumulative, which digested all cases in the volumes of the Public Utilities Reports, Annotated, since they were first issued in 1915 through 1932. In addition to classifying the cases digested under sectional numbers of the major subjects, this digest further segregates them into five "time spans"--1933 through 1939 as the prewar period; 1940 through 1947; 1948 through 1953; 1954–1958; and 1959–1962. The table of cases in volume 10 is also broken down into these five "time spans."

Periodicals

ELECTRICAL WORLD. New York: McGraw-Hill. Weekly.

The electrical industry's weekly magazine. Contains short technical articles on developments in the industry. Summarizes news items affecting the electric utilities.

LAND ECONOMICS. A QUARTERLY JOURNAL OF PLANNING, HOUSING AND PUBLIC UTILITIES. Madison: University of Wisconsin. Quarterly.

A scholarly journal containing articles, reports and comments. Published to provide an outlet for a wide variety of scholarly studies in land economics. From 1925–1947, it was known as the Journal of Land and Public Utility Economics.

PUR EXECUTIVE INFORMATION SERVICE. Washington, D.C.: Public Utilities Reports, Inc. Weekly.

A four-page letter summarizing the latest developments in the field of utilities.

PUBLIC UTILITY FORTNIGHTLY. Washington, D.C.: Public Utilities Reports, Inc. Biweekly.
> A magazine published every other Thursday. Contains articles, news items, and comments on recent cases and rulings.

UTILITY SPOTLIGHT. New York: Corporate Intelligence, Inc. Weekly.
> A four-page report giving factual, concise and prompt information on all new developments, techniques and practices in all phases of the utility industry and allied fields. All reporting is in capsule form, under such headings as: Wall Street; industry trends; advertising and public relations; construction and expansion; earnings reports; conventions and meetings; dividend changes; equipment; executive intelligence; financing calendar; financing news; forecasts; foreign news; industrial relations; legislation and politics; litigation; rate matters; and regulation.

Trade Association

The Edison Electric Institute at 750 Third Avenue, New York 17, N.Y., is the trade association for the electric industry. It was founded in 1933, has 200 members, and a staff of 125.

Members are investor-owned, electric power operating companies, and electric utility holding companies.

It has affiliated members in North, Central and South America.

The association maintains a library.

While it is not a trade association, mention must be made of the National Association of Railroad and Utilities Commissioners, 5310 ICC Building, Washington, D.C. This association was founded in 1889, has 325 members, and a staff of four. There are five regional associations affiliated with it.

This is a professional organization of state and federal regulatory commissioners, having jurisdiction over transportation agencies and public utilities.

NATURAL GAS

The gas industry is regulated by local authorities, and by both state and federal commissions. It is regulated, on the local level, through the granting of franchises. State commission control applies to the distribution phase, to transportation in intrastate commerce, and to the production of natural gas except when it is sold in interstate commerce for resale.

The federal government regulates natural gas under the Natural Gas Act of 1938. This act gives the Federal Power Commission jurisdiction over the industry, and contains provisions regarding jurisdiction, certificates of public convenience and necessity, rate control, Commission powers and proceedings, and judicial review. However, it does not give the commission authority over the securities issues of interstate gas companies.

Texts

American Gas Association Rate Committee. GAS RATE FUNDAMENTALS.
New York: American Gas Association, 1960. 357 p.
> Deals with rate making for gas utilities, both distribution and
> transmission companies. Presupposes a general knowledge of the
> history of gas industry and appreciation of the problems of the
> economics of gas production, transmission and distribution.

Falck, Edward and Welch, Francis X. FEDERAL REGULATION OF NATURAL
GAS IN THE UNITED STATES. Washington, D.C.: Edward Falck & Co.,
1958. 100 p.
> An excellent pamphlet, summarizing the Federal Trade Commission
> investigation leading to the enactment of the Natural Gas Act of
> 1938; explaining utility regulation in the United States; analyzing
> the Natural Gas Act of 1938 and amendments to it; and discus-
> sing certificates of public convenience and necessity, rate cases,
> and export and import licenses.

Kulp, Victor H. OIL AND GAS RIGHTS. Boston: Little, Brown, 1954.
916 p. Contains a 1960 supplement.
> A short comprehensive text on the law of oil and gas rights, re-
> printed from the American Law of Property.

Leeston, Alfred M. et al. THE DYNAMIC NATURAL GAS INDUSTRY. THE
DESCRIPTION OF AN AMERICAN INDUSTRY FROM THE HISTORICAL, TECH-
NICAL, LEGAL, FINANCIAL, AND ECONOMIC STANDPOINTS. Norman:
University of Oklahoma Press, 1963. 464 p.
> An excellent treatise on all phases of the natural gas industry.
> Describes the gas industry as it is, rather than as it ought to be.

McKie, James W. THE REGULATION OF NATURAL GAS. Washington,
D.C.: American Enterprise, June 1957. 49 p.
> The author explores the concept of public utility regulation, the
> highly competitive characteristics of the natural gas industry, and
> the difficulties which would be found in establishing an equitable
> rate-base to provide a fair rate of return. He explains the struc-
> ture of the industry, the relation of natural gas to other fuels,
> and the history of pipeline contracts. He also analyzes the Su-
> preme Court decision in Phillips Petroleum v. Wisconsin, which
> subjected the field price of natural gas to Federal Power Commis-
> sion control, and the various attempts in Congress-notably the
> Harris-Fulbright and Harris bills--to exempt natural gas from such
> regulation. The author concludes that there is no decisive reason
> why market competition can not generally regulate the field price
> of natural gas in the public interest.

Neuner, Edward J. THE NATURAL GAS INDUSTRY. MONOPOLY AND
COMPETITION IN FIELD MARKETS. Norman: University of Oklahoma
Press, 1960. 302 p.

A detailed investigation of the problem of field market monopoly.
Sets out the public policy decisions which have to be made in
regulating natural gas. The author is an economist, and the book
is written from that point of view.

Stockton, John R., et al. ECONOMICS OF NATURAL GAS IN TEXAS.
(Bureau of Business Research Monograph No. 15) Austin: University of Texas,
1962. 316 p.
> Chapter 8 deals with public control of the Texas natural gas in-
> dustry, covering the basis of control, and state and federal regu-
> lation.

Sullivan, Robert E. HANDBOOK OF OIL AND GAS LAW. New York:
Prentice-Hall, 1955. 556 p.
> Concerned with production and transportation, only, and with the
> aspects of taxation and financing that are peculiar to those
> branches of the industry. One section deals with the nature and
> mechanics of governmental regulation of production.

Summers, W. L. THE LAW OF OIL AND GAS. A TREATISE COVERING
THE LAW RELATING TO THE PRODUCTION OF OIL AND GAS FROM PUB-
LIC AND PRIVATE LANDS, AND THE TRANSPORTATION THEREOF, WITH
STATUTES AND REGULATIONS AND FORMS. Kansas City, Missouri: Ver-
non Law Book, 1939-1962, with 1965 supplements. 12 vols.
> Covers natural gas and natural gas pipelines, as well as oil.

Williams, Howard R., et al. CASES AND MATERIALS ON THE LAW OF OIL
AND GAS. 2nd ed. Brooklyn, New York: Foundation Press, 1964. 986 p.
> A case book prepared for use in a third year course or seminar
> in the law of oil and gas. Contains little material on the regu-
> latory aspects of the federal government.

Williams, Howard R. and Meyers, Charles J. OIL AND GAS TERMS. AN
ANNOTATED MANUAL OF LEGAL, ENGINEERING, TAX WORDS AND
PHRASES. Albany, New York: Matthew Bender, 1957. 282 p.
> The purpose of this manual is to collect in one place the words
> and phrases which persons concerned with oil and gas matters are
> likely to encounter; and to define these with accuracy, but with
> brevity and clarity. Useful for lawyers, landmen, accountants,
> investors in oil and gas properties, students, and others in the
> industry.

Williams, Howard R. and Meyers, Charles J. OIL AND GAS LAW. Albany,
New York: Matthew Bender, 1962. 7 vols.
> A study of the creation and transfer of property interests in oil
> and gas, oil and gas leases, and purchase and sale contracts.

Government Publications

Federal Power Commission. DEPRECIATION PRACTICES OF NATURAL GAS
COMPANIES. Washington, D.C.: Government Printing Office, 1961. 8 p.
> Covers depreciation practices of the large interstate natural gas
> pipeline companies under its jurisdiction. Studies 76 companies,

with annual gas operating revenues exceeding $1,000,000.

Federal Power Commission. NATURAL GAS ACT. Washington, D.C.: Government Printing Office, 1962. 50 p.
> A pamphlet with index.

Federal Power Commission. NATURAL GAS INVESTIGATION (Docket No. G-580). Washington, D.C.: Government Printing Office, 1948. Report of Commissioners Nelson Lee Smith and Harrington Wimberly in 498 pages. Report of Commissioners Leland Oles and Claude L. Draper in 158 pages.
> This investigation was undertaken by the Commission as a comprehensive examination and evaluation of national policy with respect to natural gas, particularly as related to the regulatory functions of the Commission under the Natural Gas Act. Recommendations are made, based on the investigation, some calling for amendments to the act, while others are suggestions to the state conservation and regulatory agencies, and to the producing, transporting and distributing segments of the natural gas industry.

Federal Power Commission. REGULATIONS UNDER THE NATURAL GAS ACT. Washington, D.C.: Government Printing Office, August 1, 1962. 64 p.
> A pamphlet kept up to date with supplements.

Federal Power Commission. SALES BY PRODUCERS OF NATURAL GAS TO NATURAL GAS PIPELINE COMPANIES. Washington, D.C.: Government Printing Office. Annual.
> Tables include sales by states and by pricing areas; sales to individual purchasers; and interstate pipeline companies' purchases from producers and their own production.

Federal Power Commission. STATISTICS FOR INTERSTATE NATURAL GAS PIPELINE COMPANIES. Washington, D.C.: Government Printing Office. Annual.
> Give detailed statements of the balance sheet, income and earned surplus accounts, operating expenses, operating revenues, customers and sales, gas utility plant investment, gas account and certain physical property data of interstate natural gas pipeline companies.

Federal Power Commission. STATISTICS OF NATURAL GAS COMPANIES. Washington, D.C.: Government Printing Office. Annual.
> Give detailed statements of balance sheets, income and earned surplus accounts, operating expenses, operating revenues, customers and sales, gas utility plant investment, gas account, and certain physical property data.

Federal Power Commission. UNIFORM SYSTEM OF ACCOUNTS PRESCRIBED FOR NATURAL GAS COMPANIES. Washington, D.C.: Government Printing Office, 1964
> Covers Class A and Class B natural gas companies.

Miscellaneous

BROWN'S DIRECTORY OF AMERICAN GAS COMPANIES. Duluth, Minnesota:

Moore Publishing Co. Annual.
>An alphabetical listing of operating; and of holding, operating, and service gas companies, arranged by state and city. Gives name, address, names of supervisory personnel, annual sales, and miscellaneous other information. A separate listing, in the same format, covers Canadian companies. An alphabetical list of gas companies appears at the beginning of the volume, and under the name of each state there is a list of gas companies in that state, arranged alphabetically, with a list of the communities served. At the end of the volume, there is an alphabetical list of officials and department heads.

FEDERAL POWER COMMISSION GAS DOCKET SERVICE. Washington, D.C.: FPC Gas Docket Service. 4 looseleaf volumes.
>Kept currently up to date. Intended to provide a key to Federal Power Commission and federal court decisions under the Natural Gas Act. Contains: table of cases arranged alphabetically by party involved; docket citator arranged by docket number; opinion tabulator where number of opinion is known; decision tabulator arranged in chronological order (also shows status of examiners' decisions which have not become final and are still pending); topic digest, arranged by subject; rules and regulations, arranged by section, with annotations of cases in which the section was involved; litigation log, which lists court and commission cases alphabetically; case citer, which gives citations and further developments in cases by their citations in the Federal Power Commission reports. This last section includes electric power, as well as natural gas cases.

Oakes, Curtis M. STANDARD OIL AND GAS FORMS. St. Louis, Missouri: Thomas Law Book, 1952. 611 p.
>A compilation of old, tried, and tested forms, as well as new forms recently compiled. Covers leases, rentals, conveyances, assignments, contracts, etc.

ROCKY MOUNTAIN MINERAL LAW INSTITUTE. New York: Matthew Bender. Annual. 1955 to date.
>Lectures delivered at the annual institutes, expanded beyond their lecture form, and with extensive footnotes. These Institutes are sponsored by the Rocky Mountain Mineral Law Foundation, and are held in Boulder, Colorado. The topics covered are oil and gas, public lands, and taxation.

SOUTHWESTERN LEGAL FOUNDATION INSTITUTES ON OIL AND GAS LAW AND TAXATION. New York: Matthew Bender. Annual. 1949 to date.
>Contain articles delivered as lectures in condensed form, presented at the annual Institutes held in Dallas, Texas.

Southwestern Legal Foundation. OIL AND GAS REPORTER. New York: Matthew Bender, 1952 to date.
>A publication of the cases, statutes, and administrative rulings in the field of oil and gas law, and taxation. Cases are reported in their entirety from official sources. However, headnotes and discussion notes reflect the opinion of the individual editors. Each volume has a table of cases and an index. Kept up to date

with monthly supplements.

Texas Law Review. OIL AND GAS LAW. Austin, Texas: 1922-1951. Articles, comments, case notes, and book reviews, published in the Texas Law Review from 1922 through 1951. Original page numbers are retained. An index-digest, and a table of cases is included. A supplemental volume covers the period from 1951 through 1954.

Wallach, Kate. LIST OF MATERIALS ON OIL AND GAS IN THE LOUISIANA STATE UNIVERSITY LIBRARIES. Baton Rouge: Louisiana State University, 1953.
Covers articles as well as texts.

Periodicals

OIL AND GAS JOURNAL. Tulsa, Oklahoma: Petroleum Publishing Company. Weekly.
A magazine containing short articles, usually of a technical nature, and special features. One of the features is entitled "Watching Washington," and briefly reports on what the government is doing in the field of oil and gas.

WASHINGTON OIL MEMO. Washington, D.C.: Oil News Enterprises, Inc. Weekly.
A four-page letter, highlighting government actions affecting the nation's oil and gas producers.

Trade Association

The trade association for the gas industry is the American Gas Association, 605 Third Avenue, New York, N.Y. 10016. This association was founded in 1918, has 6887 members, and a staff of about 400.

Membership is composed of producers of natural, manufactured and mixed gas; manufacturers of apparatus, appliances, equipment and supplies; and pipeline companies. Provides information on sales, finance, utilization, research, management, safety and all phases of gas transmission and distribution. Maintains a staff of experts in nearly every field of the gas industry. Develops operating and performance standards, specifications, good operating practices and standards on construction and performance of appliances and equipment. Promotes employee and public safety; conducts promotional campaigns, such as the Gold Star Range Program; carries on extensive advertising of gas and gas appliances in national consumer magazines, trade and business publications, and on television; assembles a wide variety of national and regional statistical economic, financial and market studies; publishes gas rate schedules in use for every type of service for virtually all gas companies. The association also conducts cooperative research, and development programs, which have resulted in developments, such as new improved gas air conditioners and smokeless, odorless incinerators.

The association maintains, in Cleveland and Los Angeles, National Testing Headquarters for gas appliances, under Blue Star Approval Seal requirements. It also maintains a library to answer questions, loan books, pamphlets, films and magazines; and to compile bibliographies and index reports.

Section 6

INTERSTATE COMMERCE COMMISSION

Section 6

INTERSTATE COMMERCE COMMISSION

The Interstate Commerce Commission was created in 1887, and is the oldest of the federal regulatory commissions in the field of utilities. It regulates companies which provide domestic surface transportation, including railroads, trucking companies, bus lines, barge and other inland and coastal shipping companies, oil pipelines, freight forwarders, and express companies. Its jurisdiction does not extend to transportation which is not part of an interstate or foreign movement. Rates, safety regulations, and accounting rules are prescribed by the commission.

TEXTS

Auerbach, Carl A. and Nathanson, Nathaniel L. FEDERAL REGULATION OF TRANSPORTATION. MATERIALS ILLUSTRATING PROBLEMS OF PUBLIC UTILITY CONTROL. (American Casebook Series) St. Paul: West, 1953. 1223 p.
> Presents the various aspects of utility regulation in the context of the problems of a related group of utilities--the transportation industries. Covers federal regulation only, to the exclusion of state regulation.

Bennett, H. Arnold. THE COMMISSION AND THE COMMON LAW. New York: Exposition Press, 1964. 127 p.
> The author takes up the way in which the freight forwarders have been affected by the Interstate Commerce Commission. He suggests the setting up of an advisory council to prevent errors from occurring in regulatory body decisions.

Bigham, Truman C. and Roberts, Merrill J. TRANSPORTATION. 2nd ed. New York: McGraw-Hill, 1952. 710 p.
> Deals with the economics of transportation in the United States. While giving special attention to the needs of teachers and students in universities and colleges, it is also directed to any mature reader interested in the economic aspects of transportation.

Conant, Michael. RAILROAD MERGERS AND ABANDONMENTS. Berkeley: University of California Press, 1964. 212 p.
> The author, an economist and lawyer, is associate professor of business administration at the University of California in Berkeley.

159

He has written this book as an economic criticism of the administrative regulation of resource allocation.

Among the particular topics taken up at length are: the ineffectiveness of inter-railroad competition as an impetus to the adjustment of investment to changing demand; the economic impact of recent railroad mergers; and problems presented by the reallocation of resources resulting from disinvestment in fixed plant.

Chapter III is devoted to the antitrust laws and railroad consolidation, with an economic appraisal of recent mergers.

Daggett, Stuart. PRINCIPLES OF INLAND TRANSPORTATION. 4th ed. New York: Harper, 1955. 788 p.

The author was Professor of Transportation at the University of California, before his death. This work describes all major forms of transportation in the United States; including the automobile, the inland waterway, and the airplane, as well as the railroad. It also seeks to draw attention to the facilities which traffic uses, and to the flow of traffic which carriers are organized to promote, as well as to questions with which legislators are concerned. The author describes the transportation system of the United States; surveys the agencies; discusses transportation geography; takes up relations between the carriers and the users of transportation service, rates, competition, relations of carriers with each other; and the problems and practices of regulation.

Fair, Marvin L. and Williams, Ernest W., Jr. ECONOMICS OF TRANSPORTATION. Rev. ed. New York: Harper, 1959. 684 p.

A general treatment of intercity transportation, designed as a college text. Uses a "functional" approach, primarily concerned with the place of transportation in the flow of utilities, and the distribution of resources in the economic system. Part IV deals with government regulation of transportation.

Flood, Kenneth U. RESEARCH IN TRANSPORTATION SOURCES AND PROCEDURE. Washington, D.C.: Association of Interstate Commerce Commission Practitioners, 1960. 46 p.

Author's objective was to create a practical guide for use by transportation and traffic men, who must come up with the answers to questions arising under federal regulation and control of railroads, motor carriers, water carriers, and freight forwarders.

Basically, the aim of the booklet is to describe and evaluate source of transportation information concerned with legislation, regulations, rulings, court and Interstate Commerce Commission decisions, forms, reports, and instructions; and to set out, in brief form, examples of how information on specific topics can be developed.

Frederick, John G. IMPROVING NATIONAL TRANSPORTATION POLICY. Washington, D.C.: American Enterprise Association, November 1959. 50 p.

A history of the various studies which have been made of the transportation problem. Discusses the development of the transportation industry, the background of its regulation, current transportation problems, and the danger of nationalization. Presents transportation as part of a competitive economy, and outlines the steps necessary to improve national policy.

Fulda, Carl H. COMPETITION IN THE REGULATED INDUSTRIES TRANSPORTATION. (Trade Regulation Series). Boston: Little, Brown, 1961. 533 p.
Deals with the interplay between competition and regulation, in one of the federally regulated industries--interstate transportation. This takes in railroads, motor and water carriers, airlines, and freight forwarders. The administrative decisions of the Interstate Commerce Commission, the Civil Aeronautics Board, and the Federal Maritime Board are considered.

Fuller, Burton. WATKINS, SHIPPERS AND CARRIERS. INTERSTATE COMMERCE. 5th ed. Atlanta: Harrison, 1962. 2 vols.
Designed primarily to meet the needs of practitioners who want a treatise on the Interstate Commerce Commission which gives an idea of the Interstate Commerce Act as a whole. Contains a helpful discussion of particular questions affecting shippers and carriers.

Grossman, William Leonard. FUNDAMENTALS OF TRANSPORTATION. New York: Simmons-Boardman, 1959. 280 p.
A basic textbook. Chapter IX is devoted to government regulation of transportation.

Guandolo, John. TRANSPORTATION LAW. Dubuque, Iowa: W.C. Brown, 1965. 864 p.
A discussion of the principles of law established, by the Interstate Commerce Commission and the courts under the Interstate Commerce Act and related acts, by the Civil Aeronautics Board and the courts under the Federal Aviation Act and related acts, and by the Federal Maritime Commission and the courts under the Shipping Act and related acts.

Gives full coverage to the application of the antitrust laws to common carriers.

The book is divided into the principal subject headings under which various laws applying to each mode of transportation can be found.

Designed to be used for a course in transportation law at the law school level, and as a primary reference for administrative law and transportation courses.

Healy, Kent T. THE ECONOMICS OF TRANSPORTATION IN AMERICA. New York: Ronald, 1940. 575 p.
A basic text by an authority in the field. The author was assistant professor of economics at Yale University. In this work he emphasizes economic forces and motives, presenting a picture of the changing demands for transportation, the invention of facilities, the promotion of new enterprise, and the operation and government regulation of the finished transportation facilities.
In general, the railroads are given greater space. Part IV covers

the economic regulation of transportation by the government.

Kahn, Fritz R. PRINCIPLES OF MOTOR CARRIER REGULATION. Dubuque, Iowa: Wm. C. Brown, 1958. 229 p.
The author sets forth the major principles of law governing interstate truck and bus transportation. He has endeavored to synthesize into a readable whole the more important provisions of Part II of the Interstate Commerce Act, and of the regulations promulgated thereunder together with a selection of the decisions of the Interstate Commerce Commission and the courts interpreting and applying them.

Knorst, William J., ed. INTERSTATE COMMERCE LAW AND PRACTICE. Chicago: College of Advanced Traffic, 1953. 4 vols., volume 4 (1958) being a supplement to the first three.
The purpose of this set is to clarify and assemble in a logical manner the rulings of the courts and the Interstate Commerce Commission, as well as statements of facts and points of law, of important decisions of the Supreme Court of the United States. The first volume covers the constitutional power of federal regulation, the original act to regulate interstate commerce, the transportation policy of Congress, carriers subject to the Interstate Commerce Act, territorial jurisdiction of the Act. The second volume covers the duties, prohibitions, penalties and forfeitures, and general application of the act. The third volume covers the nature, function and organization of the Interstate Commerce Commission, and practice and procedure before the Commission and the courts, as provided for in the Interstate Commerce Act and the Commission's general rules of practice and procedure.

Kolko, Gabriel. RAILROADS AND REGULATION, 1877-1916. Princeton: Princeton University Press, 1965. 264 p.
Examines the relationship of the economy to the political process in the United States, and shows how the railroad industry encouraged and relied on national politics to solve its economic problems.

Landon, Charles E. TRANSPORTATION. New York: Sloane, 1951. 618 p.
Designed for an introductory course in the field. Its object is to acquaint the reader with the principles, practices, and problems of transportation that prevail in the United States, and with the social and economic importance of transportation to the operation of our economic system. Emphasis is primarily on the organization and operation of transportation as a business, on the application of economic principles in transportation, and on the problems which must be solved in order to improve transportation. Part four discusses regulation, devoting one chapter to the federal commissions which regulate transportation.

Locklin, David Philip. ECONOMICS OF TRANSPORTATION. 6th ed. Homewood, Illinois: Irwin, 1966. 882 p.
Emphasizes the economic aspects of transportation. Covers railroad, water, and pipeline transport, with expanded coverage of highway and air transport.

Meyer, John R., et al. THE ECONOMICS OF COMPETITION IN THE
TRANSPORTATION INDUSTRIES. Cambridge: Harvard University Press, 1959.
359 p.

> The basic theme of this work is that the major reason the trans-
> portation industries have not grown and prospered as much as
> most industries is that transportation has been overregulated.
> The solution offered is to decrease the scope of government con-
> trols. The concluding chapter advocates increased competition.

Mossman, Frank H. and Morton, Newton. PRINCIPLES OF TRANSPORTATION.
New York: Ronald, 1957. 510 p.

> This book aims to present a clear and detailed description of the
> basic principles of transportation, and to illustrate the practices
> involved in carrier operation, management and regulation. The
> plan is first to treat the economic fundamentals of transportation
> generally and to cover the historic development of all major
> transport facilities. It then outlines the practices of modern
> carrier operation and management.

Nelson, James C. RAILROAD TRANSPORTATION AND PUBLIC POLICY.
Washington, D.C.: Brookings Institution, 1959. 512 p.

> The author emphasizes the competitive elements in the markets
> in which the railroads and other carriers operate; the failure of
> the railroads to deal constructively and sufficiently with their
> competitive problems; the effects of government promotion and
> regulation of transport on the distribution of traffic and revenues
> and on the outcome of the pervasive interagency rivalry; and
> the action that management and government can take to improve
> the performance and competitiveness of the railroads, and to
> contribute to over-all economy in transport as a whole. Chapter
> V deals with public regulation and the railroad problem.

Pegrum, Dudley F. PUBLIC REGULATION OF BUSINESS. Rev. ed. Homewood, Illinois: Irwin, 1965. 766 p.

> Part V, entitled "The Regulation of Transportation and Public
> Utilities," covers: (a) The Transport System; (b) The Pricing of
> Transport Services; (c) The Regulation of Transport; (d) The Na-
> tional Transport Problem; (e) The Regulation of Public Utilities;
> (f) Public Utility Rate Making; and (g) Public Ownership of
> Utilities.

Pegrum, Dudley F. TRANSPORTATION: ECONOMIC AND PUBLIC POLICY.
Homewood, Illinois: Irwin, 1963. 610 p.

> Designed as a text for undergraduate study of transportation eco-
> nomics. The author regards economic theory as the only sound
> basis for evolving a rational legislative regulatory policy for
> transportation.

Phillips, C.F. THE ECONOMICS OF REGULATION: THEORY AND PRAC-
TICE IN THE TRANSPORTATION AND PUBLIC UTILITY INDUSTRIES. Homewood, Illinois: Irwin, 1965. 783 p.

> This book resulted from a one semester course given by the
> author at Washington and Lee University. It concentrates on the
> theory and practice of regulation, and on current regulatory prob-

lems. Topics discussed are: the economic and legal concepts of public regulation; the independent regulatory commissions; accounting and financial control; operating costs; the rate base; rate of return; rate structure; service and safety regulation; regulation of transportation industries; and public policy and transportation. Separate chapters are devoted to the electric power industry, the natural gas industry, and communications.

Proctor, Charles W. AUTHORITIES AND RIGHTS OF INTERSTATE TRUCKERS. Charlottesville: Michie, 1958. 736 p. 1961 supp.

The author clarifies the rulings of the Interstate Commerce Commission, and of the courts, giving numerous case citations. The volume answers such questions as: what are the three groups of common carriers; what constitutes transportation and interstate commerce; and what interstate trucking operations are exempt from regulation? It also examines the construction of the certificates and permits issued by the Interstate Commerce Commission.

Sharfman, Isaiah L. THE INTERSTATE COMMERCE COMMISSION, A STUDY IN ADMINISTRATIVE LAW AND PROCEDURE. New York: Commonwealth Fund, 1931-1937. 5 vols.

Covers the legislative basis of the Commission's authority, the scope of its jurisdiction, the character of its activities, and its organization and procedure.

Tedrow, Joseph. REGULATION OF TRANSPORTATION, PRACTICE AND PROCEDURE BEFORE THE INTERSTATE COMMERCE COMMISSION. 6th ed. revised by M. L. Fair and J. Guandolo. Dubuque, Iowa: Wm. C. Brown Co., 1964. 445 p.

Intended as a course of study to enable the student to gain a comprehensive knowledge of the regulation of carriers and transportation.

Troxel, Emery. ECONOMICS OF TRANSPORT. New York: Rinehart, 1955. 837 p.

An introduction to transport economics, intended primarily as an undergraduate textbook. The second part of the book deals with public control, beginning with a chronology of federal legislation, and referring particularly to the work of the Interstate Commerce Commission.

Westmeyer, Russell E. ECONOMICS OF TRANSPORTATION. New York: Prentice-Hall, 1952. 741 p.

Treats of motor, domestic water, and air transportation, as well as railroads. Part 7 takes up inter-agency relationships, and the place of each, in a sound national transportation system.

Williams, Ernest W. REGULATION OF RAIL-MOTOR RATE COMPETITION New York: Harper, 1958. 247 p.

Confined to the rate aspects of the competition between rail and motor carriers, and its regulation. The analysis is based primarily on the reported decisions of the Interstate Commerce Commission, which touch on rate competition between the two types of carriers. Its intent is primarily to ascertain how the commission has exercised its expanded authority over motor carriers.

Wilson, G. Lloyd. THE ELEMENTS OF TRANSPORTATION ECONOMICS.
New York: Simmons-Boardman, 1950. 178 p.
> Presents certain economic principles which are of particular im-
> portance to transportation. It also describes and illustrates the
> interrelationships of transportation with other forms of economic
> activity.

Wilson, G. Lloyd. TRANSPORTATION AND COMMUNICATIONS. New
York: Appleton-Century-Crofts, 1954. 757 p.
> Designed for students who have not had a course in transportation
> and communications. Gives a comprehensive and factual pre-
> sentation of the structure and services of these utilities, discus-
> sing the principles of economic theory characteristic of these
> industries; sketching the development of each form of transpor-
> tation and communication; and discussing the services rendered
> by each. Also describes the bases upon which their rates are
> made, and outlines the organization and management patterns.
> The relations of the utilities with each other and the public they
> serve are taken up. Finally, the regulation of the various in-
> strumentalities of transportation amd communications, and the ad-
> ministrative control by regulatory commissions and the courts, are
> discussed through the media of statutory law, and commission and
> court decisions. References are given for further study at the
> conclusion of each part.

Wolbert, George S., Jr. AMERICAN PIPE LINES, THEIR INDUSTRIAL STRUC-
TURE, ECONOMIC STATUS AND LEGAL IMPLICATIONS. Norman: University of Oklahoma Press, 1952. 179 p.
> Discusses issues raised by vertical integration of pipelines and
> concentration of ownership.

GOVERNMENT PUBLICATIONS

Administrative Conference of the United States. Committee on Rulemaking.
THE CONDUCT OF RATE PROCEEDINGS IN THE INTERSTATE COMMERCE
COMMISSION, by Roger C. Cramton. Washington, D.C.: December 1, 1961.
109 p.
> Describes the procedures for handling rate cases in the Interstate
> Commerce Commission, and makes some suggestions for their im-
> provement. The object is to determine whether there are oppor-
> tunities for improvement in the speed and effectiveness, with
> which the commission performs its responsibilities in the field of
> rate regulation.

Administrative Conference of the United States. Committee on Licenses and
Authorizations. REPORT ON LICENSING OF TRUCK OPERATIONS BY THE
INTERSTATE COMMERCE COMMISSION, by William K. Jones. Washington,
D.C.: March 1962. 135 p. Mimeographed.
> This study considers the objectives of Congress in establishing
> licensing requirements for interstate trucking; the substantive pol-
> icies used to effectuate these objectives; the economic signifi-
> cance of truck licensing; the administrative organization and pro-

cedures for processing license applications and resolving the
litigation issues they present; the performance of the Interstate
Commerce Commission in terms of processing time and volume;
and the possibilities for improvement of the licensing process.

INTERSTATE COMMERCE. PRICE LIST 59. 46th ed. Washington, D.C.:
Government Printing Office, 1964. 13 p.
Lists material available from the Government Printing Office in
the field of interstate commerce. Reports, regulations, statistics
are covered, among other items.

Interstate Commerce Commission. ANNUAL REPORTS. Washington, D.C.:
Government Printing Office. 1887–
These reports cover the preceding fiscal year in transportation,
and then give more detailed discussion of the activities of the
carriers and the work of the commission in the major subjects in
the field of transportation. References are made to the legislative actions by the last Congress; and legislative recommendations
are made for consideration by the next Congress.

Interstate Commerce Commission. GENERAL RULES OF PRACTICE BEFORE THE
COMMISSION IN PROCEEDINGS UNDER THE INTERSTATE COMMERCE ACT
AND RELATED ACTS, WITH APPROVED FORMS. Washington, D.C.: 1962.
62 p.

Interstate Commerce Commission. INTERSTATE COMMERCE ACT, revised to
October 1, 1958. Washington, D.C.: Government Printing Office. 636 p.
A pamphlet which contains the text of the act, as well as of
supplementary acts and related sections of various other acts. It
contains no annotations, but has an extensive and detailed index.

Interstate Commerce Commission. INTERSTATE COMMERCE ACTS, ANNOTATED.
Washington, D.C.: Government Printing Office. Vol. 1– , 1930–
In 18 volumes at this time.
A compilation of federal laws relating to the regulation of carriers subject to the Interstate Commerce Act, with digests of
pertinent decisions of federal courts and the Interstate Commerce
Commission, and the text of, or reference to general rules and
regulations. Advance bulletins are issued at frequent intervals,
to provide annotations on legislation, regulations, and court and
commission decisions.

Interstate Commerce Commission. NEWS RELEASES. Washington, D.C.:
Current.
Issued several times a month, to summarize work being done by
the commission, decisions handed down, changes in personnel,
changes in organization, and general matters affecting interstate
commerce.

Interstate Commerce Commission. TRANSPORT STATISTICS. Washington, D.C.:
Government Printing Office. Annual.
Contain statistics based on the annual reports of railroads, their
lessor and proprietary companies, the Pullman Company, Railway
Express Agency, electric railways, carriers by water, oil pipelines,
motor carriers, freight forwarders and private car owners.

Incorporates statistical information formerly issued as Statistics of Railways in the United States, Summary Tables of the Statistics of Railways in the United States, and the Preliminary Abstracts of Railways Statistics.

INTERSTATE COMMERCE COMMISSION REPORTS. DECISIONS OF THE INTERSTATE COMMERCE COMMISSION OF THE UNITED STATES. Washington, D.C.: Government Printing Office. Vol. 1- , 1887-

Decisions on stock and bond issues and track abandonments are found in volumes labeled Finance Reports, and those on shipping are covered by volumes labeled Water Carrier and Freight Forwarder Reports. Until 1929, when they were issued as a separate series, the set also included decisions relating to valuation of physical property labeled Valuation Reports. Decisions relating to motor carriers are reported separately. The undesignated reports, which comprise the greater part of the series, cover tariff rates and all other matters under the jurisdiction of the Interstate Commerce Commission.

Advance sheets to the reports, in the form of separate pamphlets for each decision, are paginated to correspond with the bound volumes.

INTERSTATE COMMERCE COMMISSION REPORTS. VALUATION REPORTS. DECISIONS OF THE INTERSTATE COMMERCE COMMISSION OF THE UNITED STATES. Washington, D.C.: Government Printing Office. Vol. 22- , 1929- (Valuation reports included in series described above, though not so numbered, are regarded as volumes 1 to 21.)

Cover decisions relating to valuation of physical properties.

INTERSTATE COMMERCE COMMISSION REPORTS. MOTOR CARRIER CASES. DECISIONS OF THE INTERSTATE COMMERCE COMMISSION OF THE UNITED STATES. Washington, D.C.: Government Printing Office. Vol. 1- , 1936-

Cover decisions relating to the regulation of motor carriers engaged in interstate commerce. The set also includes odd volumes labeled Finance Reports, which are concerned mainly with the purchase of operating rights and property, and with the acquisition of control through said purchase. Advance sheets to the reports, in the form of separate pamphlets for each decision, are paginated to correspond with the bound volumes.

Interstate Commerce Commission. RAILROAD CONSOLIDATIONS AND THE PUBLIC INTEREST--A PRELIMINARY EXAMINATION. Washington, D.C.: Government Printing Office, 1962. 79 p. plus appendix.

This is a staff study by the Bureau of Transport Economics and Statistics of the Interstate Commerce Commission. It was undertaken to identify and examine the public interest criteria which the Interstate Commerce Commission has used since 1920 in considering merger proposals. It was hoped, in this way, to provide useful information to the commission to help in its evaluation of specific individual mergers from the standpoint of the public interest, especially with respect to testing the quantitative and qualitative adequacy of evidence.

Interstate Commerce Commission. Section of Reference Services. SOME RULES OF EVIDENCE DISCUSSED IN TRANSPORTATION PROCEEDINGS. Washington, D.C.: Government Printing Office, 1962–1964. 2 parts.
> Compilations of classified lists of citations to prior rulings. A descriptive word-index provides the means of locating citations on particular points.

Interstate Commerce Commission. Section of Reference Services. CONSOLIDATED INDEX-DIGEST OF REPORTS OF THE INTERSTATE COMMERCE COMMISSION INVOLVING FINANCE. Washington, D.C.: Government Printing Office.
> This publication is a consolidation of the index-digests of finance reports (both ICC and MCC) in advance sheet form. Bound volumes when published will include these index-digests. Part I is a systematically cross-indexed, short-line digest of principles of law and important conclusions of fact. Part II is a list of "Reports Cited as Controlling Precedents." Includes the titles of cases, which were either cited by popular names or cited as controlling precedents.

Interstate Commerce Commission. Section of Reference Services. CONSOLIDATED INDEX-DIGEST OF REPORTS OF THE INTERSTATE COMMERCE COMMISSION INVOLVING MOTOR CARRIER OPERATING RIGHTS. Washington, D.C.: Government Printing Office.
> This publication is a consolidation of the index-digests of reports involving motor carrier operating rights in advance sheet form. Bound volumes, when published, will include these index-digests. Part I is a systematically cross-indexed, short-line digest of principles of law and important conclusions of fact. Part II is a list of "Reports Cited As Controlling Precedents." Includes the titles of cases which were either cited by popular names or referred to as leading precedents.

Interstate Commerce Commission. Section of Reference Services. CONSOLIDATED INDEX-DIGEST OF REPORTS OF THE INTERSTATE COMMERCE COMMISSION INVOLVING RATES AND PRACTICES. Washington, D.C.: Government Printing Office.
> This publication is a consolidation of the index-digests of reports, involving rates and practices, in advance sheet form. Bound volumes of the ICC Reports will include these index-digests. Part I is a systematically cross-indexed, short-line digest of principles of law and important conclusions of fact. Part II is an index to the reports, based on the principal commodities involved. Part III is a list of "Reports Cited as Controlling Precedent." Includes the titles of cases which were either cited by popular names, or referred to as leading precedents.

Interstate Commerce Commission. UNIFORM SYSTEM OF ACCOUNTS FOR RAILROAD COMPANIES. Washington, D.C.: Government Printing Office, 1962. 129 p.

OPERATING REVENUES AND OPERATING EXPENSES OF CLASS 1 RAILROADS IN UNITED STATES. Washington, D.C.: Interstate Commerce Commission. Quarterly. Subject to revision.

Does not include switching and terminal companies.

Based on Statement Q-100, Bureau of Transport Economics and Statistics.

OPERATING STATISTICS OF LARGE RAILROADS, SELECTED ITEMS. Washington, D.C.: Interstate Commerce Commission. Quarterly. Subject to revision. Gives detailed statistics by individual company.

Based on Statement Q-200, Bureau of Transport Economics and Statistics.

TRANSPORT ECONOMICS. Washington, D.C.: Interstate Commerce Commission. Monthly, with annual index.
Comment by Bureau of Transport Economics and Statistics.

U.S. Congress. Senate. Committee on Interstate and Foreign Commerce. NATIONAL TRANSPORTATION POLICY. (87th Cong., 1st Sess.) Report No. 445. Washington, D.C.: Government Printing Office, 1961. 732 p. Prepared by a special study group. This study tries to identify fundamental problems in the transportation field--lack of adequate information, lack of continuing research, lack of a program approach; and organization in the government, and in the law, which impedes rather than assists coordination of promotion and regulation. It also indicates a complete re-direction of transportation pricing philosophy.

U.S. Congress. Senate. Committee on Interstate and Foreign Commerce. SURVEY OF ORGANIZATION AND OPERATIONS OF THE INTERSTATE COMMERCE COMMISSION. (83rd Cong., 1st Sess.) Committee Print. February 2, 1953. Washington, D.C.: Government Printing Office, 1953. 62 p. A report submitted to the Senate Committee on Interstate and Foreign Commerce by the Wolf Management Engineering Company of Chicago. The scope of the survey was to determine administrative and organizational ways and means to increase the efficiency and economy of the commission, and to make recommendations with regard to the following objectives: (1) an increase in the quantity and quality of the commission's work; (2) a simplification and clarification of its organizational structure; and (3) the safeguarding of the independence and objectivity of the commission's quasi-judicial functions. Includes the functions at the bureau level in Washington, and reports on visits to a representative cross-section of the Interstate Commerce Commission field offices throughout the country.

U.S. Department of Commerce. FEDERAL TRANSPORTATION POLICY AND PROGRAM. Washington, D.C.: Government Printing Office, March 1960. 32 p.
Identifies emerging national transportation problems, suggests a redefined federal role in meeting these problems, and recommends certain legislative and administrative steps intended to assure the balanced development of our transportation system.

U.S. Department of Commerce. RATIONALE OF FEDERAL TRANSPORTATION POLICY. Prepared by Ernest W. Williams, Jr. and David W. Bluestone.

Washington, D.C.: April 1960. 71 p.
>Issued as an appendix to the Department's publication entitled
Federal Transportation Policy and Program. It contains a bibliography of reports prepared for the transportation study of the U.S.
Department of Commerce. The report reflects the considered
views of the study staff. It takes up federal transportation policy
in general, federal economic regulation--control of operating
rights and control of rates, cost finding and census of transportation, federal investment and user charges, defense readiness, government procurement and operation, urban transportation, merchant marine problems, railroad passenger service deficits, and
transport integration and related questions.

MISCELLANEOUS

ABSTRACTS OF SUPREME COURT DECISIONS INTERPRETING THE INTERSTATE
COMMERCE ACT. Washington, D.C.: Association of Interstate Commerce
Commission Practitioners, 1954. 297 p. and pocket supplement.
>Contains abstracts of decisions deemed of importance to the Inter-
state Commerce Commission, and of those decisions most frequently
cited by the commission. Insofar as possible, the abstracts have
been arranged in accordance with the section of the Interstate
Commerce Act, to which the main point of decisions is related.

American Bar Association, Section of Public Utility Law. ANNUAL
REPORT. Chicago.
>Contains articles and reviews of the year's developments in the
field of public utilities. Includes surface transportation--motor
carriers and railroads.

Blaisdell, Ruth F., et al. SOURCES OF INFORMATION IN TRANSPORTA-
TION. Chicago: Northwestern University Press, 1964. 262 p.
>A publication intended to enable the user to find the principal
sources of information in several fields of transportation. A tool
for both beginners and candidates for the doctoral degree, as
well as for those who seek practical day-to-day answers to operating problems.

>Lists are presented under the following headings, each compiled
by a librarian who is a specialist in the field: general sources;
highways; motor carriers; metropolitan transportation; railroads;
pipelines; merchant marine; inland waterways; air transportation;
and missiles and rockets.

Booz, Allen & Hamilton. ORGANIZATION AND PROCEDURES SURVEY OF
THE INTERSTATE COMMERCE COMMISSION. New York: 1960. 3 vols.
Abridged edition in one volume.
>A survey by a management consultant firm of the Interstate Com-
merce Commission's organization and operations. The survey was
authorized by the Bureau of the Budget. Its object was to determine whether there are opportunities for improvement in the speed
and effectiveness with which the commission performs its functions,

and whether operating costs can be reduced. Covers: the roles of the commission and its chairman; the organization of the agency; management policies and practices; operating processes and procedures; and the effect of statutory procedural requirements.

Commerce Clearing House, Inc. FEDERAL CARRIERS REPORTER. Looseleaf. 3 vols.
> A guide to the regulation of motor carriers, water carriers, and freight forwarders by the Interstate Commerce Commission. Contains statutes and regulations, and current Commission and court decisions.

Commerce Clearing House, Inc. STATE MOTOR CARRIER GUIDE. Looseleaf. 2 vols.
> An operating guide to state regulation of motor carriers, with comprehensive state-by-state digests of the laws and regulations.

COST AND VALUE OF SERVICE IN RATE MAKING FOR COMMON CARRIERS Washington, D.C.: Association of Interstate Commission Practitioners, May 1951. 92 p.
> Reprint of articles previously appearing in the ICC Practitioners' Journal, supported by a digest of ruling cases.

HAWKINS INDEX-DIGEST-ANALYSIS OF DECISIONS UNDER THE INTERSTATE COMMERCE ACT. Washington, D.C.: Hawkins Publishing Company. Looseleaf.
> Digests cases before the Interstate Commerce Commission, with citations to the ICC reports. Arranged by topics, with a general index indicating the topic numbers corresponding to the subject.

MANUAL OF PRACTICE AND PROCEDURE BEFORE THE INTERSTATE COMMERC COMMISSION. Washington, D.C.: Association of Interstate Commerce Commission Practitioners, 1945 (Reprinted October, 1959). 76 p.
> There is a considerable field of additional information, that cannot be covered in the rules, and also, there are important subjects of interest to practitioners that find no place in Rules of Practice. It is in this broader field that this manual may find its value to practitioners.

Metcalf, Kenneth N. TRANSPORTATION INFORMATION SOURCES. Detroit: Gale Research, 1965. 307 p. Management Information Guide: 8.
> An annotated guide to publications, agencies, and other data sources concerning air, rail, water, road and pipeline transportation.

Moody's Investors Service. MOODY'S TRANSPORTATION MANUAL. New York. Annual, with semiweekly supplements.
> This publication covers railroads, airlines, steamship companies, electric, railway, bus and truck lines, oil pipelines, bridge and canal companies. It is designed primarily for the use of the individual and institutional investors purchasing securities for investment. The information on individual companies includes a history of the company, a list of its officers, its financial statements, a history of its financings, and a description of its operations.

National Association of Railroad and Utilities Commissioners. ANNUAL RE-
PORTS. Washington, D.C.: 1964-

>   Reports on what is happening, collectively, in the field of regu-
>   latory commission activity; what projects they are working on   as
>   a group; and how they are organized to carry out such work.

>   Contains a list of NARUC officers and committee members   and
>   chairmen and their state regulatory affiliation.   Also describes
>   the function of each commission.

>   Activities in the Washington office of the NARUC are a valuable
>   feature.

National Association of Railroad and Utilities Commissioners. PROCEEDINGS.
Washington, D.C.: Annual.

>   Papers presented at the annual meetings of the association, which
>   consists of commissioners on both the federal and state level
>   who head commissions regulating public utilities.   On the federal
>   level, the Interstate Commerce Commission, the Federal Commun-
>   ications Commission, the Federal Power Commission, the Securities
>   and Exchange Commission, and the Civil Aeronautics Board are
>   represented.

ORGANIZATION OF DIVISIONS AND BOARDS AND ASSIGNMENT OF WORK
OF THE INTERSTATE COMMERCE COMMISSION WITH ORGANIZATIONAL
CHART (Rev. to January 1, 1959). Washington, D.C.: Association of Inter-
state Commerce Commission Practitioners. 22 p.

OUTLINE OF STUDY COURSE IN PRACTICE BEFORE THE INTERSTATE COM-
MERCE COMMISSION. (3rd and rev. ed., 1959.) Original text by Warren
H. Wagner. Revised text by Robert B. Einhorn. Washington, D.C.: Associa-
tion of Interstate Commerce Commission Practitioners, 1959. 30 p.

SELECTED READING LIST OF BOOKS HELPFUL IN THE STUDY OF THE PRIN-
CIPAL LAWS WITHIN THE JURISDICTION OF THE INTERSTATE COMMERCE
COMMISSION. (3rd and rev. ed.) Washington, D.C.: Association of Inter-
state Commerce Commission Practitioners, 1957. 97 p.

>   Arranged by sections of the Interstate Commerce Act.   Under each
>   section cites to the volume (where applicable) and pages of text-
>   books, periodical articles and the Interstate Commerce Act, an-
>   notated, which discuss that particular section.

PERIODICALS

ICC PRACTITIONERS JOURNAL. Washington, D.C.: Association of Interstate
Commerce Commission Practitioners. Monthly, except July and August.

>   Contains articles, book reviews, summaries of recent court deci-
>   sions, and an index to current Interstate Commerce Commission
>   decisions.

RAILWAY AGE WEEKLY. New York: Simmons Boardman. Weekly.

>   A magazine primarily devoted to railroads and their problems.
>   Gives coverage of the Interstate Commerce Commission as the
>   regulatory body over the industry.

TRAFFIC WORLD. Washington, D.C.: The Traffic Service Corp. Weekly.
This periodical contains very short articles and news items on the
Interstate Commerce Commission and the Maritime Administration
as well as the Civil Aeronautics Board. It summarizes the work
of these agencies during the preceding week, listing orders issued,
hearings, etc., as well as news items.

TRANSPORTATION BUSINESS REPORT. Washington, D.C.: Federal Publications. Biweekly.
A four page report designed for transportation industry executives,
their legal and technical representatives, and government officials.
It covers significant developments, present and prospective, and
contains briefings on the effects of those developments on carriers and their users. Railroads, motor carriers, airlines, barge
lines, and pipelines are covered. Sources used for information
are the regulatory agencies of the federal government (Interstate
Commerce Commission, Civil Aeronautics Board and Federal
Aviation Administration), the federal departments concerned with
transportation, state planning agencies, the courts, Congress, and
top men in government and industry.

TRADE ASSOCIATIONS

The trade association for the transportation industry is the Transportation
Association of America, 1710 H Street, N.W., Washington 6, D.C. It was
founded in 1935, has 1216 members, and a staff of 30.

Members are representatives of all sections of the transportation industry:
users, investors, airlines, freight forwarders, highway carriers, pipelines, railroads, and water carriers.

Its purpose is "to resist all trends which may lead to government ownership
or operation of any form of transportation." It brings together divergent groups
to resolve conflicts, so that unified policies in the national interest can be
developed; and conducts a broad educational and research program.

The Association of Interstate Commerce Commission Practitioners, 1112 ICC
Building, 12th and Constitution Avenue, N.W., Washington 25, D.C., is a
professional organization of lawyers, and transportation and traffic specialists,
admitted to practice before the Interstate Commerce Commission. It publishes
the ICC Practitioners' Journal, manuals, and other documents relating to transportation, traffic, and related matters.

While it is not a trade association, mention must be made of the National
Association of Railroad and Utilities Commissioners, 5310 ICC Building, Washington, D.C. This association was founded in 1889, has 325 members, and a
staff of four. There are five regional associations affiliated with it.

This is a professional organization of state and federal regulatory commissioners having jurisdiction over transportation agencies and public utilities.

Section 7

SECURITIES AND EXCHANGE COMMISSION

Section 7

SECURITIES AND EXCHANGE COMMISSION

The Securities and Exchange Commission was created by the Securities Exchange Act of 1934. It is an independent, bipartisan, quasi-judicial agency of the United States government, which administers the federal securities laws.

Beginning in 1933, Congress enacted the "truth in securities" laws to protect investors in the purchase and sale of securities. These laws cover companies which wish to acquire new capital by the issuance of securities to the public, and persons in the business of buying and selling securities. They also govern investment advisers, holding companies, and investment companies.

The Securities and Exchange Commission issues its orders and decisions, as well as other material, in mimeographed form under each of the acts which it administers. These acts are: the Securities Act of 1933; the Securities Exchange Act of 1934; the Public Utility Holding Company Act of 1935; the Trust Indenture Act of 1939; the Investment Company Act of 1940; and the Investment Advisers Act of 1940. The commission also issues pamphlets containing each of these acts, and the regulations thereunder, revised at intervals.

Other publications of the commission are listed in the publications list, which can be obtained by writing to the commission in Washington, D.C.

TEXTS

Baum, Daniel J. and Stiles, Ned B. THE SILENT PARTNERS: INSTITUTIONAL INVESTORS AND CORPORATE CONTROL. Syracuse, N.Y.: Syracuse University Press, 1965. 192 p.
> Contents include: 1. The Evolution of a Proletarian Capitalism;
> 2. The Nature and Functions of Institutional Investors; 3. Institutional Concentrates and Market Impact; 4. Some Uses of Institutional Power; 5. Present Legal Restraints on the Uses of Institutional Power; 6. Some Possible Antitrust Aspects: The Stigma of Bigness; and 7. Power and Responsibility.

> Daniel J. Baum, an associate professor at the Indiana University School of Law, has served on the Federal Trade Commission. Ned B. Stiles was formerly on the staff of the Securities and Exchange

Commission.

Bosland, Chelcie C. VALUATION THEORIES AND DECISIONS OF THE SECURITIES AND EXCHANGE COMMISSION. New York: Simmons-Boardman, 1964. 89 p.

The author, Eastman Professor of Political Economy at Brown University, has made an extensive study of the decisions of the Securities and Exchange Commission with regard to determining the value of a going business concern.

During the years from 1940 to 1950, a large number of simplification proceedings, under the Public Utility Holding Company Act, gave the commission many opportunities to set out its theories and practices in valuation cases. In the same period, a number of decisions under the Investment Company Act of 1940 involved the valuation of ownership interests where transactions between affiliated persons raised questions of the fairness and adequacy of the prices paid. The author considers the decisions of the commission during this period, and in a later chapter takes up valuation decisions handed down from 1956 to 1960, to see if the principles evolved earlier were still being applied. The final chapter sums up the author's conclusions as to the commission's standards in determining valuation.

Bradley, Joseph F. FUNDAMENTALS OF CORPORATION FINANCE. Rev. ed. New York: Holt, Rinehart, 1959. 644 p.

Intended for the serious student, stressing the viewpoint of management. Chapter 25 deals with government regulation of the issuance of corporate securities.

Burtchett, Floyd F. and Hicks, Clifford M. CORPORATION FINANCE. 3rd ed. Lincoln, Nebraska: Johnsen, 1959. 712 p.

Chapter 24 of this general text deals with the regulation of securities and banks.

Childs, John F. LONG TERM FINANCING. Englewood Cliffs, New Jersey: Prentice-Hall, 1961. 369 p.

Designed as a practical guide and working tool for the men who have to raise the money for their companies. An outgrowth of a financial seminar for corporate executives, run by the author in Wall Street.

Choka, Allen D. AN INTRODUCTION TO SECURITIES REGULATION. Chicago: Twentieth-Century, 1958. 165 p.

An introductory work in the field.

Cohan, Avery B. COST OF FLOTATION OF LONG-TERM CORPORATE DEBT SINCE 1935. Chapel Hill: University of North Carolina School of Business Administration, 1961. 89 p.

The purpose of this study is to measure and explain those changes which have occurred since 1935 in the cost of selling corporate debt to the public.

Cooke, Gilbert W., et al. FINANCIAL INSTITUTIONS. New York: Simmons-Boardman, 1962. 501 p.

Written for students on both the graduate and undergraduate level.
The chief emphasis is on the source of funds and the financial
intermediaries which supply them. Financial institutions are studied
from the viewpoint of the user of the funds, rather than from that
of the saver. Part V deals with the capital market, and discusses
the regulation of securities.

Cooke, Gilbert W. THE STOCK MARKETS. New York: Simmons-Boardman,
1964. 540 p.
This volume covers the techniques and processes in the marketing
of capital stock. It also discusses the rules and regulations governing such markets. Emphasis is on the financial aspect, rather
than on the theoretical economic relationship. Part I deals with
the securities industry; Part II is concerned with the over-the-
counter markets arising from the distribution of new issues and
the trading in issues off the exchanges; part III covers the operations on organized exchanges; and part IV discusses the factors
which affect changes in market prices. References to the Special
Study of Securities Markets are appended to the chapters where
pertinent.

Cormier, Frank. WALL STREET'S SHADY SIDE. Washington, D.C.: Public
Affairs Press, 1962. 198 p.
Discussion of unethical, fraudulent and criminal activities, per-
petrated in the securities markets since the establishment of the
Securities and Exchange Commission in 1934.

Press accounts of stock market wrongdoing necessarily have dealt
with the situation on a piecemeal basis, hitting the high points of
first one case, then another. Many of the details which offer
valuable insights into the significance of market problems have
not been published at all. Aim of this book is to present a detailed, cohesive account of some of the most significant and in-
teresting cases, emphasizing information that has not been published
before.

Author, a press association reporter since 1951, has been reporting
on day-to-day activities of the Securities and Exchange Commission for a leading press association since early 1958.

De Bedts, Ralph F. THE NEW DEAL'S SEC. THE FORMATIVE YEARS. New
York: Columbia University Press, 1964. 226 p.
Considers not only the historical origins and antecedents of the
SEC, but also its growth and formative years in the lights of
the financial and political happenings of the times and in relation-
ship to the many individuals involved.

Dewing, Arthur Stone. THE FINANCIAL POLICY OF CORPORATIONS. 5th
ed. New York: Ronald Press, 1953. 2 vols.
The regulation of issues of securities, on both the federal and state
levels, are taken up briefly in chapter 34. The bulk of the
treatise is devoted to the question of financing corporations.

Donaldson, Elvin F. and Pfahl, John K. CORPORATE FINANCE. POLICY
AND MANAGEMENT. 2nd ed. New York: Ronald, 1963. 759 p.

Chapter 14 discusses the Federal Securities Act of 1933.

Guthmann, Harry G. and Dougall, Herbert E. CORPORATE FINANCIAL POL-
ICY. 4th ed. Englewood Cliffs, New Jersey: Prentice-Hall, 1962. 776 p.
Chapter 19 of this general text deals with securities exchanges
and markets.

Hazard, John W. and Christie, Milton. THE INVESTMENT BUSINESS. New
York: Harper & Row, 1964. 436 p.
The authors have shortened and condensed the official government
study of the securities markets, preserving the sense, the spirit
and the recommendations of the original. Reference tables refer
from the chapters of this book to the chapters and page numbers
of the Special Study, as published by the Government Printing Office.

Israels, Carlos L., chairman. TRANSCRIPT OF PLI FORUM ON SEC PROB-
LEMS OF CONTROLLING STOCKHOLDERS AND IN UNDERWRITINGS. New
York: Practising Law Institute, 1962. 318 p.
Participants in this panel discussion included: Commissioner Man-
uel F. Cohen, of the Securities and Exchange Commission; Charles
E. Shreve, Esq., counsel for the Corporation Finance Division of
the Commission; and fifteen experienced lawyers, who regularly
advise controlling stockholders, investment bankers, brokerage
houses, and others on problems of the type under discussion.

Israels, Carlos L. and Duff, George M., Jr., ed. WHEN CORPORATIONS
GO PUBLIC. TAKING A CORPORATION'S SECURITIES TO THE PUBLIC
MARKET. New York: Practising Law Institute, 1962. 391 p.
Panel and editorial discussions, illustrative agreements and other
forms are presented in this volume. It contains substantially
the entire text of a forum discussion on the subject, supplemented
by editors' notes based on practical experience in the field, and
on other courses. It includes a section "On Drafting a Prospectus."
Special emphasis is given to methods and techniques for finding
workable solutions to the financial and legal problems usually
encountered when corporations bring their securities to market
for the first time, particularly by counsel for the issuing corporation. The volume offers expert guidance on the preparation of a
registration statement, with specimen texts illustrating the treatment
of typical problems in well-drawn prospectuses.

Jennings, Richard W. and Marsh, Harold, Jr. SECURITIES REGULATION.
Brooklyn, New York: Foundation, 1963, with 1966 supplement. 992 p.
A collection of cases and materials for a course in securities regulation. It speaks as of September 1962. The main topics are:
regulation of the distribution of securities; regulation of trading
in securities; and regulation of investment companies.

Leffler, George L. THE STOCK MARKET. 3rd ed. Rev. by Loring C. Far-
well. New York: Ronald, 1963. 654 p.
A study of the stock market as it operates and functions today.
Takes up the work of the stock exchanges, the work of the securities houses, investing practices and special instruments, and regu-

lation. Chapter 28 is devoted to the Securities Exchange Act.

Loll, Leo M., Jr. and Buckley, Julian G. THE OVER-THE-COUNTER SECURI-
TIES MARKET. Englewood Cliffs, New Jersey: Prentice-Hall, 1961. 343 p.
Designed to help anyone who wishes to enter the securities business.
The material goes beyond the basic facts necessary to the prospective securities salesman in his preparation for the NASD Qualification Examination. Provides useful tools with which to solve
the complex investment problems which confront the securities
salesman. Chapter 12 deals with federal and state securities regulations.

Loss, Louis. SECURITIES REGULATION. 2nd ed. Boston: Little, Brown,
1961, with 1962 supplement. 3 vols.
The outstanding work in this field. The author has had three purposes in mind: to tell the story of government regulation of those
aspects of the world of finance having to do with securities; to
paint a picture of administrative law in action in one important
field; and to provide a teaching tool. The scope of the work
takes in state statutes and decisional law, the special legislation
in the securities field administered by other federal agencies, the
foreign experience, and the common law background, in such
fields as fraud and civil liability. The author provides the most
thorough coverage of the decisions of the Securities and Exchange
Commission that exists at the present time.

Loss, Louis and Cowett, Edward M. BLUE SKY LAW. Boston: Little, Brown,
1958. 503 p.
The authors' primary purpose in writing this treatise was to produce
a survey of blue sky law, as it is administered and practiced
throughout the country as a whole. It is based on the Harvard
Law School Study of State Securities Regulations, which was
started in 1954 at the request of the National Conference of
Commissioners on Uniform State Laws, and which resulted in the
Uniform Securities Act. It is not intended to be a treatise on
the law or practice in any particular jurisdiction.

McCarthy, George D. ACQUISITIONS AND MERGERS. New York: Ronald,
1963. 353 p.
The author is a partner in Price Waterhouse & Co. The book is
intended to offer a comprehensive guide and useful reference work,
to show the factors to be considered, and the steps to be undertaken in effecting corporate acquisitions and mergers. Among the
topics discussed are: types of business combinations; financial
and accounting information needed before effecting the deal; management, marketing, and operating information needed before
effecting the deal; how to value a company; how to account for
a "purchase" or a "pooling of interests"; financial and other provisions of business combination agreements; federal tax aspects;
SEC filing requirements; financial data required in SEC filings; and
stock exchange listing requirements.

Mundheim, Robert H., ed. CONFERENCE ON SECURITIES REGULATION.
Chicago: Commerce Clearing House, 1965. 248 p.

Papers presented at the Duke University School of Law conference on securities regulation which dealt with regulation of the broker-dealers. The 16 papers presented are grouped under the two major topics of the new high standards of conduct imposed on the broker-dealer community, and the impact on the institutional investor of raising broker-dealer standards.

Osborn, Richard C. CORPORATION FINANCE. New York: Harper, 1959. 637 p.

Designed for undergraduate students. Chapter 13 deals with the regulation of trading in securities.

Practising Law Institute. HOW TO COMPLY WITH THE NEW SEC RULES. New York: 1965. 376 p.

Materials prepared for a forum held March 10-12, 1965, in New York City. Include forms, notes, questionnaires, SEC releases, and other valuable source materials.

Practising Law Institute. HOW TO COMPLY WITH THE NEW SEC RULES. Edited Forum Transcript. New York: 1965. 451 p.

Forum was held March 10-12, 1965 at the Statler-Hilton Hotel, New York City.

Forum dealt with the Securities Acts Amendments of 1964, and the rules thereunder which, among other things, extend the registration, periodic reporting, proxy solicitation, and insider reporting and trading provisions of the Securities Exchange Act of 1934 to a significant portion of the securities traded in the over-the-counter market; and which, in addition, endeavor to strengthen the standards of entrance into the securities business, and the disciplinary controls of the Securities and Exchange Commission, and the self-regulatory organizations of the industry, over brokers, dealers and associated persons.

Practising Law Institute. HOW TO COMPLY WITH THE NEW SEC RULES: BROKER-DEALER PROBLEMS. Edited Transcript. New York: 1965. 424 p.

Forum was held March 12, 1965, in New York City.

Focuses upon broker-dealer problems, including examination and registration requirements, standards of conduct and responsibility, personnel training, intra-firm supervision, investigations, and disciplinary proceedings. A "Materials Appendix" to the volume contains forms, SEC releases, statutory provisions and amendments, suggested procedures for effecting compliance, and other pertinent source materials.

Rappaport, Louis H. SEC ACCOUNTING PRACTICE AND PROCEDURE. 2nd ed. New York: Ronald, 1963. Each chapter separately paginated.

The author is a partner in Lybrand, Ross Bros. & Montgomery. The volume aims to present, in a systematic manner, all of the requirements of the Securities and Exchange Commission relating to: accounting principles and practices; auditing standards and procedures; form and content of financial statements, including summaries of earnings and pro forma statements; certification by independent public accountants; and accounts' independence. It is designed as a guide, not only for accountants, but also for corporation officials, investment bankers, security analysts, and lawyers engaged in securities work. It tries to show how these requirements have been complied with in actual practice by numerous illustrative examples and comments based on experience and observation.

Ritchie, Robert F. INTEGRATION OF PUBLIC UTILITY HOLDING COMPANIES. Ann Arbor: University of Michigan Law School, 1954. 339 p.
Takes up the ways in which the Securities and Exchange Commission has met, and resolved, the problems of geographical and economic integration arising under the "death sentence" provisions of the Public Utility Holding Company Act. The author examined and studied the legislative history of the act; contemporaneous legal, economic, and political comment; all court decisions concerning the problem of integration; and all official releases of the Securities and Exchange Commission issued under the Public Utilities Holding Company Act of 1935, through release 11606, dated November 28, 1952.

Robinson, Gerald J. GOING PUBLIC. SUCCESSFUL SECURITIES UNDERWRITING. New York: Clark Boardman, 1961. 353 p.
Intended as a practical guide, introductory in nature. The mechanics of a public issue are presented; the underwriting contract is discussed; applicable federal and state securities laws are dealt with; and federal income tax problems connected with going public, are described.

Rohrlich, Chester. ORGANIZING CORPORATE AND OTHER BUSINESS ENTERPRISES. 3rd ed. New York: Bender, 1958, with 1964 supplement. 534 p.
Chapter X deals with initials capitalization and financing. Chapter XI takes up marketing securities, covering methods of distribution, e.g. private sale, public offering, "best efforts" sale, fraud in the sale of securities, Blue-Sky laws, and the Federal Securities Act of 1933.

Sarnoff, P. THE WALL ST. THESAURUS. New York: Obolensky, 1963. 250 p.

Shultz, Birl E. THE SECURITIES MARKET AND HOW IT WORKS. Rev. ed., edited by Albert P. Squier. New York: Harper, 1963. 372 p.
Deals mainly with the workings of the New York Stock Exchange, but takes up the relationship of the Securities and Exchange Commission where pertinent.

Sobel, Robert. THE BIG BOARD. A HISTORY OF THE NEW YORK STOCK MARKET. 1965. 395 p.
Traces the development of the financial district and shows how different pressures--political and social, as well as economic and financial--have affected the New York money market.

Sowards, Hugh L. THE FEDERAL SECURITIES ACT. ANALYSIS, PROCEDURES, FORMS. New York: Bender, 1965. Paginated by sections.

Primarily concerned with the Securities Act of 1933. Emphasis is on dealing with conditions as they presently exist. Treats each exemption in the act in detail, and makes specific recommendations as to obtaining those exemptions. Also treats the actual preparation of both Regulation A filings and registered offerings.

Chapter 8 deals with the Securities Acts amendments of 1964.

Thomas, Eliot B. FEDERAL SECURITIES ACT HANDBOOK. Philadelphia: Joint Committee on Continuing Legal Education of the American Law Institute and the American Bar Association, 1959. 181 p.
Intended to help the general practitioner determine whether, in a particular situation, action before the Securities and Exchange Commission is necessary or advisable; to guide him in taking such action; to alert him to possible pitfalls; and to provide him with some basic information on subjects closely related to the public offering of securities. Discusses the statutes, rules, and regulations as of November 1, 1958.

Weiss, Ezra. REGISTRATION AND REGULATION OF BROKERS AND DEALERS. Washington, D.C.: Bureau of National Affairs, 1965. 361 p.
The author is Regional Counsel for the Securities and Exchange Commission in New York City.

This book explains the rules governing the conduct of the business of brokers and dealers under the Securities and Exchange Act. It outlines in detail the reporting requirement, financial responsibility requirements, special anti-fraud requirements, hypothecation rules, short sales, etc. It includes remedies available to the regulatory agencies for censure, denial, suspension, and revocation of registration. The rules and responsibilities of securities exchanges and registered securities associations are listed and explained.

Wiesenberger, Arthur. INVESTMENT COMPANIES. New York: Arthur Wiesenberger & Company. Annual.
A compendium of information about mutual funds and investment companies. Explains their functions and their various uses to the investor. Includes data on the background, management policy, and salient features of all leading companies. Also covers management results, income and dividend records, price ranges and comparative operating details, and year-end portfolio holdings.

Winter, Elmer L. A COMPLETE GUIDE TO MAKING A PUBLIC STOCK OFFERING. Englewood Cliffs, New Jersey: Prentice-Hall, 1962. 269 p.
Analyzes the problems facing executives who wish to have their corporation "go public" for the first time. Written in non-legal terms. The role of the Securities and Exchange Commission is discussed in detail.

Young, Harold H. FORTY YEARS OF PUBLIC UTILITY FINANCE. Charlottesville: University of Virginia Press, 1965. 224 p.
The author, an investment banker specializing in public utilities, narrates his experiences in the field. Events relating to the passage of the Public Utilities Holding Company Act and its admin-

istration are described, as well as the collapse of the Insull empire.

GOVERNMENT PUBLICATIONS

COMPILATION OF DOCUMENTARY MATERIALS AVAILABLE IN THE SEC. Washington, D.C.: Securities and Exchange Commission, 1957. 12 p.
Lists the documents filed with the Commission pursuant to the acts administered by it, and the sections of the acts pursuant to which they are required to be filed. Only the titles of these documents are given, without annotations.

Securities and Exchange Commission. ANNUAL REPORTS TO CONGRESS. Washington, D.C.: Government Printing Office, 1935-
These reports survey the work of the Commission for the preceding year, and outline proposals for the coming year.

Securities and Exchange Commission. COST OF FLOTATION OF CORPORATE SECURITIES, 1951-1955. Washington, D.C.: Government Printing Office, June 1957. 76 p.
Presents current data on the cost of floating new issues of securities. Covers registered securities and private placements in the years 1951, 1953, and 1955. Data are shown for other exempt offerings, with the exception of small issues exempt under Regulation A. Brings up to date material presented in two earlier reports by the Commission--"Cost of Flotation of Registered Issues, 1945-1949"; and "Privately-placed Securities--Cost of Flotation," covering 1947-1950.

Securities and Exchange Commission. COST OF FLOTATION-PRIVATELY-PLACED SECURITIES. Washington, D.C.: Government Printing Office, September 1952.
A study of privately placed issues in 1947, 1949, and 1950.

Securities and Exchange Commission. DECISIONS AND REPORTS. Washington, D.C.: Government Printing Office. Vol. 1- , 1938-
These bound volumes collect the opinions and decisions of the Commission, which have appeared previously in mimeographed form.

Securities and Exchange Commission. DIRECTORY OF COMPANIES FILING ANNUAL REPORTS WITH THE SECURITIES AND EXCHANGE COMMISSION UNDER THE SECURITIES EXCHANGE ACT OF 1934. Arranged alphabetically and by industry groups. Washington, D.C. Annual.
The following groups are excluded: investment companies registered under the Investment Company Act of 1940; governments and political subdivisions thereof; registrants incorporated in a foreign country, other than a North American country or Cuba; banks and trust companies; issuers of voting trust certificates, and stockholders' and bondholders' protective committees; and employee stock purchase plans.

Securities and Exchange Commission. NEWS DIGEST. Washington, D.C.: Government Printing Office. Daily.

SECURITIES AND EXCHANGE COMMISSION

A daily summary of actions taken by the commission on applications by individual companies, personnel appointments, form 8-K filings, registrations and effective dates, notices of new rules and regulations, etc.

Securities and Exchange Commission. OFFICIAL SUMMARY OF SECURITY TRANSACTIONS AND HOLDINGS. Washington, D.C.: Government Printing Office. Monthly.

Lists (by issuer, the security involved, and the reporting person) changes in beneficial ownership of: (a) equity securities of issuers having such securities listed and registered on a national securities exchange, reported to the commission by officers, directors and principal stockholders; (b) securities of registered public utility holding companies and their subsidiaries, reported by officers and directors; and (c) securities of registered closed-end investment companies, reported by officers, directors, principal securities holders, members of advisory boards, investment advisers, and affiliated persons of investment advisers of such investment companies.

Securities and Exchange Commission. QUARTERLY FINANCIAL REPORTS. MANUFACTURING. Washington, D.C.: Government Printing Office. Quarterly.

Reports beginning with the third quarter of 1955, presenting quarterly balance sheet and income data for all United States manufacturing corporations. A joint study of the Securities and Exchange Commission and the Federal Trade Commission.

Securities and Exchange Commission. REPORT OF THE SPECIAL STUDY OF SECURITIES MARKETS. (88th Cong., 1st Sess.) House Doc. 95. Washington, D.C.: Government Printing Office, 1963-4. 6 parts.

This examination of the securities markets, and the writing of this report, were done by a separate group established in the commission designated the Special Study of Securities Markets, under the supervision of Milton H. Cohen, Director. The functions of the report, and of any changes proposed, are to strengthen the mechanisms facilitating the free flow of capital into the markets, and to raise the standards of investor protection. Part 6 is an index.

Securities and Exchange Commission. SECURITIES TRADED ON EXCHANGES UNDER THE SECURITIES EXCHANGE ACT OF 1934. Washington, D.C. Annual, with quarterly supplements.

An alphabetical list, by issuers, of all securities admitted to trading on stock exchanges under the Securities Exchange Act of 1934, except securities exempted under section 3(a) (12) of the act, such as obligations of the United States government, states, and political subdivisions thereof.

Securities and Exchange Commission. STATISTICAL BULLETIN. Washington, D.C.: Government Printing Office. Monthly.

Supplies data on new securities offerings, registrations, trading on exchanges, stock price indexes, round-lot and odd-lot trading,

special offerings, secondary distributions, and other financial
series, including those released under classifications 11 to 14 and
16.

Securities and Exchange Commission. THE WORK OF THE SECURITIES AND
EXCHANGE COMMISSION. Washington, D.C.: August 20, 1957. 27 p.
Outlines the laws administered by the commission and briefly describes the functions of the various offices in the administrative
set-up. Lists publications.

Securities and Exchange Commission. Division of Trading and Exchanges.
REPORT ON PUT AND CALL OPTIONS. Washington, D.C.: August 1961.
125 p.
A report concerned principally with a factual presentation of statistical data. It does not touch on regulatory or legal problems,
which are to be the subject of further study.

Securities and Exchange Commission. Division of Trading and Exchanges.
Special Study of Securities Markets. STAFF REPORT ON ORGANIZATION,
MANAGEMENT, AND REGULATION OF THE AMERICAN STOCK EXCHANGE.
Washington, D.C.: Government Printing Office, January 3, 1962. 61 p.
A staff report on the organization, management, and regulation of
the conduct of members of the American Stock Exchange. The
commission ordered its staff to make an investigation of the facts,
conditions, and practices related to the conduct shown by the
record in the case of Re, Re & Sagarese, registered specialists on
the American Stock Exchange. The investigation was also to cover
the adequacy for the protection of investors of the rules, policies,
practices, and procedures of the exchange, concerning the regulation and conduct of specialists and other members.

Securities and Exchange Commission. Office of the General Counsel. JUDI-
CIAL DECISIONS. Washington, D.C.: Government Printing Office. Vol.
1- , 1941-
These bound volumes contain all the court decisions, reported and
unreported, in civil and criminal cases, involving statutes administered by the Securities and Exchange Commission, except decisions in cases arising under Chapter X of the National Bankruptcy
Act. Volume 5, the latest issued, covers October 1, 1946 to
December 31, 1948.

U.S. Congress. House. Special Subcommittee on Legislative Oversight of
the Committee on Interstate and Foreign Commerce. HISTORY OF NATIONAL
ASSOCIATION OF SECURITIES DEALERS, INC., ITS ACTIVITIES, MEMBER-
SHIP DATA, SANCTIONS IMPOSED, MEMBERS EXPELLED, FINANCIAL
STATEMENTS, LIAISON AND SUPERVISION BY SEC FROM 1936 TO NOVEM-
BER 30, 1958. Prepared by National Association of Securities Dealers, Inc.
(Wallace H. Fulton, Executive Director) for the use of the above special sub-
committee. (85th Cong. 2nd Sess.) Subcommittee Print. Washington, D.C.:
Government Printing Office, 1959. 38 p.

U.S. Congress. House. Committee on Interstate and Foreign Commerce.
STUDY OF THE SECURITIES AND EXCHANGE COMMISSION. (82nd Cong.
2nd Sess.) Report No. 2508. December 30, 1952. Washington, D.C.: Gov-

ernment Printing Office, 1952. 152 p.

> Report is based on hearings, which covered an examination of the
> commission and its staff, relative to the commission's powers,
> duties, and functions, under the various acts administered by it.
> Also considered were the Busbey bill, private or direct placements,
> the Tucker and Kaiser-Frazer registration statements, the reorgani-
> zation of United Corp. and the divorcement of the West Kentucky
> Coal Co. from the North American system. Other problems in-
> vestigated were the rapid turnover of commissioners of the Securi-
> ties and Exchange Commission, the fraudulent sale of Canadian
> securities in the United States, the commission's personnel prob-
> lems, the practice of former SEC members and staff before the
> commission, and the problem of missing security holders.

U.S. Congress. Senate. Committee on Banking and Currency. INSTITU-
TIONAL INVESTORS AND THE STOCK MARKET, 1953-55. Staff report to
the above committee (84th Cong. 2nd Sess.) Committee Print. December 28,
1956. Washington, D.C.: Government Printing Office, 1956.

> Restricted to open-and-closed-end investment companies, corporate
> pension funds, life-casualty and fire-insurance companies, and
> bank-administered trust funds. For a substantial segment of each
> institutional group, information is provided on their overall trad-
> ing activity in common stocks, and of their trading in a selected
> list of stocks, for every month from January 1953 through October
> 1955, as well as their stock holdings at the beginning and end
> of the 34-month period.

U.S. Congress. Senate. Committee on Banking and Currency. STOCK MAR-
KET STUDY. (84th Cong., 1st Sess.) Report No. 376. Washington, D.C.:
Government Printing Office, 1955. 18 p.

> A report on the hearings held to investigate the meaning of the
> 16 months' stock-price rise, from September 1953 to January 1955.
> Aimed at determining whether a rapidly rising stock market was
> likely to threaten economic stability.

U.S. Congress. Senate. Committee on Banking and Currency. FACTORS
AFFECTING THE STOCK MARKET. (84th Cong., 1st Sess.) Committee
Print. Washington, D.C.: Government Printing Office, 1955. 201 p.

> A staff report issued as a committee print, presenting background
> materials on major factors affecting the stock market, including
> the operations and regulations of the exchanges, and the over-the-
> counter market. It was intended to lay the ground work for the
> initial phases of the committee's inquiry.

U.S. Congress. House. Committee on Interstate and Foreign Commerce. A
STUDY OF MUTUAL FUNDS. Prepared for the Securities and Exchange Commission by the Wharton School of Finance and Commerce. (87th Cong., 2nd
Sess.) Report No. 2274. Washington, D.C.: Government Printing Office,
1962. 595 p.

> Covers a description of the structure of the industry, the growth
> of investment companies, the performance and market impact of
> the funds, and the relationship between the funds and their invest-
> ment advisers.

MISCELLANEOUS

Commerce Clearing House, Inc. FEDERAL SECURITIES LAW REPORTER. Chicago: 4 vols. Looseleaf.
> Covers all the acts administered by the Securities and Exchange Commission, and the regulations thereunder. Also reports new cases and rulings, and new developments in the field.

Commerce Clearing House, Inc. BLUE SKY REPORTER. Chicago: 3 vols. Looseleaf.
> Contains the Blue Sky laws of each state; legal investment laws; and rulings, decisions, and cases.

Dunton, Chester, comp. LEGAL BIBLIOGRAPHY ON FEDERAL SECURITIES REGULATION. Fairfax, Va.: Coiner Publications, 1965. Looseleaf bound.
> Includes a 50 year bibliography of proposed and enacted legislation, a table of cases on federal securities regulation, and legal bibliographies on the Securities Act of 1933, the Securities Exchange Act of 1934, the Public Utility Holding Company Act of 1935, and the Investment Company and Investment Advisers Act of 1940. Will be kept up to date.

FEDERAL UTILITY REGULATION ANNOTATED. Washington, D.C.: Public Utilities Reports. Volume 1, Public Utility Holding Company Act of 1935. 1942. 858 p.
> This volume contains an analytical summary of the work of the Securities and Exchange Commission in the administration of the Public Utility Holding Company Act of 1935. Events leading to the enactment of that act are summarized. Each section of the act is extensively annotated. Rules and regulations under the act are in full text. A table of registered public utility holding company systems, and a table of cases decided by the commission are included.

> A supplemental volume A, dated 1951, summarizes the work of the Securities and Exchange Commission, and related court action, since the original volume was issued. Monthly supplements are issued, with annual indices.

National Association of Railroad and Utilities Commissioners. PROCEEDINGS. Washington, D.C.: Annual.
> Papers presented at the annual meetings of the association, which consists of commissioners on both the federal and state level who head commissions regulating public utilities. On the federal level, the Interstate Commerce Commission, the Federal Communications Commission, the Federal Power Commission, the Securities and Exchange Commission, and the Civil Aeronautics Board are represented.

National Association of Securities Dealers, Inc. A GUIDE TO SUPERVISION PROCEDURES. Washington, D.C.: May, 1965. 89 p.
> A guide to establishment and maintenance of written supervision procedures and record-keeping required under revised sections 15, 21, 27, and other sections, of Article III of the NASD's Rules of Fair Practice.

NASD NEWS. Washington, D.C.: National Association of Securities Dealers, Inc. 1940- . Irregular.
>A four-page letter containing news about the association and its activities. Emphasis is generally on current developments in the field of securities regulation.

National Association of Securities Dealers, Inc. REPORTS. Washington, D.C.: Annual.
>Summarize work of the association for the past year. Survey developments in the securities field. List committees and members. Financial statement for the year, and membership statistics, are included.

New York Stock Exchange. COMPANY MANUAL. New York. Current.
>Codifies policies, requirements, procedures and practices of the New York Stock Exchange relating to listed companies and their securities. Also contains specific requirements which may be applicable with respect to the Securities and Exchange Commission.

Prentice-Hall, Inc. SECURITIES REGULATION. Englewood Cliffs, New Jersey: 2 vols. Looseleaf.
>Contains the texts of the acts administered by the Securities and Exchange Commission, the regulations thereunder, and current material.

TRADE ASSOCIATION

The trade association for the securities dealers is the National Association of Securities Dealers, 888-17th Street, N.W., Washington, D.C. It was founded in 1939, has 4800 members, a staff of 160, and is divided into 13 regional divisions.

Members are investment brokers and dealers, authorized to conduct transactions of the investment banking and securities business under the federal and state laws.

It was organized under federal law to enable its members to enforce standards of ethical conduct, by self regulation, in the over-the-counter securities market.

APPENDIX

APPENDIX

LEGAL BIBLIOGRAPHIES

The following bibliographies, while not devoted exclusively to titles relating to government control of business, do include lists covering and related to this subject matter.

BUSINESS LAW ARTICLES. Chicago: Commerce Clearing House, Inc., 1965- . Looseleaf. Monthly.
> Describes new articles, notes, and comments published in business and professional journals. The papers of published proceedings of business institutes and professional meetings are also included.
> Among the topics covered are: Administrative Law; Foreign Business-Common Market; Securities; Trade Regulation--Antitrust; and Utilities--Transportation--Natural Resources.

CURRENT PUBLICATIONS IN LEGAL AND RELATED FIELDS. South Hackensack, N.J.: Fred B. Rothman. Vol. 1-   , 1953-   . Monthly except July and September.
> A non-profit service, endorsed by the American Association of Law Libraries. Coverage of new publications is world-wide and includes all books and monographs in the English language. One part lists all new supplements and continuations. Beginning with volume 13, No. 1 (April, 1965) descriptive annotations are included, wherever possible. Although entries are arranged by author, this service can be used to update Law Books in Print.

Harvard Law School Library. ANNUAL LEGAL BIBLIOGRAPHY, A SELECTED LIST OF BOOKS AND ARTICLES RECEIVED BY THE HARVARD LAW SCHOOL LIBRARY. Vaclav Mostecky, ed. Cambridge: Supplemented by a monthly Current Legal Bibliography.

The Annuals constitute a ready reference tool for locating representative materials on many legal subjects including government
controls. The monthly supplements provide an up-to-date list of
new books and articles.

INDEX TO LEGAL PERIODICALS. New York: H.W. Wilson Co. in cooperation with The American Association of Law Libraries. Issued monthly except
September. Cumulated in bound volumes at intervals.
   A comprehensive index of articles, comments, and notes appearing
   in law school reviews and journals. Also includes a list of ab-
   breviations used for the periodicals indexed, a table of cases,
   and a book review index.

Jacobstein, J. Myron and Pimsleur, Meira G., eds. and comp. LAW BOOKS
IN PRINT. Consolidated ed. Dobbs Ferry, N.Y.: Glanville Publishers,
1965. 2 vols. (Cumulative supplements to be issued annually).
   Includes books in print as of December, 1964. Entries are arranged
   by author, and may also be found by reference to one or more
   subjects, subdivided geographically. There is also a listing wher-
   ever appropriate, under joint author, editor, translator, compiler,
   series, and title. Another feature is a section devoted to publishers and distributors of law books, Publication does not include statutes, law reports, digest, citators, loose-leaf services,
   government publications, periodicals, or annuals.

Mersky, Roy M. and Jacobstein, J. Myron, ed. and comp. INDEX TO
PERIODICAL ARTICLES RELATED TO LAW. Stanford, California: Stanford
University Law Library. Quarterly, with cumulative issue at the end of each
year.
   Lists articles related to law from scholarly journals and magazines
   throughout the world. Articles covered by the Index to Legal
   Periodicals are excluded.

Price, Miles O. and Bitner, Harry. EFFECTIVE LEGAL RESEARCH. New
York: Prentice-Hall, 1953. 633 p.
   Although this book is designed primarily to assist and instruct the
   law student and the attorney in their problems of legal research,
   it is included here because of the valuable bibliographic materials
   it contains. Of interest to those concerned with government regulation is a comprehensive list of law reports on special subjects
   such as railroads, trade marks, bankruptcy, antitrust, and labor.
   In addition, the appendix sets forth all federal administrative decision reports.

Price, Miles O. and Bitner, Harry. EFFECTIVE LEGAL RESEARCH. Student
rev. ed. Boston: Little, Brown, 1962. 496 p.
   Written for law students. Covers same ground as parent book
   (see preceding entry) but in a more simplified form. Bibliographical
   appendices have been omitted.

GENERAL SOURCES

The primary source materials for federal laws affecting business are found in the acts passed by Congress. They appear first as separate sheets or pamphlets called slip laws. These are republished in volumes of the United States Statutes at Large, which present the laws passed by each session of Congress chronologically. Most of the Public Laws are then codified into the United States Code, a publication of the United States Government, and into the United States Code Annotated, published by the West Publishing Company in the same text but with extensive annotations citing cases and other materials under the various sections. Another edition of the Code is the Federal Code Annotated published by Bobbs-Merrill Co.

For regulations issued by the various agencies, the primary source is the Federal Register, a daily publication of the federal government, which sets out the President's Executive Orders and Proclamations, and the regulations promulgated or proposed by the administrative agencies and federal departments. These are later codified into the Code of Federal Regulations.

For information relating to the organizational structure of the federal government, the best source is the United States Government Organization Manual, published in the legislative, judicial, and executive branches, and supplies information in the legislative, judicial, and executive branches, and supplies information about quasi-official agencies, and selected international organizations. Charts of the more complex agencies and appendices listing abolished or transferred agencies are also included. Representative publications of departments and agencies of the federal government are listed in the appendix.

Andriot, John L. U.S. GOVERNMENT SERIALS & PERIODICALS. McLean, Virginia: Documents Index, 1964. 2 vols.
> Volume 1 covers current serials and periodicals of the various government agencies located in the Washington, D.C. area. Volume 2 covers the same agencies, setting out the releases and other ephemeral material issued by each.
>
> The judicial and legislative branches of the government are also covered. In the section covering Congress, material issued by the various committees is listed.
>
> In general the bibliographical information is set out in box form. There is also a considerable amount of descriptive material.

CODE OF FEDERAL REGULATIONS. Washington, D.C.: Government Printing Office. Cumulative supplements issued annually except Title 46, parts 146-149, which is issued semiannually.
> Contains codification of documents previously appearing in Federal Register of general applicability and future effect; with ancillaires and index.

CONGRESS AND THE NATION 1945-1964. Washington, D.C.: Congressional Quarterly Service, 1965. 2014 p.
> A review of government and politics in the postwar years. Covers among other things the following: Politics and National Issues; Economic Policy; Federal-State Relations; Government--Congress, Executive, Courts; Lobbies; and Investigations.
>
> A Directory of Persons and Events (Part II) includes: sections on Congresses and Their Leaders; Committee Chairmen; Presidents and

Their Cabinets; Major Supreme Court Cases; and Regulatory Agency
Membership for the postwar period.

Council of State Governments. THE BOOK OF THE STATES. Chicago:
Biennial.

A source of information on the structures, working methods, financing and functional activities of the state governments. It deals
with their legislative, executive and judicial branches, their intergovernmental relations, and the major areas of public service
performed by them. Two pamphlet supplements give comprehensive
listings of administrative officials, classified by functions; and of
state elective officials and the legislatures.

ECONOMIC REPORT OF THE PRESIDENT. Washington, D.C.: Government
Printing Office. Annual.

Reports are prepared and transmitted to Congress pursuant to the
requirement of Section 3(a) of the Employment Act of 1946. The
Council of Economic Advisers assists and advises the President in
the preparation of these reports, and members of the Cabinet and
heads of independent agencies assist the council.

The reports survey the economic situation of the country, and
make recommendations for the coming year.

FEDERAL CODE ANNOTATED. Indianapolis: Bobbs-Merrill, 1937- . 38
vols. Supplements plus regular monthly service, entitled Current Public Laws
and Administrative Material.

Organized by United States Code Titles. Sets out language of
the law as carried in the Statutes at Large. When interpretations
are necessary, bracketed words or references are inserted or ex-
planatory notes written. History of each section is shown, together
with amendment notes tracing the development of the law.

FEDERAL HEARING EXAMINERS' SEMINAR. Proceedings of the Federal Hearing Examiners' First Annual Seminar, September 23-25, 1963 at Washington,
D.C. Washington, D.C.: Ward & Paul, 1963.

MOODY'S INDUSTRIAL MANUAL. New York: Moody's Investors Service.
Annual with semi-weekly supplements.

A comprehensive source of information on industrial corporations
and enterprises. A Capital Structure Table follows the titles of
the more important companies and gives highlights of outstanding
bond and stock issues with Moody's Bond Ratings. Following the
Table are details of the history, background, mergers and acquisitions, subsidiaries, business and products, principal plants and
properties. Names and titles of officers and directors are shown
as well as the general counsel, auditors, date of the annual meeting, latest number of stockholders and employees, and the address
of the corporation. Financial statements are shown for the more
important companies.

Office of the Federal Register, National Archives and Records Service, General
Services Administration. FEDERAL REGISTER. Washington, D.C.: Government Printing Office. 1936- , Vol. 1- , Daily, Tuesday through Saturday
(no publication on Sundays, Mondays, or on the day after an official federal
holiday.)

The regulatory material appearing in the Federal Register is keyed to the Code of Federal Regulations.

Office of the Federal Register. National Archives and Records Service. General Services Administration. UNITED STATES GOVERNMENT ORGANIZATION MANUAL. Washington, D.C.: Government Printing Office. Revised annually.

The official organization handbook of the federal government. Describes the agencies in the judicial, legislative, and executive branches. Supplemental information following these sections includes: (1) brief descriptions of quasi-official agencies and selected international organizations; (2) charts of the more complex agencies; (3) a listing of executive agencies and functions of the federal government which have been abolished, transferred, or terminated (Appendix A); (4) a description of representative publications of departments and agencies of the federal government (Appendix B); and (5) an alphabetical list of assignments of departments and agencies of the federal government in the Code of Federal Regulations (Appendix C).

Public Affairs Information Service, Inc. BULLETIN OF THE PUBLIC AFFAIRS INFORMATION SERVICE. New York: weekly except in August when issued fortnightly. Cumulated five times a year, and annually.

The PAIS lists by subject current books, pamphlets, periodical articles, government documents, and other useful library material in the fields of economics and public affairs. Includes publications of all kinds printed in English. Emphasis is on factual and statistical information.

Schmeckebier, Laurence F. and Eastin, Roy B. GOVERNMENT PUBLICATIONS AND THEIR USE. Rev. ed. Washington, D.C.: Brookings Institution, 1961. 476 p.

Describes the basic guides to government publications; indicates the uses and limitations of available indexes, catalogs, and bibliographies; explains the systems of numbering and methods of titling; calls attention to certain outstanding compilations, or series of publications; and indicates how the publications may be obtained.

A classic reference work.

STANDARD & POOR's CORPORATION RECORDS. New York: Standard & Poor's Corporation. 7 vols. Looseleaf.

Covers capitalization, corporate background, subsidiaries, officers and directors, bond descriptions, stock data and earnings, and finances for the many corporations listed. Kept up to date by the Daily News Section which has a weekly cumulative index and a supplementary daily cumulative index. Main volumes are revised when annual reports are received or essential data released.

UNITED STATES CODE. United States Code, Containing the general and permanent laws of the United States, in force on January 3, 1965, (1964 ed.) Washington, D.C.: Government Printing Office, 1965.

UNITED STATES CODE ANNOTATED. St. Paul, Minn.: West Publishing Co.
Format and coverage same as entry above, but with the addition
of extensive annotations and other materials.

U.S. CODE CONGRESSIONAL AND ADMINISTRATIVE NEWS. St. Paul:
West, 1942- . Semimonthly pamphlets during sessions of Congress, and
monthly pamphlets when Congress is not in session. Later cumulated in bound
volumes.
Public laws enacted by Congress are reported promptly in the
advance sheets (later cumulated in bound volumes) which also
contain official committee reports explaining the background,
history, and purpose of the legislation. Current federal tax regulations, also appearing in these pamphlets, are integrated into
special bound volumes of Federal Tax Regulations.

U.S. Congress. Joint Economic Committee. ECONOMIC INDICATORS.
Washington, D.C.: Government Printing Office. Monthly.
Prepared for the above committee by the President's Council of
Economic Advisers. Contains charts and statistics on factors
affecting the nation's economy, including production and business
activity, prices, and business sales and inventories.

A supplement contains selected charts and historical tables, along
with a description of the derivation, limitations, and uses of each
indicator.

U.S. Congress. House. Antitrust Subcommittee (Subcommittee No. 5) of the
Committee on the Judiciary. INDEX OF ANTITRUST SUBCOMMITTEE PUBLI-
CATIONS. 81st Congress (January 1949) through 89th Congress, 1st session
(December 1965). 89th Cong. Committee print. Washington, D.C.: Gov-
ernment Printing Office, 1966. 72 p.

U.S. Congress. House. Select Committee on Small Business. LIST OF PUB-
LICATIONS. HEARINGS, REPORTS, STAFF STUDIES, AND DOCUMENTS.
77th-88th Congresses (1941-63). (88th Cong.) Committee Print. November,
1963. Washington, D.C.: Government Printing Office, 1963. 23 p.
Completely indexed alphabetically and also by Congresses.

U.S. Congress. Senate. Special Committee to Study Problems of American
Small Business. FUTURE OF INDEPENDENT BUSINESS. Progress report of
the chairman of the above committee. (79th Cong., 2nd Sess.) Committee
Print No. 16. January 2, 1947. Washington, D.C.: Government Printing
Office, 1947. 379 p.
Includes lists of small business committee publications during 77th,
78th and 79th Congresses.

U.S. Congress. Senate. Committee on Government Operations. SELECT
LIST OF PUBLICATIONS ISSUED BY SENATE AND HOUSE COMMITTEES.
Committee Prints, Staff Studies, Reports, and Documents; 80th to 86th Congresses (1947-60 inclusive). (87th Cong., 1st Sess.) Committee Print. December 15, 1961. Washington, D.C.: Government Printing Office, 1961.
427 p.

A list of Senate and House reports, documents, committee prints, and staff studies printed, released, or prepared for committee use, on subjects relating to governmental operations, or legislative proposals, considered to be of general interest. Compiled for the use of committees and members of Congress.

U.S. Department of Commerce. UNITED STATES DEPARTMENT OF COMMERCE PUBLICATIONS. Washington, D.C.: Government Printing Office. Basic volume covers publications issued from 1790 to October 1950. 1951-52 supplement covers publications issued from October 1950 through December 1952. Supplements from 1953 are annual.
A catalog and index of selected publications of the Department and its predecessor agencies. Cumulates issues of the Business Service Checklist, a weekly list of Department publications. Section I lists depository libraries for U.S. Government publications. Section II is a list of publications arranged by bureau and office. Section III is a subject index.

U.S. Department of Commerce. Bureau of the Census. ANNUAL SURVEY OF MANUFACTURES. Washington, D.C.: (A series of individual reports are published in advance of bound volumes).

U.S. Department of Commerce. Bureau of the Census. BUSINESS CYCLE DEVELOPMENTS. Washington, D.C.: Government Printing Office. Monthly. Brings together many of the available economic indicators for analysis and interpretation by experts in business cycle analysis. About 70 principal indicators and over 300 components are used for the different measures shown.

U.S. Department of Commerce. Bureau of the Census. CURRENT INDUSTRIAL REPORTS (formerly Facts for Industry). Washington, D.C.: Monthly and quarterly issues.
About 100 series on the output of many important manufactured products and other aspects of industry.

U.S. Department of Commerce. Bureau of the Census. 1958 CENSUS OF MANUFACTURES. Washington, D.C.: Government Printing Office, 1961. Results of the 1958 Census of Manufactures are published in three volumes: Volume I, Summary Statistics, shows comparative statistics for industries, states, and principal metropolitan areas for the more important measures of the activity of manufacturing establishments--employment, payrolls, inventories, capital expenditures, value added by manufacture, important materials consumed, etc.; Volume II, Industry Statistics, is a consolidation of reports for the 80 groups of industries, and shows detailed information on individual industries and products; Volume III, Area Statistics, shows for each state, and its important metropolitan areas and counties, general statistics (number of establishments, number of employees, payrolls, value added by manufacture, and capital expenditures) for each of the industries or industry groups of consequence in that State, or in its smaller areas.

U.S. Department of Commerce. Bureau of the Census. STATISTICAL ABSTRACT OF THE UNITED STATES. Washington, D.C.: Government Printing Office. Annual.

Statistics on the industrial, social, political, and economic organization of the United States. Compiled from both governmental and non-governmental sources.

U.S. Department of Commerce. Office of Business Economics. SURVEY OF CURRENT BUSINESS. Washington, D.C.: Government Printing Office. Monthly, with four page weekly statistical supplement.

U.S. Federal Trade Commission. PROFIT RATES OF MANUFACTURING CORPORATIONS. 1947-62. Washington, D.C.: 1963.
Tabulation of profit rates of 63 industry and size groups of manufacturing corporations compiled from past issues of Quarterly Financial Report for Manufacturing Corporations.

U.S. Federal Trade Commission. RATES OF RETURN FOR IDENTICAL COMPANIES IN SELECTED MANUFACTURING INDUSTRIES, 1953-1962.
Part A - Rates of Return on Stockholders' Investment for 374 Identical Companies in 23 Selected Manufacturing Industries, 1953-1962. Part B - Rates of Return of the 12 Largest Companies in 39 Industries, 1961 and 1962.

UNITED STATES GOVERNMENT PUBLICATIONS: MONTHLY CATALOG. Washington, D.C.: Government Printing Office. Monthly.
An excellent source for locating the materials printed by the Government Printing Office. Covers publications of all federal administrative agencies, and departments of the government. Congressional documents, hearings, and reports are listed. An invaluable tool for those doing research in government regulation of business. In 1953, all issues between January, 1941 and December, 1950 were indexed in a volume entitled "A Decennial Cumulative Index 1941-1950."

U.S. House of Representatives Library. INDEX TO CONGRESSIONAL COMMITTEE HEARINGS IN THE LIBRARY OF THE UNITED STATES HOUSE OF REPRESENTATIVES PRIOR TO JANUARY 1, 1951. Compiled by Russell Saville, Librarian, under the Direction of Lyle O. Snader, Clerk of the House of Representatives. Washington, D.C.: Government Printing Office, 1954. 485 p.

U.S. House of Representatives Library. SUPPLEMENTAL INDEX TO CONGRESSIONAL COMMITTEE HEARINGS, JANUARY 3, 1949, TO JANUARY 3, 1955--81st, 82nd, AND 83rd CONGRESSES IN THE LIBRARY OF THE UNITED STATES HOUSE OF REPRESENTATIVES. Compiled by John A. Cooper, Librarian under the direction of Ralph R. Roberts, Clerk of the House of Representatives. Washington, D.C.: Government Printing Office, 1956. 127 p.

U.S. Superintendent of Documents. NUMERICAL LISTS AND SCHEDULE OF VOLUMES OF THE REPORTS AND DOCUMENTS (for sessions of Congress). Washington, D.C.
Published at the end of each session of Congress. Useful for determining the subject matter of Senate and House reports and documents, when only report number or document number and the particular Congress are given.

U.S. Superintendent of Documents. PRICE LIST 10. LAWS - RULES AND REGULATIONS. Washington, D.C.: Government Printing Office.

U.S. Superintendent of Documents. PRICE LIST 62. COMMERCE--BUSINESS, PATENTS, TRADEMARKS AND FOREIGN TRADE. Washington, D.C.: Government Printing Office.
> Issued by the Superintendent of Documents. Lists all publications available as of the date of the pamphlet and certain out-of-print items.

U.S. Senate Library. INDEX OF CONGRESSIONAL COMMITTEE HEARINGS (NOT CONFIDENTIAL IN CHARACTER) PRIOR TO JANUARY 3, 1935 IN THE UNITED STATES SENATE LIBRARY. Washington, D.C.: Government Printing Office, 1935. 1056 p.

U.S. Senate Library. CUMULATIVE INDEX OF CONGRESSIONAL COMMITTEE HEARINGS (NOT CONFIDENTIAL IN CHARACTER) FROM 74TH CONGRESS (JANUARY 3, 1935) THROUGH 85TH CONGRESS (JANUARY 3, 1959) IN THE UNITED STATES SENATE LIBRARY. Washington, D.C.: Government Printing Office, 1959. 823 p.

U.S. Senate Library. QUADRENNIAL SUPPLEMENT TO CUMULATIVE INDEX OF CONGRESSIONAL COMMITTEE HEARINGS (NOT CONFIDENTIAL IN CHARACTER) FROM 86TH CONGRESS (JANUARY 7, 1959) THROUGH 87TH CONGRESS (JANUARY 3, 1963) TOGETHER WITH SELECTED COMMITTEE PRINTS. Washington, D.C.: Government Printing Office, 1963. 762 p.
> The above hearings are indexed by subject, Senate committees, House committees, joint, select and special committees and by bill number. A very useful tool when researching the legislative history of a bill or law.

The Quadrennial Supplement contains an appendix which lists Congressional Committee Prints by title and by committee.

UNITED STATES STATUTES AT LARGE. (1789-1873) Boston: Charles C. Little and James Brown, Vols. 1-17.

UNITED STATES STATUTES AT LARGE (1874 to date). Washington, D.C.: Government Printing Office, Vols. 18-
> Contain public laws, reorganization plans, private laws, concurrent resolutions, proclamations, and proposed amendments to the Constitution.

ECONOMIC PERIODICALS

Excellent articles pertaining to government regulation of business, particularly the antitrust aspects, often appear in economic periodicals. A selective list of these periodicals follows:

THE AMERICAN ECONOMIC REVIEW. Evanston, Ill: Northwestern University, American Economic Association. Published in March, May, June, September and December.
> May issue covers proceedings of the American Economic Association. Extensive book reviews.

AMERICAN JOURNAL OF ECONOMICS AND SOCIOLOGY. New York: American Journal of Economics and Sociology, Inc. Quarterly.

CARTEL. London: International Cooperative Alliance. Quarterly.
   Review of monopoly developments and consumer protection.

ECONOMIC JOURNAL. London: Royal Economic Society. Quarterly.

JOURNAL OF ECONOMIC ABSTRACTS. Chicago. Vol. 1-   , 1962-
Quarterly.
   An international journal published cooperatively by the contributing
   journals under the auspices of The American Economic Association.
   Designed to acquaint economists throughout the world with the methods
   and conclusions currently being reported in the general economic periodicals. Contains abstracts of articles submitted by contributing journals, and of articles originally printed in those journals.

JOURNAL OF LAW & ECONOMICS. Chicago: University of Chicago Law
School. Annual.
   Contains articles dealing with the economic aspects of the law.

JOURNAL OF POLITICAL ECONOMY. Chicago: University of Chicago
Press. Bimonthly.

QUARTERLY JOURNAL OF ECONOMICS. Cambridge: Harvard University
Press. Quarterly.

QUARTERLY REVIEW OF ECONOMICS AND BUSINESS. Champaign, Ill.:
Bureau of Economic and Business Research. Quarterly.

THE REVIEW OF ECONOMICS AND STATISTICS. Cambridge: Harvard University Press. Department of Economics. Quarterly.

AUTHOR INDEX

AUTHOR INDEX

A

Abbot, Lawrence 45
ACA News 131
Adams, George P., Jr. 45
Adams, Walter 45
Adelman, Morris 45
Administrative Conference of the U.S. 23, 32, 128, 165
Administrative Law Review 25
Air Transport Association of America 40
Air Transportation 39
Allen, C. L. 46
Allen, Frederick L. 46
American Aviation 39
American Bar Association, Section of Antitrust Law 44, 46, 47, 121
American Bar Association, Section of Public Utility Law 37, 130, 146, 170
American Economic Review 45, 201
American Enterprise Institute for Public Policy Research 47
American Fair Trade Council 47
American Gas Association 155
American Gas Association Rate Committee 151
American Journal of Economics and Sociology 201
American Management Association 47
American Marketing Association 120
Anderson, Ronald A. 47
Anderson, Thomas J. 47

Andrews, P. W. S. 48
Andriot, John L. 195
Anshen, Melvin 48
Antitrust and Trade Regulation Newsletter 121
Antitrust and Trade Regulation Report 44, 121
Antitrust Bulletin 121
Antitrust News Service 122
Arthur Anderson & Co. 147
Association of Interstate Commerce Commission Practitioners 170, 172, 173
Association of the Bar of the City of New York 120
Association of the Bar of the City of New York. Special Committee on Antitrust Laws and Foreign Trade 48
Attorney General of the United States 95, 96, 119
Attorney General's National Committee to Study the Antitrust Laws 44, 96
Auerbach, Carl A. 159
Austern, H. T. 48
Austin, Cyrus 44, 48
Aviation Daily, including international Aviation 39
Aviation Law Reporter (CCH) 37
Aviation Week & Space Technology 39

B

BNA's Antitrust and Trade Regulation Report 121

Backman, Jules 48, 49, 57
Bain, Joe S. 49
Baldwin, William L. 49
Bar Association of the District of
  Columbia 16
Barger, Harold 49
Barnard, Robert C. 49
Bary, Constantine W. 137
Bauer, John 137
Baum, Daniel J. 49, 177
Bennett, H. Arnold 16, 159
Bergh, Louis O. 49
Berle, Adolf A. 50
Bernstein, Marver H. 16, 50
Bigham, Truman C. 159
Billyou, de Forest 29
Bitner, Harry 194
Blachly, Frederick 17
Blaisdell, Ruth F. 37, 170
Bliss, James J. 50
Blue Sky Reporter (CCH) 189
Bluestone, David W. 169
Blum, Eleanor 130
Boarman, Patrick M. 50
Bock, Betty 50, 51
Bonbright, James C. 138
Booz, Allen & Hamilton 170
Bosland, Chelcie C. 178
Boulding, Kenneth E. 89
Bowie, Robert R. 51
Boyer, William W. 17
Bradley, Joseph F. 178
Brady, Gerald P. 44, 90
Brems, Hans 51
Brewster, Kingman 51
Briggs, Edwin W. 52
Bronfen, George B. 84
Brown's Directory of American Gas
  Companies 153
Bryan, Leslie A. 32
Buckley, Julian G. 181
Bulletin, American Bar Association,
  Section of Antitrust Law 121
Bureau of National Affairs, Inc. 52, 121
Burn, Duncan L. 52
Burns, Joseph W. 52, 57
Burtchett, Floyd F. 178
Burton, Jr., John F. 54
Business Law Articles (CCH) 193
Byse, Clark 19

C

Callman, Rudolf 44, 52
Campbell, Alan 52
Carriers Reporter, Federal (CCH) 171
Cartel 202
Carter, William A. 72
Cassady, Ralph 52
Cassady, Ralph, Fr. 53
Cassady, Ralph, III 53
Caves, Richard E. 29
Caywood, Russell E. 138
Chamber of Commerce of the United
  States 53
Chamberlin, Edward 45
Chamberlin, Edward H. 53, 54
Cheney, Frances 121
Cherington, Paul W. 29
Chicago Bar Association, Special Sub-
  committee on Illinois Antitrust Laws 54
Childs, John F. 178
Choka, Allen D. 54, 178
Christie, Milton 180
Civil Aeronautics Board 32-35
Clabault, James M. 54
Clark, Dodge & Co. 147
Clark, John M. 54
Clemens, Eli W. 125, 138
Cleveland, Frederick W., Jr. 92
Cochran, C. L. 54
Code of Federal Regulations 195
Cohan, Avery B. 178
Commerce Clearing House, Inc. 55
  Aviation Law Reporter 37
  Blue Sky Reporter 189
  Business Law Articles 193
  Federal Carriers Reporter 171
  Federal Securities Law Reporter 189
  State Motor Carrier Guide 171
  Trade Regulation Reporter 122
  Utilities Service 147
Commission on Organization of the
  Executive Branch of the Government
  23
Company Manual 190
Conant, Michael 55, 159
Congressional Quarterly Service 195
Conyngton, Thomas 49
Cook, F. H. 55
Cook, Franklin H. 138
Cook, Paul W. 55
Cooke, Gilbert W. 178, 179
Cookenboo, Leslie 55

Cooper, Frank 17, 18
Cormier, Frank 179
Cotter, Cornelius P. 56
Council of Economic Advisers 196, 198
Council of State Governments 196
Cowett, Edward M. 181
Cramton, Roger C. 165
Cravath, Swaine and Moore 56
Cross, James 56
Crowley, Joseph R. 56
Current Business Studies 56

D

Daggett, Stuart 160
Davidson, Ralph K. 57, 138
Davidson, Sidney 138
Davies, R. E. G. 30
Davis, J. P. 57
Davis, Kenneth C. 18
Davison, James F. 19
DeBedts, Ralph F. 179
DeChazeau, Melvin G. 56, 57
Devitt, Edward J. 74
Dewey, Donald 57
Dewhurst and Associates, J. Frederic 57
Dewing, Arthur Stone 179
Dietz, Arthur T. 58
Diplock, Sir Kenneth 58
Directory of Electric Utilities 147
Dirlam, Joel B. 58, 99
Dixon, Brian 58
Donaldson, Elvin F. 179
Dougall, Herbert E. 180
Drayton, Clarence I., Jr. 58
Duff, George 180
Dunton, Chester 189

E

Eastin, Roy B. 197
Eaton, Frederick M. 56
Economic Indicators 198
Economic Journal 202
Economic Report of the President 196
Edelman, Murray 126
Edison Electric Institute 148, 150

Edwards, Corwin D. 56, 59
Eiteman, Wilford J. 59
Electrical World 149
Elkouri, Frank 60
Ellsworth, Catherine C. 71
Emery, Edwin 126
Emery, Walter B. 126

F

Fainsod, Merle 60
Fair, Marvin L. 160, 164
Falck, Edward 151
Federal Aviation Agency 34
Federal Bar Association, Antitrust Committee 60
Federal Bar Association of New York, New Jersey and Connecticut, Trade Regulation Committee 60
Federal Code Annotated 196
Federal Communications Bar Journal 131
Federal Communications Commission 125-133
Federal Hearing Examiners Seminar 196
Federal Power Commission 137 - 156
Federal Power Commission Gas Docket Service 154
Federal Trade Commission 95 - 96, 99, 120, 200
Federal Register 196
Federal Utility Regulation Annotated 148, 189
Feldman, George J. 61
Fisher, Burton R. 61
Fisher, W. E. 61
Fishman, Betty G. 61
Fishman, Leo 61
Fixel, Rowland W. 30
Fleming, Harold 61
Flood, Kenneth U. 160
Flynn, John J. 62
Forkosch, Morris D. 19, 62
Foster, J. Rhoads 139
Foulke, Roy A. 62
Frederick, John G. 160
Frederick, John H. 30
Friday, Frank A. 48
Friendly, Henry J. 19
Fuchs, Victor R. 62

Fugate, Wilbur L. 62
Fulda, Carl H. 62, 161
Fuller, Burton 161
Fuller, J. G. 63

G

Gable, Richard W. 70
Galbraith, John K. 63
Galgay, John J. 57
Garfield, Paul J. 126, 139
Garwood, John D. 139
Gas Docket Service 154
Gellhorn, Walter 19
Giddens, Paul H. 63
Glaeser, Martin G. 139
Glover, John D. 63
Goldberg, Milton S. 63
Goldstein, Ernest E. 64
Gort, Michael 64
Goss, Bert C. 64
Gray, Horace M. 45
Greenberg, Joshua F. 65
Greenleaf, William 64
Grimshaw, Austin 64
Grossman, William Leonard 161
Grundstein, Nathan D. 19
Guandolo, John 30, 64, 161, 164
Guthmann, Harry G. 180

H

Hale, George 64
Hale, Rosemary D. 64
Hamilton, Daniel C. 65
Hamilton, Walter 65
Handler, Milton 44, 65
Hardwicke, Robert E. 65
Harms, John 65
Harvard Law School Library 193
Hauser, Gustave M. 65
Hauser, Rita E. 65
Hawkins Index-Digest-Analysis to
   Civil Aeronautics Board Reports 37
Hawkins Index-Digest-Interstate Com-
   merce Commission 171
Hayes, James V. 56
Hazard, John W. 180
Head, Sydney W. 126
Heady, Ferrel 19

Healy, Kent T. 161
Hector, Louis J. 34
Herling, John 66
Hicks, Clifford M. 178
Hidy, Muriel E. 66
Hidy, Ralph W. 66
Hoffman, M. A. 66
Hollander, Stanley C. 120
Honig, Frederick 66
Hoover Commission 23
Howard, Marshall C. 66
Hunt, Florine E. 148
Hurst, James W. 66

I

I.C.C. Practioners Journal 172
Index to Legal Periodicals 194
International Air Transport Association
   40
International Bar Association 67
Interstate Commerce Commission
   159-173
Isaacs, Asher 67
Israels, Carlos L. 180

J

Jackson, Elmo L. 67
Jacobstein, J. Myron 194
Jaffe, Louis L. 19, 20
James, C. M. 61
Jennings, Amy 120
Jennings, Richard W. 180
Johnson, Arthur M. 67, 68
Jones, William K. 32, 128, 165
Joskow, Jules 68
Journal of Air Law and Commerce 39
Journal of Broadcasting 131
Journal of Economic Abstracts 45,
   202
Journal of Law & Economics 202
Journal of Political Economy 45, 202
Judicial Conference of the United
   States 68
Jurow, E. F. 80

K

Kahn, Alfred E. 57, 58
Kahn, Fritz R. 162
Kamerman, Michael 68
Kaplan, A. D. H. 68
Kaysen, Carl 69
Kefauver, Estes 69
Keyes, Lucile Sheppard 30
Kintner, Earl W. 44, 69
Kirsch, William 69
Kittelle, Sumner S. 70
Knauth, Oswald W. 56, 69
Knorst, William J. 162
Kolb, Burton A. 140
Kolko, Gabriel 162
Koontz, Harold 70
Kreps, T. 70, 99
Krislov, Samuel 70
Kronstein, Heinrich D. 70
Kulp, Victor H. 151

L

Labor Research Association 70
Lamb, George P. 70
Land Economics 149
Landau, Henry 71
Landis Report 25
Landon, Charles E. 162
Lane, Robert E. 71
Lanzillotti, Robert F. 71
Latham, Earl 71
Laurent, Lawrence 127
Learned, Edmund P. 71
Leeston, Alfred M. 151
Leffler, George L. 180
Leftwich, Richard H. 71
Legal Periodicals, Index to 194
Levin, Harvey J. 72, 126
Library of Congress 121
Lilienthal, David E. 72
Lindahl, Martin L. 72
Lipstreu, Otis 140
Little, Arthur D., Inc. 72
Locklin, David Philip 31, 162
Loescher, Samuel M. 72
Loll, Leo M., Jr. 181
Loss, Louis 181
Lovejoy, Wallace F. 126, 139
Lyons, Barrow 72

M

Machlup, Fritz 73
MacIntyre, Malcolm A. 31, 72
Mansfield, Edwin 73
Marsh, Harold, Jr. 180
Martin, David D. 73
Marx, Daniel, Jr. 74
Mason, Edward S. 74
Massel, Mark S. 74
Mathes, William C. 74
Maurer, Herrymon 74
Mayall, Kenneth L. 74
McAllister, Harry E. 73
McCarthy, George D. 73, 181
McFarland, Carl 20
McGill University, Institute of Air
  and Space Law 38
McKeage, Everett C. 140
McKie, James W. 73, 151
McKinsey and Company, Inc. 38
McMahon, Robert S. 130
Means, Gardiner C. 75
Mergers & Acquisitions 122
Mersky, Roy M. 194
Metcalf, Kenneth N. 171
Meyer, John R. 163
Meyer, Walter E., Research Institute
  of Law 121
Meyers, Charles J. 152
Miller, John P. 75
Millstein, Ira M. 50
Minow, Newton N. 127
Monthly Catalog, U.S. Government
  Publications 200
Moody's Investors Services
  Industrials 196
  Public Utilities 148
  Transportation 171
Morton, Herbert C. 75
Morton, Newton 163
Mossman, Frank H. 163
Mostecky, Vaclav 193
Motor Carrier Guide, State (CCH)
  171
Mund, Vernon A. 44, 75
Mundheim, Robert H. 181
Murphy, Blakely M. 140
Musolf, Lloyd D. 20, 70

N

Nathanson, Nathaniel L.   20, 159
National Association of Attorneys,
   General Antitrust Committee 76
National Association of Broadcasters
   133
National Association of Manufacturers
   76
National Association of Railroad and
   Utilities Commissioners 38, 131,
   149, 150, 172, 173, 189
National Association of Securities
   Dealers, Inc. 187, 189, 190
NASD News 190
National Bureau Committee for
   Economic Research 76
National Industrial Conference Board
   76, 77, 78, 121
National Wholesale Druggists'
   Association 78
Neale, A. D. 78
Nelson, Dalmas H. 20
Nelson, James C. 163
Nelson, Ralph L. 79
Neuner, Edward J. 79, 151
New York State Bar Association,
   Section on Antitrust Law 44, 79,
   80, 122
New York Stock Exchange 190
New York Stock Exchange Guide
   (CCH) 189
New York University School of Law
   20
Newman, Philip C. 80
Nichols, Ellsworth 140
Nicholson, Joseph L. 31
Norbye, O. D. K. 80
Nordhaus, R. C. 80
Northwestern University School of Law
   80
Nutter, G. Warren 81

O

Oakes, Curtis M. 154
Oatman, Miriam E. 17
Oberdorfer, Conrad W. 81
Oil and Gas Journal 155
Oil and Gas Law 155
Oil and Gas Reporter 154

Operating Statistics of Large Railroads
   169
Oppenheim, S. Chesterfield 44, 81
Osborn, Richard C. 182
Organization for Economic Co-operation
   and Development 81, 82
Oxenfeldt, Alfred R. 82

P

Packer, Herbert L. 121
Palamountain, J. R., Jr. 82
Papandreou, Andreas G. 82
Parker, Reginald 21
Patman, Wright 44, 83
Peck, Merton J. 83
Pegrum, Dudley F. 44, 83, 140, 163
Pfahl, John K. 179
Pfiffner, John M. 21
Phillips, Almarin 83
Phillips, Charles F., Jr. 31, 84, 127,
   141, 163
Phillips, Joseph D. 84
Pike & Fischer 25, 131
Pimsleur, Meira G. 194
Pollzien, Gotz M. 84
Potter's Supreme Court News Service
   122
Power Survey, National 143
Practising Law Institute 182
Prentice-Hall, Inc.
   Securities Regulation 190
Presthus, Robert V. 21
Prettyman, E. Barrett 21
Price, Miles O. 194
Proctor, Charles W. 164
Proxmire, William 84
Public Affairs Information Service, Inc.
   197
Public Utility Fortnightly 131, 150
Public Utilities Reports, Inc. 148,
   149
PUR Executive Information Service
   149
Purdy, Harry 84

Q

Quarterly Journal of Economics 45, 202

Quarterly Review of Economics and Business 202

Quinn, Theodore K. 84

R

Radio & Television Weekly 132
Radio Regulation 131
Radio Television Daily 132
Railway Age Weekly 172
Rappaport, Louis H. 182
The Record of the Association of the Bar of the City of New York 44, 120
Redford, Emmette S. 21, 85
Reed, Stanley Foster 122
Restrictive Practices Commission 85
Review of Economics and Statistics 202
Richmond, Samuel B. 31, 85
Ritchie, Robert F. 183
Roberts, Merrill J. 159
Robinson, Gerald J. 183
Robinson, Joan 45, 85
Rocky Mountain Mineral Law Institute 154
Rodey, Bernard S. 139
Rohlfing, Charles C. 86
Rohrlich, Chester 183
Ross, R. 54
Rowe, Frederick M. 44, 85
Rozwenc, Edwin C. 86

S

Sage, George H. 86
Sarnoff, P. 183
Sawyer, Albert E. 86
Scharf, Charles A. 86
Schmeckebier, Laurence F. 197
Schmidt, Heinz 87
Schulman, John 22
Schwartz, Bernard 22
Schwartz, Louis B. 87
Securities and Exchange Commission 177-190

Securities Law Reporter, Federal (CCH) 189
Sharfman, Isaiah L. 164
Shipman, William D. 141
Shubik, Martin 87
Shultz, Birl E. 183
Simmons, Andre 87
Simon, William 87
Slesinger, Reuben E. 44, 67
Smith, Blackwell 56
Smith, G. Ralph 87
Smith, Hilda 87
Smith, Howard R. 87
Sobel, Robert 183
Society of Business Advisory Professions, Inc. 56
Southwestern Legal Foundation 87, 154
Sowards, Hugh L. 183
Speiser, Stuart M. 31
Squier, Albert P. 183
Standard & Poor's Corporation Records 197
State Bar of California. Committee on Continuing Education of the Bar 88
Stein, Eric 88
Steiner, George A. 88
Stelzer, Irwin M. 68, 88
Stickells, Austin T. 88
Stigler, George J. 45, 89
Stiles, Ned B. 177
Stocking, George W. 89
Stockton, John R. 152
Sullivan, Robert E. 152
Summer Institute on International and Comparative Law. University of Michigan 90, 127
Summers, W. L. 152
Surrey, Stanley S. 57
Sutton, Francis X. 90
Suviranta, Bruno 90
Swenson, Rinehart John 22
Swope, Gerard, Jr. 57

T

Taggart, Herbert F. 90
Task Force on Legal Services and Procedures 23
Tedrow, Joseph 164
Telecommunications Reports 132

Telephone Engineer & Management
132
Telephony 132
Television (report) 130
Television Age 132
Television Quarterly 132
Temporary National Economic Com-
mittee 97-98
Texas Law Review 155
Thomas, Eliot B. 184
Thompson, George C. 44, 90
Thorelli, Hans B. 91
Till, Irene 69
Timberlake, E. Compton 91
Toulmin, Harry A., Jr. 91
Trade associations
Air Transport Association of America
40
American Gas Association 155
Edison Electric Institute 150
International Air
Transport Association 40
National Association of Broadcasters
133
National Association of Securities
Dealers 190
Transportation Association of America
173
United States Independent Telephone
Association 133
Trade Regulation Reporter (CCH) 44,
122
Traffic World 39, 173
Transportation Association of America
173
Transportation Business Report 40, 173
Travis, William P. 91
Troxel, Emery 164
Tun, Thin 92
Turner, Donald F. 69
Tuthill, W. C. 139
Twentieth Century Fund 139

U

U.S. Advisory Committee on Cost
Justification 119
U.S. Attorney General 119
U.S. Aviation Reports 38

U.S. Code 197
U.S. Code Annotated 198
U.S. Independent Telephone Association
133
U.S. Code Congressional and Admini-
strative News 198
U.S. Commission on Organization of
the Executive Branch. Task Force
on Water Resources and Power 146
U.S. Congress 96
U.S. Congress Committee Hearings,
Index 200-201
U.S. Congress Reports and Documents.
Numerical List 200
U.S. Congress. Joint Economic
Committee 99, 198
U.S. Congress. House. Committee on
Government Operations 23
U.S. Congress. House. Committee
on Interstate and Foreign Commerce
129, 187, 188
U.S. Congress. House. Committee on
Interstate and Foreign Commerce.
Subcommittee on Legislative Over-
sight 24, 130, 187
U.S. Congress. House. Committee on
the Judiciary. Antitrust Subcommittee
(Subcommittee No. 5) 35, 105-108, 198
U.S. Congress. House. Committee on
the Judiciary. Subcommittee on the
Study of Monopoly Power 108
U.S. Congress. House. Select
Committee on Small Business 113-
116, 198
U.S. Congress. House. Select
Committee on Small Business. Special
Subcommittee 116
U.S. Congress. House. Select
Committee on Small Business.
Subcommittee No. 1 117
U.S. Congress. House. Select
Committee on Small Business.
Subcommittee No. 3 117
U.S. Congress. House. Select
Committee on Small Business.
Subcommittee No. 4 117
U.S. Congress. House. Select
Committee on Small Business.
Subcommittee No. 5 118

U.S. Congress. House. Select
Committee on Small Business.
Subcommittee No. 6 119
U.S. Congress. Senate. Committee
on Banking and Currency 188
U.S. Congress. Senate. Commerce
Committee 36
U.S. Congress. Senate. Committee
on Government Operations 198
U.S. Congress. Senate. Committee
on Interstate and Foreign Commerce
130, 169
U.S. Congress. Senate. Committee
on the Judiciary. Subcommittee on
Administrative Practice and Procedure
25
U.S. Congress. Senate. Committee
on the Judiciary. Subcommittee on
Antitrust and Monopoly 100–105
U.S. Congress. Senate. Committee
on the Judiciary. Subcommittee on
Patents, Trademarks, and Copyrights
108–109
U.S. Congress. Senate. Select
Committee on Small Business 36,
109–111
U.S. Congress. Senate. Special
Committee to Study Problems of
American Small Business 112–113,
198
U.S. Congress. Senate. Select
Committee on Small Business.
Subcommittee on Monopoly 36,
111–112
U.S. Department of Agriculture 119
U.S. Department of Commerce 120,
169, 199
U.S. Department of Commerce.
Bureau of Census 199
U.S. Department of Commerce.
Office of Business Economics 200
U.S. Department of Justice 25, 95–96
U.S. Government Organization
Manual 197
U.S. House of Representatives Library
200
U.S. Senate Library 201
U.S. Statutes at Large 201
Universities National Bureau Committee
for Economic Research 92
University of California Extension.
Department of Continuing Education

of the Bar 72
University of Chicago, Graduate School
of Business 67
University of Michigan Law School.
Summer Institute on International
and Comparative Law 90, 127
Utilities Service (CCH) 147
Utility Spotlight 150

V

Van Cise, Jerrold G. 44, 92
Vanderbilt, Arthur T. 20
Vennard, Edwin 141

W

Wade, H. W. R. 22
Waer, David K. 92
Wallace, Donald H. 92
Wallach, Kate 155
Walter E. Meyer Research Institute
of Law 121
Walton, Clarence C. 92
Warner, Harry P. 127
Warren, George 20
Washington Oil Memo 155
Watkins, Myron W. 89, 99
Weiler, Emanuel 93
Weiss, Ezra 184
Welch, Francis X. 141, 142, 151
Wernette, John P. 93
Westmeyer, Russell E. 164
Weston, John F. 93
Wheeler, John T. 82
White, William R. 93
Whitney, Simon N. 93
Wiesenberger, Arthur 184
Wilcox, Clair 44, 94, 127
Williams, C. Arthur, Jr. 94
Williams, Ernest W., Jr. 160, 164,
169
Williams, Howard R. 152
Wilson, G. Lloyd 32, 127, 165
Winard, A. I. 66
Winter, Elmer L. 184
Withey, Stephen B. 61
Wolbert, George S., Jr. 165
Wolf Management Engineering Co.
169

Wolfe, Thomas   32
Woll, Peter   22
World Airline Record   38
World Aviation Directory   39
Wright, David McCord   94
Wormuth, Francis D.   48

Y

Yamey, B. S.   94, 95
Young, Harold H.   184

Z

Zorn, Burton A.   61

INDUSTRY INDEX

INDUSTRY INDEX

A

A & P
  Study in price cost 45

Adams dairy companies (Missouri)
  Case study 102

Aluminum
  Case study 45
  Competition 83
  Small business problems 117

American (industries)
  Antitrust policies; American
  experience in twenty industries 93
  Concentration 102
  Diversification and integration 64
  Merger movements 79
  Structure 45

American Airlines, Incorporated
  Merger 108

American Telephone & Telegraph Co.
  Connection with Western Electric
  Co. 107

Asphalt roofing
  Administered prices 100

Automobile
  Administered prices 69, 100
  Case study 45
  Case study of General Motors
  Corporation 101

Aviation
  Structure and functions – antitrust

committee report 105
  Case study 45
  Competition 110
  Merger of Eastern Airlines and
  American Airlines 108
  Need for better definition of
  standards 19
  Regulation and competition 85

B

Banking
  Chain banking 113
  Concentration 111, 113
  Corporate and bank mergers 107
  Interlocks in corporate management
  107
  Mergers 83
  Mergers and concentration of
  facilities 106
  Structure 110

Batteries
  Distribution 118

Bituminous coal
  Price fixing 61

Bread
  Administered prices 69, 100

Broadcasting 125–133
  Regulation and joint ownership 72
  Television 105

Brokers 177–190

Brown Shoe Co.
  Merger 47

Burlington Industries, Inc.
  Merger 108

Business Advisory Council for the
  Department of Commerce 106

C

Cans
  Competition 73

Cartels (See also European Common
  Market, foreign commerce)
  Cartel law of the European Economic
  Community 66
  Cartels and trusts 87
  Cartels, combines and trusts,
  bibliography 121
  Common market cartel law 81
  Competition, cartels and their
  regulation 75
  Foreign legislation concerning
  monopoly and cartel practices 111
  International cartels: economic and
  political aspects 74
  International petroleum cartel 112
  International shipping cartels 74

Cement
  Basing-point pricing 72

Chemical
  Case study 45
  Competition 48

Chrysler Corp.
  Administered prices 100

Coal
  Price fixing 61

Columbia Broadcasting System
  Applicability of antitrust laws to
  television broadcast activities 56

Communications 125-133
  Economics of regulation 141

Construction
  Antitrust cases 112

Consumers
  and antitrust 68
  British 95

Case Study 45

Containers
  Case Study 45

D

Dairy
  Price discrimination 116
  Small business problems 116
  Study of incipient monopoly 102

Dealers in securities 177-190

Discount-house
  Operations 109

Dixon-Yates Contract 103
  Power policy 104

Drugs
  Administered prices 69, 100

E

E.I. du Pont de Nemours & Co.
  Antitrust in perspective 65
  Interlocks in corporate management
  107

Eastern Air Lines, Inc.
  Merger 108

Electric power
  Competition 54

Electric utilities 137-150
  Tax amortization 104

Electricity
  Price discrimination in selling 57

Electrical equipment
  Price-fixing charges 63, 66, 92

European Common Market (See also
  cartels, foreign commerce)
  American enterprise 88
  Antitrust and European communities
  46
  Antitrust developments 101
  Antitrust structure 56
  Cartel law 66, 81
  Common market antitrust 92
  Edinburgh conference 67
  Guide to doing business 65

New antitrust rules 54
Restrictive trading agreements 52

F

Flat glass
Dual distribution 111

Floor covering
Study of market structure and
competition 71

Food
Distribution 118
Ownership changes 119
Retailing – competition and price
making 52

Ford Motor Co.
Administered prices 100

Foreign Commerce (See also cartels,
European Common Market)
American enterprise and Scandinavian
antitrust law 64
Antitrust and American business
abroad 51
Antitrust problems of expanding
business abroad 77
Control of restrictive business
practices 67
Doing business abroad 71
Edinburgh conference. Antitrust
problems 67
Foreign commerce and the antitrust
laws 62
Foreign licensing agreements 77
Foreign trade conferences 103
Guide to legislation on restrictive
business practices 81
International licensing agreements 84
Mission report on restrictive business
practices 80
National security and foreign policy
in application of antitrust laws 48
Public control of business. An
international approach 80
Register of research on restrictive
business practices 82
Restrictive business practices 104
Restrictive business practices,
comparative summary of legislation
82

Sherman Antitrust Act and foreign
trade 87
Trade regulation overseas 59

Fur
Economics 62

G

Gas
Economics of regulation of natural
gas 141
Monopoly and competition 79
Oil or gas pools 65
Price discrimination in selling 57

Gas utility
Price discrimination 137-150

Gasoline
Demand 73
Pricing 71

General Electric Co.
Interlocks in corporate management
107

General Motors Corp.
Administered prices 100
Bigness and concentration of
economic power 101
Interlocks in management 107

Glass
Dual distribution 111

H

Hydroelectric
Water resources 146

I

Insurance
Aviation and ocean marine –
regulation 103
Interlocks in corporate management
107
Price discrimination in property and
liability insurance 94
Rates – state regulation 103

Investment bankers 177-190
Investment companies 177-190

Iron and steel
Basing-point pricing 89

L

Luria Bros. & Co. Inc.
Concentration and control of scrap
steel industry 110

M

Manufacturing (industries)
Barriers to new competition 49
Concentration 50, 79, 102
Quarterly financial report 95
Rates of return for identical
companies 95
Ratios 102

Metal container
Case study 45

Milk
Incipient monopoly in distribution
102

Motion picture
Antitrust suit 53, 55

Motor carriers 159-173

Mutual Funds 177-190

N

Natural gas 150-156
Economics of regulation 141
Monopoly and competition 79

New York Great Atlantic and Pacific
Tea Co.
Price-cost behavior 45

Newsprint
Antitrust 108

O

Oil
Crude oil pipe lines and

competition 55
Gulf Coast refinery market 65
Oil or gas pools 65
Oil pipe line consent decree 107
Standard Oil Company (Indiana) 63
Standard Oil Company (New Jersey)
66
Vertical integration 56

P

Packaging
Truth in 105

Patents
Antitrust in exploitation of 106
Licensing 108
Research and development 109

Pencil
Pricing practices 85

Petroleum
Antitrust laws and government
policy 104
Case study 45
Development of pipe lines 67
Distribution practices 118
Integration and competition 57
International cartels 112
Oil or gas pools 65
Small business problems 118
West Coast Oil case 115

Pipe lines
Crude Oil 55
Development of petroleum pipe
lines 67
Oil pipe line consent decree 107

Poultry
Small business problems 119

Power
Alleged monopoly 103
Dixon-Yates contract 104
Puget Sound Power and Light Co.
and Washington Water Power Co.
attempted merger 104

Public utility holding companies 183,
184

Puget Sound Power and Light Co.
Attempted merger 104

R

Radio broadcasting 125-133
  Need for better definition of
  standards 19

Railroad 159-173
  Mergers and abandonments 55

Regulated (industries)
  Rapid amortization 104

Residential construction
  Case study 45

Retailers
  Cooperative advertising 115
  Impact of shopping centers 109
  Regulations affecting 50

Roofing
  Administered prices 100

Rubber
  Synthetic - competition 84

S

Scrap steel
  Monopoly and technical problems
  110

Securities 177-190

Shipping
  International cartels 74

Shoe machinery
  United Shoe Machinery Corporation
  Antitrust case 69

Shopping centers
  Impact on independent retailers 109

Small business 109-119

Standard Oil Co.
  Integration 112

Standard Oil Co. (Indiana)
  History 63

Standard Oil Co. (New Jersey)
  History 66

Steel
  Administered prices 69, 101
  Basing-point pricing 89

Case study 45
Pricing power and public interest 75
Scrap - monopoly and technical
problems 110
Study in competition and planning
52

Stock Market 177-190

Supermarkets
  Competition and price making 52
  New York Great Atlantic and
  Pacific Tea Co. 45

Synthetic rubber
  Competition 84

T

Telecommunications 125-133

Telephone 125-133

Television broadcasting 125-133
  Application of antitrust laws 56
  Need for better definition of
  standards 19
  Study of industry 105

Textile
  Merger movement 108

Textron American, Inc.
  Merger 108

Tin can
  Competition 73

Tin plate
  Competition 73

Tires
  Distribution 118

Tobacco
  Pricing 67

Trade associations
  Law and practice 70

Transamerica Corp.
  Clayton Act proceeding 111

Transportation 159-173
  Antitrust laws 64
  Competition 62
  Mergers 83

U

Utilities   137–156
  Price discrimination   57
  Public Utility Holding Company
  Act   112
  Tax amortization   104

United Shoe Machinery Corp.
  Antitrust case   69

United States Steel Corp.
  Integration   112
  Interlocks in corporate management
  107

W

Washington Water Power Co.
  Attempted merger   104

West Coast Oil case
  Consent decree   115

Western Electric Co., Inc.
  Connection with American Tel.
  107

GOVERNMENT REPORTS INDEX

GOVERNMENT REPORTS INDEX

A

Administered prices
Asphalt roofing 100
Automobiles 100
Bread 100
Compendium on public policy 100
Drugs 100
Steel 101

Administrative Conference of the
United States 15, 23, 25, 32

Administrative organization
Procedure and practice 23

Administrative Procedure, President's
Conference on 15

Administrative Procedure Act
Attorney General's Manual 25

Advertising
FTC advisory opinion on joint ads
115
Self regulation 120

Air laws and treaties of the world 36

Air transportation
Licensing 32
Role of competition in commercial
36

Airlines (industry) 35–6
Antitrust report 105

Aluminum (industry)
Small business 117

American Stock Exchange 187

Amortization
Regulated industries 104

Antitrust activities
Statistics 116

Antitrust laws
Compilation 105
Complaints 113
Development 112
Enforcement 112, 113

Antitrust policy
Relation to economic growth, full
employment and prices 99

Antitrust subcommittee
Publications 198

Attorney General's Manual on
Administrative Procedure Act 25

Attorney General's National Committee
to Study the Antitrust Laws 96
Small Business Committee report 115

Aviation goals
Report of Task Force 34

Aviation (industry)
Competition 36–7
Materials relative to competition 110

Aviation study 36

B

Banking
  Chain   113
  Concentration in the United States
  111
  Concentration and small business   113
  Developments in structure   110
  Mergers   107
  Mergers and concentration   106

Bidding, identical
  Public procurement   119

Broadcast facilities
  Licensing   128

Broadcasting
  Network   129
  Regulation   129

Business Advisory Council for
  Department of Commerce   106

C

CAB and independent regulatory
  commissions   34

Cartels
  Foreign legislation   111
  International petroleum   112

Chain banking   113

Commissions, regulatory   24, 25
  CAB and   34

Concentration in American industry
  102

Concentration ratios in manufacturing
  industry   102

Congress and the monopoly problem
  114

Consent decrees
  Program of Department of Justice
  106
  West Coast oil case   115

Construction (industry)
  Antitrust cases   112

Corporate and bank mergers   107

Cost justification

Report to Federal Trade Commission
  119

D

Dairy (industry)
  Small business problems   116

Directors
  Interlocking   115

Discount-house operations
  Small business study   109

Discrimination
  Refusal to sell to small business   110

Distribution practices
  Petroleum industry   118

Dixon-Yates contract   103, 104

Dual distribution
  Flat glass industry. Small business
  report   111
  Impact on small business   117

E

Economic freedom
  Antitrust laws – a basis for   105

Economic power
  Concentration   97
  Concentration (Case study of General
  Motors Corp.)   101

European Common Market
  Antitrust developments   101

European Productivity Agency Mission
  104

F

Fair trade   109
  Problems and issues   114

FTC advisory opinion on joint ads   115

Federal Trade Commission
  Antitrust complaints   113
  Antitrust law enforcement   113
  Investigations   99

Flat glass (industry)
Dual distribution   111

Food (industry)
Ownership changes by purchase and
merger   119
Small business problems in distribution   118

Foreign legislation concerning
monopoly and cartel practices   111

Foreign trade conferences   103

G

Government policy
Competition and private pricing   99
Petroleum, the antitrust laws   104

H

Hoover Commission reports   15, 117

I

Independent business
Future. Small business report   112

Interstate Commerce Commission
Organization and operations   169

Institutional investors and the stock
market   188

Insurance
Aviation, ocean marine and state
regulation   103
Rates, rating organizations and
state regulation   103

Interlocking directors   115

Interlocks
Corporate management   107

Interstate Commerce Commission
Organization and operations   169
Rate proceedings   165

Investors, institutional
And the stock market   188

J

Japanese Restrictive Business Practices
Study Team   104

Judicial doctrine of primary jurisdiction
as applied in antitrust suits   107

Jurisdiction, primary
Judicial doctrine as applied in
antitrust suits   107

L

Landis report   15, 25

Leases
Small business guarantees   111

Legal services and procedure   23

Legislative histories
Trusts (Sherman Act)   96

M

Manufacturing (industry)
Quarterly financial reports   95
Rates of return for identical
companies   95

Mergers
Airlines   108
Banks   106, 107
Puget Sound Power & Light and
Washington Water Power Co.   104
Textile industry   108

Mergers and acquisitions   102
Research and development factor   109

Mergers and superconcentration   115

Milk
Incipient monopoly in distribution
102

Mutual funds
Study   188

N

National Association of Securities

Dealers
History 187

National power survey 143

Natural gas
Investigation 153

National transportation policy 169

Network broadcasting 129

Network monopoly 130

Newsprint
Antitrust report 108

O

Ownership changes by purchase and merger in selected food industries 119

P

Packaging
Truth in 105

Patents
Antitrust problems in exploitation 106
Compulsory licensing under antitrust judgments 108

Petroleum (industry)
Antitrust laws and government policies 104
Distribution practices 118
International petroleum cartel 112
Small business problems 118
West Coast oil case 115

Poultry (industry)
Small business problems 119

Power (industry)
Monopoly 103
National survey 143
Power policy Dixon-Yates contract 104
Water resources and power 146

Price discrimination
Distribution of dairy products 116
Small Business Committee report 115

Pricing
Administered 100-101
Competition and private pricing 99
Employment, growth and price levels 99
Government policy 99

Primary jurisdiction
Judicial doctrine as applied in antitrust suits 107

Procurement, public
Identical bidding 119

Public Utility Holding Company Act
Small business study 112

Put and call options 187

R

Railroad consolidations and public interest 167

Rapid amortizations
Regulated industries 104

Rate proceedings, federal
Improvement in the conduct 23
Conduct (Interstate Commerce Commission) 165

Regulatory commissions 24, 25
CAB and regulatory commissions 34
Effect on small business 117

Research and development factors
Mergers and acquisitions 109

Restrictive business practices 104

Right to buy
Denial to small business 110

Robinson-Patman Act
Distribution of dairy products 116
Small Business Committee report 115

S

Scrap steel
Monopoly and technical problems 110

Securities markets
Report of special study 186

Securities and Exchange Commission
 Study 187

Shopping centers
 Impact on independent retailers 109

Small business
 Aluminum industry 117
 Dual distribution and vertical
 integration 117
 Effect of regulatory commissions 117
 Food distribution 118
 Law enforcement activities affecting
 117
 Lease guarantees 111
 Monopolistic practices 112
 Petroleum industry (tires, batteries,
 and accessories) 118
 Poultry industry 119
 Private antitrust enforcement in
 protecting 110
 Problems in dairy industry 116
 Right to buy 110

Small Business, Select Committee on
 List of publications 115

Steel
 Monopoly and technical problems
 110

Stock market
 And institutional investors 188
 Factors affecting 188
 Study 188

Suburban shopping centers
 Impact on independent retailers 109

T
Telecommunications 129

Television broadcasting
 Antitrust study 105

Television inquiry 130

Transportation
 Federal policy and program 169
 National policy 169
 Rationale of federal policy 169

Truck operations
 Licensing by I.C.C. 165

Truth in packaging 105

U
U.S. Department of Justice
 Antitrust law enforcement 113

Utilities
 Attempted merger of Puget Sound
 Power & Light Co. and Washington
 Water Power Co. 104

V
Vertical integration
 Impact on small business 117

W
Water resources
 And power 146
 Appraisals for hydroelectric licensing
 146

WOC's and Government advisory
 groups 108